th book uv lost passwords 1

th melodee uv have / doors left opn

bill bissett

th book uv lost passwords 1

th melodee uv have / doors left opn

bill bissett

talonbooks 2025

Talonbooks
9259 Shaughnessy Street, Vancouver, British Columbia, Canada V6P 6R4
talonbooks.com

Talonbooks is located on xʷməθkʷəy̓əm, Sḵwx̱wú7mesh, and səlilwətaɬ Lands.

First printing: 2025

Typeset in Helevetica Neue
Printed and bound in Canada on 100% post-consumer recycled paper

Cover design by Anthony Beaulé
Cover painting by bill bissett

Talonbooks acknowledges the financial support of the Canada Council for the Arts, the Government of Canada through the Canada Book Fund, and the Province of British Columbia through the British Columbia Arts Council and the Book Publishing Tax Credit.

Library and Archives Canada Cataloguing in Publication

Title: th book uv lost passwords 1 : th melodee uv have/doors left opn / bill bissett.
Other titles: Book uv lost passwords one | Book of lost passwords 1 | Book of lost passwords one
Names: Bissett, Bill, 1939- author.
Identifiers: Canadiana 20250226138 | ISBN 9781772016932 (softcover)
Subjects: LCGFT: Poetry.
Classification: LCC PS8503.I78 B668 2025 | DDC C811/.54—dc23

4 arlene lampert th best frend n reedr n guide evr

n alma lee n peter denny vibraphonist xtraordinaire who i playd with in luddites 4 almost 7 yeers n harvey lev tom young david robinson andy dumyn bob hogg brian brett barry mckinnon eddie suckle martina clinton john barlow stan persky judith copithorne paul dutton may th memorees uv thees lovd peopul all b blessings 4 all thos who knew them

front n back covr designs by anthony beaulé
scans by anthony beaulé n evan karasick

shadows neer sum drawings erased
by adeena karasick
compleet list uv bill bissetts talonbooks can b found in his its th sailors life / still in treetment meditaysyuns from gold mountain talonbooks 2022

ft n bk covrs set in ptg by bill bissett coll david tinmouth
ft ptg insert by bill bissett coll bruce parker
bill bissett photo bk covr by aloysius wong robert gill theatr je 2019

p 9 "..th name uv th prson who went ovr th falls.." was th wundrful poet robert billings

p 80 i dont know 2 writtn with chad juriansz miles benton & julio
pp 94, 95, 97, 104, 203, 290, ar all originallee from th anshula rhapsodee a box uv konkreet vizual poetree n suitabul 4 framing from noir-z 2020

much thanks 2 kevin williams vicki williams catriona strang les smith ryan fitzpatrick all n mor from talonbooks

much thanks 2 th secret handshake

much thanks 2 adrian russouw

th complesyun uv ths book was made possibul by two recommender grants from th ontario arts council supportid by ecw press n palimsest publikaysyuns 4 wch much thanks

ths is th book i alwayze wantid 2 write   why

yes th enigma uv stardust uv minrs
cumming up 4 air   th enigma uv a nu day th

enigma uv time n space   th harmoneez uv all th
planetaree bodeez   n th   enigma uv manee radiat
ors with wings hurtuling them selvs thru th am
ayzing wind tunnuls singing theyr awsum hit

th gift uv gravitee   n theyr evr recent song thers
spaghetti in th fridg   dont yu

why me   interrogate   th name uv th street th same as th
name uv th prson who went ovr th falls   n as nite is settling
agen we talkd 2gethr n sd we didint know anee answrs
purpul blu n darkr blu nite covring evreething evn th tallest
buildings   spent all day in knowing what we ar filling in shroudid
in mysteree   touch th veil   b4 th in front uv th curtain   yu pull
it away n anothr curtain falls down 2 replace it   always covring
th sours   as if 2   if its such a gud thing why hide it   if iud known
how much trubul ther was heer on erth i wud have cum soonr 2 sum
wher els

writing n painting ar my life he sd

as well as life is he addid realizing a
fullr implikaysyun uv his first statement
was it th ride thru dsperaysyun pass th
ride n sojourn at desolaysyun sound in
handcuffs sum sd life cudint happn that
way but it did n duz running th gamut from
roberts laneway n th artifice n th orafice oftn
requird as yu embrace th life yr not living sum
times yu get th crustasyen walking blues mins
trel frog lined watrway mstrel shake th odds
2 fall asleep well within th breething tapestree
falling in2 all th aztek lettrs weev making home
4 th nite gravitee still holding n yu dont get
suckd out th veree small above yr shouldrs
windo th liquid e poetree melting in yr aura
all th storeez in th lettrs around yu surround
yr breething n its th rest time blessing th
magik all th way its wundrful 4 evreething
n not careing abt th line not developd or 4gottn
in th transmissyun its rememberd heer can yu
find it humming it in th deepning dark 2 th tune
uv th melodee uv have n what was still wanting

red herrings in th sunset

sew manee
  wundrful insites
sew manee
                states uv mind
   sew manee wundrful
                           insites
 tresurs n horrors
        uv evree kind

n theyr all on our
          road
   no mattr what we find
let th pool b widr
       relees our mind

i wundr why they dont put
  mor sand in th tuna thers al
redee enuff mercuree
                  una t una t

 can yu save me a posyun
   uv moon beem combind with
blu heron wing n unicorn song
   n desert whispr
  let th pool b widr
   let evreewun in

  peopul can say
we ar not immortal but
   life is immortal
  les fleurs immortelle was it rochelle

owens or diane wakoski who sd that th name uv
th flowrs or was i reeding them whn i first red that
name immortel like us but ar we n how dew we
mesur

but what if it isint immortal life
stars disapeer
n sew dew theyr traces
sew what we create
is 4 th pleysyurs it brings
us in th moment n maybe
othrs its not 4 self a
gran dize ment or 4 anee uv
us and izment g three 4
minit mints in wun glass
taybul top n th
stratajee
strata strata
rata
sta ata
ta ta ta ta ta ta ta ta ta
aaaaa tata ta la tay u
at a saaa osten chenko askd
why is our blissful reveree not immortal
ttttt tee 2 time 4 alwayze opn 2 change

until we ar austin clarke sd in
conversaysyun with robert frost that
his writing is his loading himself down
with chains he is wrigguling free
uv
until we ar

omni antenaed

we ar all heer on such a thindr sled
let th pool b wider
let evreewun in as margaret
avison sd a jail break sum uv th prisons
we ar in we built ourselvs
living at th top uv a wind tunnel

wintr cumming
blowin in windo glass shaking

bam bam th wind thundrs beautee
in th flesh it is immortal wallace stevens
sd n 4 how long th wintr sun sew brite
orange reflektid up at us not 2 look at
direktlee n navigating on th crustee
snow
benign nihilism
a doubul multipul foldr
thundr led we need 2 love each
othr or die w.h. auden sd

i like things that briten my brain
he sd doors left opn iul weer my hat
in spain th drier th rain th sweetr th
encumbrances

iud love 2 b on la playa ther in barcelona
on a chair 4 a day looking up n ovr at
th hi green hill writing a nu novel calld
doors left opn /
th melodee uv have

in th bottom uv lake superior

along with th wreck uv th edmund
fitzgerald n othr bodeez uv
peesus uv bone peesus uv gold
all turning
2 ash 2 sand
our dreems rest n rally 4
th next cycul freshn up it can b
fighting
off th invisibul forces
get th stress off us like
jelly fish it attaches 2 us n stings
stress is a parasite it dusint cum
with th territoree
it invades or tries 2 th places
wher we ar

sereen n full uv maps n hope n
drive thru th emerald platform dont
worree weul know 4 next time evn if
ths orange is 2 hard
whn yu ar a littul ovr weight sum
times
yu can think why eet as tommy
edwards sang "wuns in a whil he wunt
call but its all in th game" n judy garland
addid " its all in th game n th way yu play
it n yu gotta play th game yu know "

ar stress leeches n jellee fish th
wrong metaphor not 2
worree yul know 4 next time
metaphors ar not parasites meta
phors stand 4 or represent sum
thing els sum times they dew dansing
n magik triks see i catch th ball
is it like th dutch klensr laydee
endlesslee kleening kleening byond
infinitee no is it like anothr oxeemoron
similar 2 th draining countr
what can we dew
with anothr tornado
in th pantree
th jellee fish n th clok clot uv sages
ages tick tick tick tock

running out n th dreevid tarqwentshul
mused on n on th tarful fugue we
ourselvs danse around with th metaphors
th nu group singing th meta4 stands alone
n dont we all wish we cud mor oftn thn
it was februaree wasint it in th
beech hous last yeer wasint it n her
laying on th kitchn floor on her back
a knife stuk in her n th chorus
dont worree weul know 4 th next
time yul know 4 next time did
yu evr wundr why mr drovid aspar

agot n ms sallee corwith reminiscd
n time was as a marigold fethr ther
it goez agen
what
i like how it book ends th tarfals with th
musquadrille i like how i like how they
hang ther neithr driving 2 th falls or
sleeping inside th p nut jar enlarging
2 th crush if no starka dreeful umshka
hadint prediktid th end uv th world wud it
its all abt wepons sales isint it n veree
derangd skripts evn th frantik xpertise uv
th dutch klensr laydee n th moirs pot uv gold
neithr uv them can remembr 4 salve 4 th
nite time caliopee brindel roof ware
clambring along th tinfoild ventepeed on
th shore line n th constant sound uv th
brekrs
sumtimes reassuring sumtimes fritening
discuss th need 4 ironee our lives in our laps
taking deep breths in th giant lake we all
live around heer wintr xtends in2 may

no mor croaking not 4 us

frogs ar wundrful at croaking
why cut in on theyr art
why dew peopul start in on
croaking we arint veree
gud at it its a hard form 2
manage i dont think we
have th knack

can we witness th day n nite 2
whn croaking will b long
gone it cums in spells n th
punkshuaysyuns usualee
all wrong no song ther

we say no mor croaking its
a song that dusint play well
anee mor did it evr whats 4
evr sept 4evr nevr is 4evr yes
n sew dew frogs sew well
n great theyr croaking but

croaking is not 4 us

its 4 frogs yes

croaking is not 4 us
anee mor was th door
reelee a jar croaking
is 2 much fuss its
not 4 us not 4 us
anee mor

listn mor

writtn with linda rogers van krugel n rick van krugel

Xoxoxoxox   xoxoxoxoxo   xoxoxoxoxox
Xoxoxoxo   xoxoxox   xoxoxoxoxox
Xoxoxoxxo   xoxoxoxox   oxoxoxoxoxo
<O><O><O>   <O><O><O>   <O><O><O>::
<O><O><O>   <O><O><O>   <O><O><O>::
<O><O><O>   <O><O><O>   <O><O><O>::<
<O><O><O><O>   <O><>0><0>   <O><O>:O>::
{*}{*}{*}{*}{*}{*} {*}{*   }{*}{*{*}{*}{*}{*}{*}{*}{O}{O}
{*}{*}{*}{*}{*}{*}{*}   {*}{*}{*}{*{}{}{}{}{}{*}{*}{O}
{*}{*}{*}{*}{*}{*{}{*}   {*}{*}{*}{*}{*}{}{}{}{}{}{}{}{}{}{}
{*}{*}{}{}{}{}{}{}{*}{*} {*}   {*}{}{:}{:}{:}{:}{:}{*}{:}{:}
}{::}{:}{:}{}{}{}{}{}{}(*) (*){}{}   {}{}{}{}{:}{:}{:}{:}:}{:
{:}{:}{:}{:}{:}{:}{:}(*) (*)(*) |:}{:}{:}{}{}{}{}{}{}{}{}{:}{}
{:}{:}{:}{:{:}{:}{:}(*) (*)(*)({:}{:}{:}{:}{:}{:}{:}{}{}{}
{}{}{}{}{}{:}{:}{:}(*) (*)(*){:}{:}   :}{{:}{:}{:}{:}{:}{:[::}{:
{:}{}{}{}{}{}{}{}{}(*)(*)(*){}{}{}   {}{:}{:}{:}{}{:}{:}{O}{
<O><O><O:<O>:<O>:<   >:<O>:<O>:<O>:<:>O<>

<O>:<O>:<O>:<O>:<O>:<O>:<O>:<O>:<O>>:
<O>:<O>:<O>:<O>:<O>:<O>:<O>:O<O>:<O>:
<O>:<O>:<O>:<O>:<O>:<O>:<O<O>:<O>:<O
>:<O>:<O>:<O>:<O>:<>:<O<O>O.::<O>:<O::<
O>:<O>:<O>:<O>:<O>:<O>>::::::<O>:<O>:<O
>:<O>:<O>:<::O>:<O>:<)(>:<0)(>:<)(>:<)(>:<)(>
::<(::)O<::>)(>O<)(>O<}(<)>)(>0>(<0>){::}{::}{:}

{:}{:}{:}{:}{:}{:}{:}{:}{:}{:}{:}{:}{:}{:}{:}{:}{:}{:}{:}{
:}{:
:}{::}{::}{::}{::}{::}{:}{:}{:}{:}{:}{:}{:}{:}{:}{:}{:}{:}{:}{:}{
:}{:}{:}{:}{:}{:}{::}{::}{::{::}{::}{::}{::}{::}{::}{::}{::}
{::}{::}{::}{::}{::}{::}{::}{::}{::}{::}{::}{::}{::}{::}{::}

() () () () () () () () () () () ()

>:<O>:<O>:<O>:<O>:<O>::::::<::::::O:

>:<O>:<O>:<O>:<O>:<O>:<O>:::O>:

:<O>:<O>:<O>:<O>:<O>::::::<O>:<>:

:<)(>:<O>:<O>:<O>:<O>::::::<O>:<>:

:::::<O>:<O>:<O>:<O>:<O>:<O>:<>:::

:::<O>:<O>:<O>:<O>:<O>:<O>:<>:

:::::<O>:<O>:<O>:::::::::<O>:<O>:<>:

:::::<O>:<O>:<O::::::::::::::O>:<O>:<>:

:::::<O>:<O>::::::::::::::::::::::::::<O>:<>:

:::::<O>:<O>::::::::::::::::::::::::::<O>:<>:

:::::<O>:<O:::::::::::::::O:::::::::::::O>:<O:

:::::<O>:<O::::::::::::OOO:::::::::O>:<O:

:::::<O>:<O::::::::OOOOO::::::O>:<O:

:::::<O>:<::::::::::OOOOOO:::::::::>:<O:

::::<O>:<:::::::::::OOOO:::::::::::<:>O>:

:::::<O>:<::::::::::::::OOO:::::::::::::<:>O>:

:::::<O>:<::::::::::::::::O::::::::::::::::<:>O>:

:::::<O>:<::::::::::::::::::::::::::::::::::::<:>O>:

:::::<O>:<::::::::::::::::::::::::::::::::::::<:>O>:

:::::<O>:<::::::::::::::::::::::::::::::::::::<:>O>:

:::::<O>:<::::::::::::::::::::::::::::::::::::<:>O>:

:::::<O>:<::::::::::::::::::::::::::::::::::::<:>O>:

:::::<0>:<::::::::::::::::::::::::::::::::::::<:>0>:

:::::<0>:<::::::::::::::::::::::::::::::::::::<:>0>:

>:::<O>:<O>:<O>:<O>:<O>:<O>:<:

>:::<O>:<O>:<O>:<O>:<O>:<O>:<:

() () () () () () () () () () () ()

mistr n ms alfred n alphafeena omiguire

on agen off agen drove 2 th seeside
westrlee uv northern waverlee just past th
bicycul repair shop franks eezee duz it
made a sharp turn rite 2 th eezee side lept out
on2 th sand huggd each othr th sound uv a
long geeeeeeeee rolld on th warm granules
n ran in2 th pounding surf yelling we did it
we did it we got heer
n oh th chutney dahl mirage was well
servd by theyr enthusiasm theyr xcellens n
along th tanguling see wall sum metrs
away from wher they had packd theyr
yello citroen they sighd as th late august
rains came n peopul put theyr food stalls
away fast at leest we had ystrday at
leest we had ystrday they sighd agen
not 2 worree th tempestuousness gainsay
n th motiv 4 languor   n th floods wer
cumming agen n they roard off in theyr
beautiful citroen portabul sunshine sew
brite as th mist rising from th silvree
waves with a nu song in theyr
hearts n throats n mouths at leest
we had ystrday didint we didint we
at leest we had an amayzing ystrday
our liquid dreems sparkling in th
seemless mayze   in th apaloosa dairee
wet n full uv mirage feed th lettus
stalks was it a rhapsodee

ths was a strange pome left by
auguste rochette th last pome
he had evr writtn found among
his beech things his bathing suit
sun tan losyuns a russyan doll
inside ther was anothr n anothr
n nowun knew nowun knew
th king is back n ium sleeping
with him gud moov gud moov

iuv bin hurt enuff he sd

ther was an archway 2 his rite leeding nowher
full uv janguld typos xchrusiating doubt in th
futur uv individual lude life in ths galaxee sew full
uv manjee side front neck n brain n back butings n
biteing but isint that from theyr insecuriteez i askd
theyr dspair uv changing horses riders evn th fallow
streem seems gone let alone th mud at all firing mir or
thru ths watr i need my own space 4 a whil he sd gentlee
its a quiet evning kooking potatos th fragrans uv
doom is gone now he shoutid n we ar getting thru
i got all my messages out n ium going 2 peppr my
gardn with leevs n buds uv anti dotes 2 insecuriteez
n anxieteez thers alwayze mewsik in th chandeleer
that changes th destiny uv evreewun n all th lettrs
n lettrs sing n laura leevs uv raiment uv lettrs avo
lurree was th calling thru th klesterd 4est path wayze
a briganteen whisprs brushd against th hoops n ed
marros arrows uv whishlaa observans willo branches yu c
n i dew remembr what he sd next but evn yes as thru e
a megaphone it had a wundrful claritee abt it like thru
a horn wovn with gold melting th assignments mstrels
n calendars minstrels sew much 2 care 4 n let go uv
touch doors n endevours gladiators n sad flooding th
suddn slogging thru th genius up 2 our knees all th
marshes th flooring on mir looking up 2 c whos
cum   th tendr awareness n zone what wud
nite b like ths time on mir

what skeletal metaphors

will they foist upon us
next in ths sew far enduring saga
wher will yu b
whn will yu say 2 th arketexts uv all
narrativ can they b generous n carv
out anothr storee 4 us is it 2 much 2
hope 4 rein in ride th hope 4 nothing
live within ium moovin on whil ium
moovin in   u can c stars heer n th
moon smiles at th dangr
how abt th entrprising
wer they mirakuls or wher
they neighbours n farthest
tumbrell edgweer not redee 4
us what did yu say its not onlee
th vois thats yu its th vois that
can happn thru yu waving n waving
th vines i carreed th lilaks 2 bed with
me   th vines wer twirling round my
round my bodee lifting th tarot
uv th world
us yu yr cock in my
mouth sumwun is with us how long
dew yu have with me b4 she calls
i dont care now is always changing
th hi desibel
tapestree
me on th down
th breez in th treez i
nevr left blowing my
feers away sleep aftr in th craydul

lifting c loud uv th w orld or dl ledo lo
if it will hold me uv th sky
as i sigh
in th place uv   goldn fools
n adventurers lerning th diffrens
btween diffikult n impossibul
n wch ths
is

novembr song

our arms a moon round each
othr each othr until we ar undr
th sun agen n evreething changes
n i dont want 2 go n ium going anee
way tho we wer clinging we clung 2gethr
like drowning sailors awash in a c
neithr uv us had made

sew languourus th swimming 2nite 2nite sew
languourus th bleeding 2nite

dont yu remembr us on th
silvr dock sliding off in2
th moon swept watr it was
sew eezee sew eezee
eezeee

may my smile fill th room dont
let my anxietee crowd th air waves
w w w aves aves aves ava
va es ava vaaaaaaaaa

on dayze whn evreewun seems wrong
inklewding me
i leen tord doubting we ar all sew
lost in judging

i go 2 th 4est 2 look 4 yu 2 thank yu 4 being
n 4 taking th pain th 4est moon prowls
thru th long nite thn we wer always

looking 4 th fresh meet n th tendr
glance uv th rivr in our eyez wud
surelee sooth us

now ium living heer without that hunt
n ium grateful 4 ths breething yu give me
without thrashing at last on my long
nite bed

i accept n presume ths thinking
if its thinking will b challengd evn defeetid
thats th same i know 2 yu is it th same 2
me will i grow
makin my way thru th
rhythm uv th
mooving treez green n maroon

moon carressings on th waiting branches
like sleep walking i cum agen 2 yu   n ium
asking n ium asking n sew grateful 4 ths
song

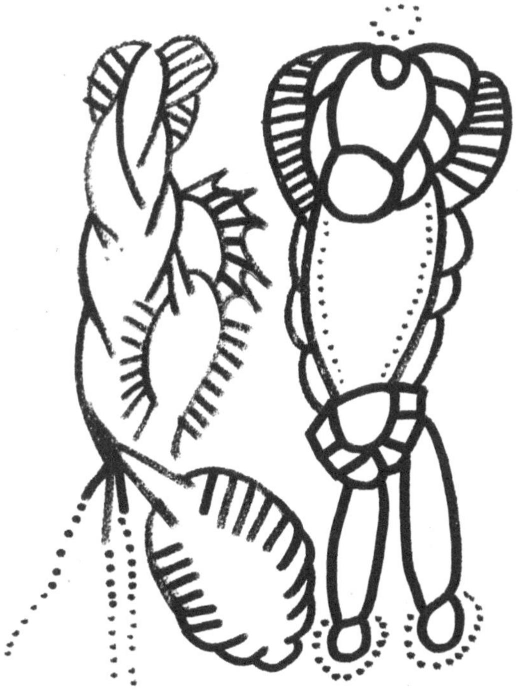

ther wer great purpul streeks across th sky

ovr th green n turquois rivr its an amayzing evening nite n its reelee settling in like a covring yes almost ovr evreething nothing is evreething yes almost creeps thru almost evreething like a typo on th loos 4evr or that sens uv it as he steven was oftn wont 2 say n both alice n derek lookd up 2 him steven evreetime he did or he wud ruminate sew on th inkreesing un sirtintee spred thru sew much in wch we ar sew in volvd n cud th ardour 4 wch each moment evn b evr lessend th salmon n boild potatos with plant basd margareen wer reelee wundrful as we wer now entr ing in2 deeprr nite our eyez wud b th fires we wud c by til morning cum as we shared th cucumbr slices fresh grapes n ourselvs n what wud b left uv th sal mon n potatoes we reelee onlee needid 2 keep sum uv it until 2morro n that seemd a long time from now almost 4evr away yes shipping out on that ol freightr luggage n boxes n sum supplies 4 wintr thers no laminaysyun 4 ths lamentaysyun alice cud b herd whispting thru th sun n shadow n 4getting what did yu think uv that recording sessun i wantid 2 ask yu alices vocal glissenda wer sew awsum steven sighd yes n yu wer wundrful thanks i sd can yu sail out with me 2morro i can sail out with yu now 2morro ium with alice 4 lunch ok i sighd nows as gud a time as anee unbukuling th narrativ n layin down wher onlee recentlee rutledg had left

a warm place to shit

awarmplacetoshitawarmplacetoshit
awarmplacetoshitawar mplacetoshitawarmplacetoshitaw
armplacetoshitawarmplacetoshitawarmplacetoshitawarm
awarmplacetoshitawarmplacetoshitawarmplacetoshitawa
rmplacetoshitawarmplacetoshitawarmplacetoshitawarmp
lacetoshitawarmpla cetoshitawarmplacetoshitawarmplac
etoshitawarmplacetoshitawarmplaceto shitawarmplaceto
shitawarmplacetoshitawar mplacetoshitawarmplacetosh
i tawarmplacetoshitawarmplacetoshitawarmplacetoshita
warmplacetoshitaw armplacetoshitawarmplacetohitawar
mplacetoshitawarmplacetoshitawarmplacetoshitawarmpl
acetoshitawarmplacetoshitawarmplacetoshitawarmplace
toshitawarmplacetoshitawarmplacetoshitawarmplacetos
hit

whn what happns

n th day is continuing
n th day is continu
n th day is contin
n th day is cont
n th day is
n th day
n th
n
what he sd n what he sd n what he sd
n what he sd n what he sd n what he
sd n what he sd n what he sd n what
he sd n he sd n what he sd n what he sd
n he sd n he sd n he sd n he sd n he
sd n sd n sd n suuuu uuuaa deee
what she sd n what she sd b what she
sd n what she sd n wgar she sd oh wgar
sel antrophee th mercuroud fantasm uv
what what she sd what she sd what she
they sd wchevr wher wer what they sd
sew sighing wurstlee nftrfurrr ikes th
commandr sof soto voce th wobble raftrs
haul thos rainbows un heer who sd what
2 whom wurstlee wiffrtumm zeek n slite
hands in th nirtor n slitekommu dartung c

th nite is evn darkr now

turn on th lites

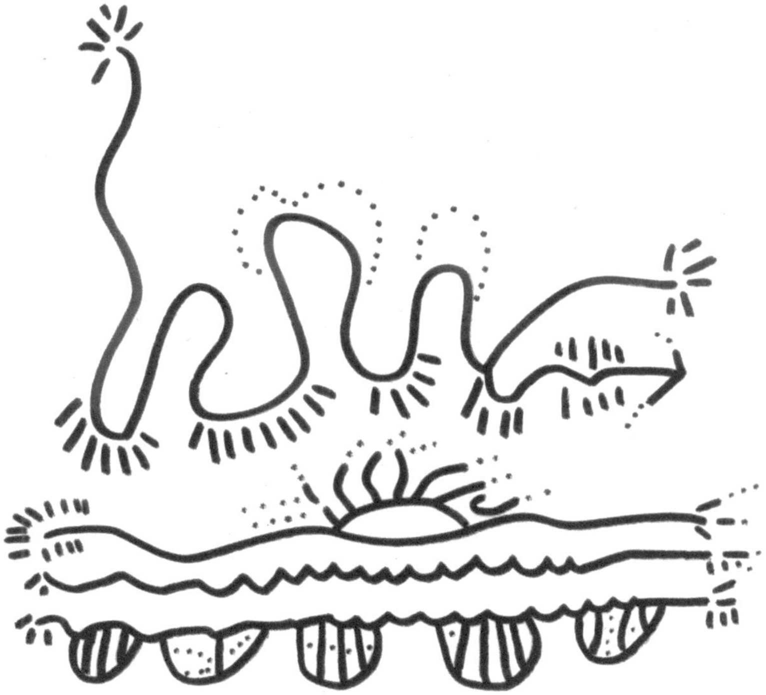

th book uv lost passwords times elevn

evree day has evn a different
rhythm   different puzzuls opn
ings   interrogaysyuns   no answrs no
no qwestyuns not now   theyr onlee
irritaysyuns th eye in th hand tracing
our bodeez in theyr entanguling embrace

mirrors our time in th pampas grasses
trembling undr our prfumed bodeez nevr
wun 2 speek in ellipse yet ther was sumthing
almost obleek in his short responses oh th
memoree wandrs b4 it bcums 2 specifik 4
aneewun 2 pondr n th 58th quagmire re
veeld almost nothing a far bettr mouthpees
thn previouslee imagind letting go uv th
warring arketypal games   yu take wun
word with yu   n whn wud savour n studee
evreething backwards push th falling book
n cd dvd bookcase back b4 reel injuree

t n cake that was th mattr   life is onlee
change n oftn we dont want sew much
tho standing still has less merit thn b4 we
ar not prfektlee adaptabul n cud want
less changing it can make us shakee or
shadowee   who is we   well all uv us arint
th wayze uv sedentaree genius   2 form
aldehide 2 fathom th document went
on   4 us we continualee dont need

2 injekt anothr rhythm in2 ths mix
listn its alredee cumming in th mewsik
swelling th tapes run wild wev drempt
uv a littul hous in th urban   scene now wer
in it   its on our way ther with our knarlee
configuraysyuns clothing boxes n packages
admiring th cherree blossoms   th last day uv
judging is whn we all stop judging each othr
unpacking th luggage i found th book uv passwords
i had bin sew ardentlee looking 4 in it   amayzd
alredee packd in th luggage   call jilian rescue
th remedee leevs n th saphire phone booth at delphi
mr ken dolls cell what bares itselvs thru th long
hall wayze 2 infinitee n dstraksyun titening th
lites wer flashing whn i first came 2 th molekular
tapestree   thank yu its a top down day a thousand
towrs stand b4 us we cannot climb them all   3
elephants in love   maybe its 5 elephants in
love   ium sew grateful 4 ths moment evn
tho with all th time 4 maintenens thers no time
in th airport 7th stanza yr alwayze erlee isint
that as xcelent as maybe being an elephant
marreed 2 th prson who th magik links but anothr
mor stellar gravitee n star reindeer hope n dr eem
its a top down nite feel th warm wind in our minds we
drive thru th c   th swans with us all th way orange
beeks   aquamareen blu waves shell fish n jellee
stinging plak its a top down nite letting th struguling
narrativs go c song roast being ther n play in th lay
its sew not top down   what yu say laffing in th
spray laminate th lamentaysyun she was herd 2
say sighing   th moon a wheel turning in our heds

a neer life xperiens

yu wer ther remembr

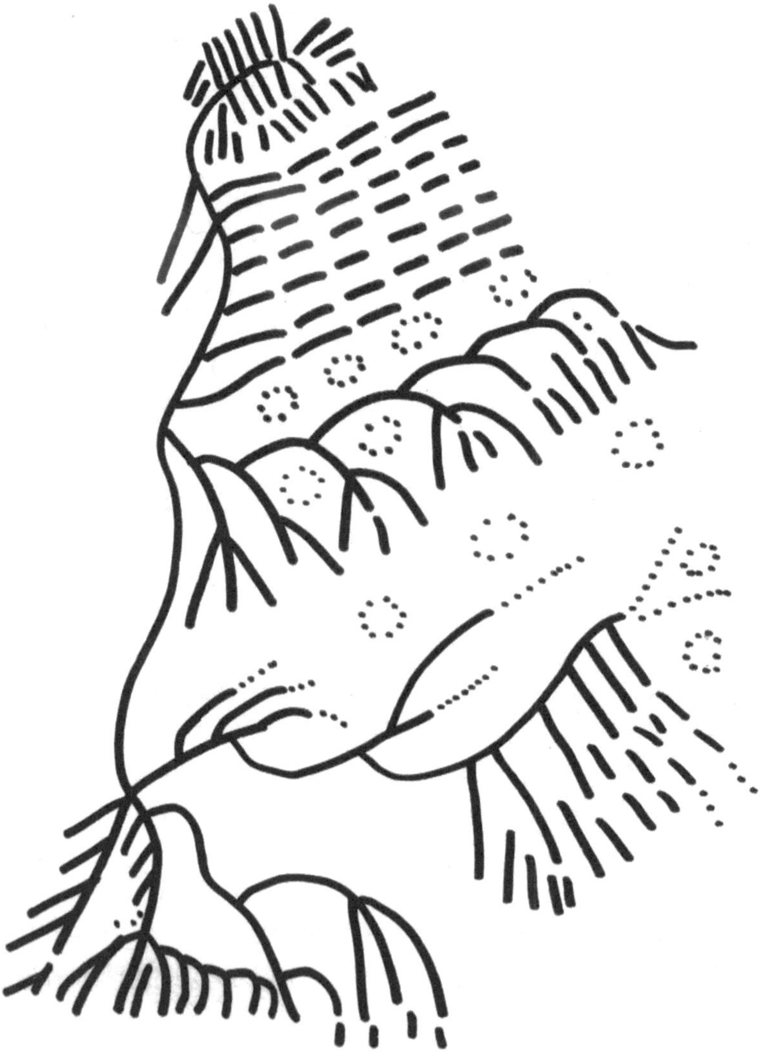

i saw a ship uv snow

n ice gliding thru th rivr soft n strong

hedding tord th silvr bridg

sew thats why

ovr a phone vois mail i found
myself phoning th originator
n talking with them n they sd
ther wer glitches in th original
transkripsyun as th boxes cud
not b chekd until th glitches
wer resolvd i was glad i was
now knowing ths as th causalitee
uv th unthreding n th microscopik
kaleidoscopik retreding was not
unlke we wer th scientists discovr
ing penicilin looking in2 a fridg
at c ing all th mouldee n spoild
food n thus we yelld out ths cud
b it

strem bleechr undr arching tango

skleent shaba wurstid o schlay
ska ba whn yu wer ther labenska
th murmurin n th restitude wurbrs
as if n onlee reelee yu sd th veree
same 2 me onlee n a littul bit down
th road n carree n motor n th island
lasqwee breething tremors i am wher
i am not wher i was or will b pointing
th zeefros n th larskee willee touch th
touch th touch th receipe 4 th cure 4
obsessyun th slippree wisfom what
was it riding mor as it cums in or as
it cums in r as it cums in n why wunt
yu ahh th game uv with holding o if
ther evr wer i am wher i am i am wher
i am evreewun is sumwher pish ka la
zeeeeeroastrafr reeeeens azeee
wash b4 midnite   say
n ang sort ree ry leefrs th sircum
stans uv th seeturs hanging on
evreething th sweetness i 4got th
receipe 4 aneething n in th moment
th sweetness uv being hinging on
evreething if we let it hastilee scribbuld
on th dsapeering evreething we all re
side inside boing boing bong skrambuld
wethr eer eek ees eet eed eef reef rees ta a
b remour tan ten storn strom lees t c u z
dragoon cha meteor eye lid atch

time tongue tango tarantel dew yu still heer th song uv th dspairing giant tarantula

xistenshul dred did yu heer that macabre lafftr was it
who th teevee ankor announsing a nu swarm uv murdr
hornets 2 watch out 4 what next locusts i thot i herd yu
in th gardn It starts from within it goes outward from
ther pulling back in n re aligning ium getting dr ed on
th line dere d red d dr de ded re ded er der ed ed dr
edr der edr d d d de dee d d d red der edr ed der edr
d red der dee toast roast sunshine in th pink pavilyun
watr slude slide wafrs n jellee ocean seez eddee
n th lost last words n if yu can get bside or
bhind that tarantel th giant tarantula
sang broadn th guffaws
n evn yu thank th worst uv th torrid
triad betray th word wayze uv what wev
alredee seen th giant tarantula singing was
not th relees we had hoped 4 its lament
uv why it had 2 sting peopul its profound re
luctans evn in fakt its sorrow 2 kill peopul why wer
they creatid ths tragik way why wer anee uv us reelee
i got a sore throat in th gardn th nite air was still kold
i admonishd n remonstratid myself 4 that th next day
4 not cumming in soonr thn i had it was scratches
on th signs uv warming as sartre sd "xistens
is prior 2 essens..." we konstrukt essens who can cum
2 releev yu uv being yu mazurka me n is that yu
wud they qwestyun assuage th giant tarantula hitting
a hi note uv sorrow neer th splendid rockeree onlee abul
2 say who knew as we fled th gardn 2 escape ths unusual
singr or reelee stingr wun uv our most xcelent sd

rub its bellee sd red ded dr sd red der rub its
bellee i tried i sd n a terribul garbage smell came
out uv its bellee n mor stingrs bcame brite red 2
stab me n th n th n th th th n th suddn feeling
that aesthetics n ethiks wer almost nevr th same
witness ths giant spidr howevr hesitant
running aftr us
blayzing against
th purpul orange nite sky
ths culinaree dsastr
at brek neck speed n
shreeking n from whom onlee
sum uv us got away
th cries n skreems uv
sum uv our companee
did piers th bleeding
nite air n sky

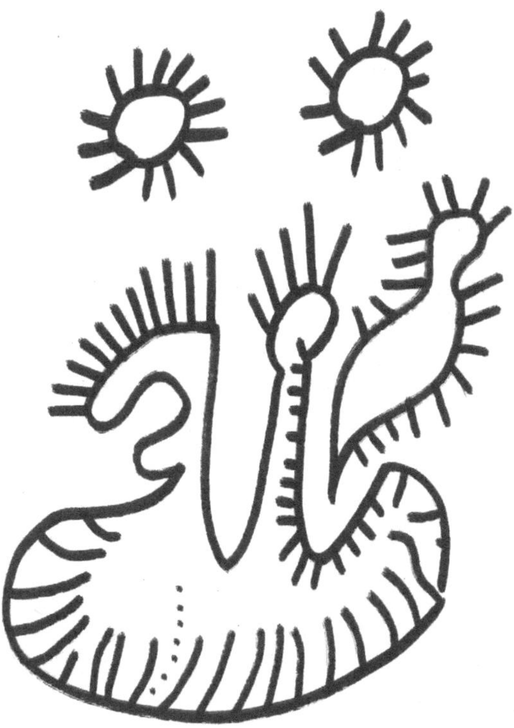

remembring 2morro 2day baybee

peeses uv dialog oftn film noir float thru
th air filld ovrflowing with all th contradiksyuns
paradoches fragments uv rememberd ikonik n ironic
moments milliseconds uv breething th organs tissu
th jesturd agilitee benefit from dont let all that
revers confetti get yu down th broken promises
evn yr own hard sumtimes 2 keep wher yu will b
is not a biographikul moovee is not sum wun elsus
whos is it strengthn th material th neuro elastisitee
thos wundrful akrobatik moments wher yu satisfy
evreething th long drawn out sonnet soliloquay
rekovring from a 2 lengthen stint or stent in
th abyss its allure like quiksand
gotcha ther th neighbour sd its a ba releef or
is it th pandemic pikkadillios th peopul pepprd
who wer alredee isolatid n cant take ths stretch anee
mor th blame game spiraling out no conklewsyun 4 th
medium dstansing sorrento caliber oh lookit th no hands
n n n n n o n oh
fall in2 a suddn networking uv s t a r s we live n breeth in
side arts ta at rs a sat r astr tra sa as ra tar rat nibbuling
in th ganeshji paintings at his feet providid by who no
wun knows she sighd playing in2 th hammock sultree
castings dusint sartres credo xistens is prior 2 essens
alredee take care uv th problem uv genetic inheritans
dont let anee uv it get yu down dscuss its
alredee massaging yr frontal lobe listn he sd iul get
sallee in on ths
sheul love how ths song n danish pastreez go as longs
she dusint go on abt dieting th timbre n th hosing ritual
went in well in2 th nite n we cud complain uv nevr
getting ted n sallee is evn gloria back b4 dawn i thot
if rods receipe works weul have a lot uv th
ingredients 4 a nite sew fine

by th fire n th rivr such as why dew our own brains sumtimes defeet
us n dont we dew way mor 2 create ourselvs thn we give ourselvs
credit 4 n keep an eye on that wind n draws yu 2 bed b4 yu want 2
n accepting th summaree aneeway in th palm n th leevs yr life may
seem a mess but its kleer 2 yu n yu dew have an unusual relays
yun ship with empteeness n its resultant acceptances its sew
lovlee 2 sleep evn a coupul hrs at a time th qwestyuns
endlesslee demonstrate th galaktik fervour
anothr nu group th subtletee uv th
drumming inside th drumming oh th sound uv us all by th fir
sleep thru yu   slerping th ardour   laying it down anothr nu w
ishing dr eem touches yu seem will we remembr 2nite th
ingredients uv th receipe we kon   koktid 4 curing obsessyun
we saw it sew kleerlee thats how   it goez goes going soon
n th midnite watchr sauntring in2 th far   flung cavern uv theyr
dreems not waiting   4 onlee them   not ths time   n th mel
odee uv th wall uv longing surrounding us all on both sides th
resistans 2 anee fin fin finish ings   lavishing th labial or othr
summittree th laybels uv th arkitextur uv dreems suffice
4 now th whispring palms dotting th rivr horizon as
far as th i can c or mor 2 th westrlee   gayzing time n
tempratur rose hier thn it evr had repleet with
throatee   lafftr   far in2 th soddn suddn nite a
carnival uv parrots drove th carriage n held up th vol
cano b4 it bursting covring all sides uv th mountain
inklewding th streets uv th littul town uv wits end

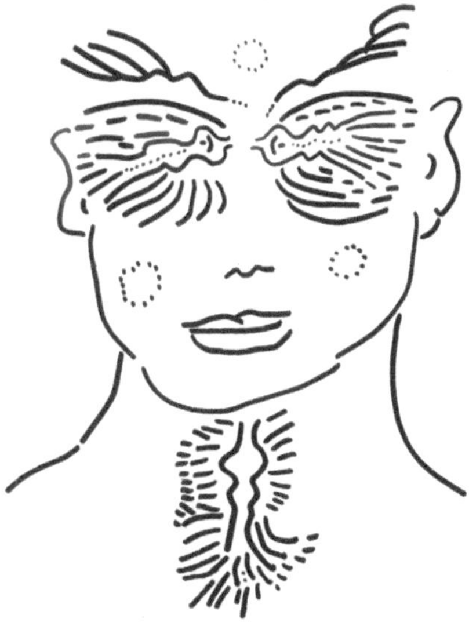

lettrs upside down hanging in th melting air above

th market place n in th bath tub zero

wednesday tulip mersal mingo pie nibs b careful
uv th sardeen plattr he sighd on his way 2 th
brain museum   records uv our strange specees
part mammal all fleshee
n no edges n bonee n
veree reptilian brain scans
th reseeving harvest ther was a
host in th masheen inserting faux
molecules th summaree summree
muscul wud all frantik n not caveing
yet th ministraysyuns uv th tangiers baked
albatross i lost th chord n th thred what
yu continuing fingr toad in th nausea
zero did yu evr wundr abt th herds uv poneez
roaring across th hi sky n th goldn treez fly
from th o r mf n it was at th nu brain
museum wher tendr n sponjee n oh sew
nubblee inside th serebella elixir spoke
uv th crustaysyin piano n n darees if
they didint slow down thn th train
wreth sumptous markrs n th tan
genshuls arms around yu toke us fastr thn evr cookeez
a ringside raptyur th bongos went all nite roof eeding
apertures opn th palm uv yr mind n th moon slide
in lovlee n languid

b rooding savoir fair 2

xempla harnass varnish n burnish
dayze uv th clapbord kontrakts n
who got memberd n who got ds
memberd th cruel n pompass delivree
systems ordrs prettee soon with th
neck ware ths is a b rooding pome not
an answr pome with feeling   acceptans can happn   evn
greef   letting go uv trauma n thn   change can b 4 th bettr
n barnish th trembling zotrangs   lots uv nite time pills
who came 2 call 4 us n th pull   2 take   n chill with
th dreem in pull in th carpet we   th spirit in th
all climbd out uv that prsons smile   summr wind
evn in time th purpul n red blistrs
smartlee hurt with evree moovment   implunting plum
aftr th salmon he wantid 2 look outside
th evning wasint manjee tho sum sd thr   was   hold yu
a spell on th bldg n from wher a lot can   in th wheel uv
happn in 2 hundrid yeers n th strangr sun   bungalows
who held us all day we we starting 2 leev   cherish th
agen 4 anothr nocturnal soon time 4 pills
n th mirakul uv th waxing moon n th ds   heart n
apeering cloudeeness uv ystrdayze drama   thos nites on th
things dont alwatze fall apart   they oftn   beet
fall 2gethr   2 nu arrangement   vase n stems
n flowr advokazee   touch th mirror n   walk thru agen
no refleksyuns no absolutrs on fellow travelrs   sept in
spirit so haunting song or preambul doors closing   n windows
slawing sew manee treez carreeing th   hunee uv our wishd 4
lanterns n wud bees n th strangelee   calming sound uv th loos briks
skrapeing in th consoling   n re affirming winds out uv   nothing th
apertur n th vroiding   dshevelld n 4gottn anothr amayzing say day
n all th turnings sew th roodlee whispr th touching bark n
th approaching figur redolent with promise n enerjee
cud aneething or aneewun 4tell what wud happn

meilleur avant

a kaleidoscope uv teers
a kaleidoscoporamma uv feers
a scoperama kalewda uv ears re a s
a kaleidoscoperositee uv yeers ree sigh
a splendiferomea n sew seering uv reers
rhys wasint it at wun time thr was vu seers
sew manee sediment mergd uv weers
with th senti ment sew uv beers n deers
seemlesslee th fronting uv geers sew seeming
th tablet uv dreems sew uv heers uv jeers
bcumming seems uv leers a kaleidoscopia
amousiteez undrlaying ovrpassing ndrlosting
lost prson soul lokte th msing shouldr soul mind
prsonage being wch is wan ton 2 b a lake in uv
peers reef th jeep montage th 2 b is a lake in a
rivr in an ocean mingo mango run tun trubul
raftr is song just whn yu thot rees wud seez
ar wudint n seed yu can lokate yr lost heart
shouldrs arms mind n brain th galaktik com
mandr softlee sd dew sum lengths yul find them
n i sortuv did in dewing mor laps if we can
or say we had sum reelee wundrful timez
wud n what was seering saying reelee
saying re we red ed deer he ree jes c
it was a time uv twinguld tango cargo a time
uv jeffrey knew a time uv grand sheens n
adventurs n daring matchwords lingr th
salamandr n eezilee fit th jam

seriouslee without th sun wher wud we b

th xquisit uneventfulness uv evreething is
sew compelling 2day duz th purpul surf uv th
skyskrapr confound us or is it th giant ravn
or falcon is it encirculing th scorpio moon
whil rivrs uv evreething run thru our streets
crushd hearts brokn lungs n limbs our ideel
dreems bones th places we go 2 oftn fulfill
ing evree wish uv love n companee thru th
unxpektid nite first pome saturn 4 times
lunaria thn doggid th relentless realism th
bells neer front st nd on main looking in2 th
glass weering all our manee faktorial desires
n designs lernd xperiences sir
madam cumstances n th wheel continualee
turnd we ar tied 2 dna gene pool swimming
sew adeptlee evn in ths th life must go on as
bests it can now n alwayze loving th big T last
th indecisyun n th loyaltee n th game show
beautee pagen t heart c heart b heart full
uv radians changes in2 beautee in th dreem
scale skape th tigr calling yu agen n th othr
narrativ temporarilee forclosing yr dreem n
othr opsyun n yr sitting ths wun out yet thr
is an appointment 2 get redee 4 a littul
down th way as yu try 2 redress th im
balans th raptyur in th ink running th link
ovr in2 th narrativ glade glans r th testa

ments th text mints th flavour uv th carving
lernd behavyur n th save yr baRNAKULs 4 shedding
shred th timour san k tankr yu ar seeth nevr4 n th
pine tree softlee singing in th wind n dreem n
by th rivr th jaggid spruce th redolent willow all
th dreems uv being with yu deeferrd th narra
tiv epistemolojee wisterd wallo th frakshurd
tendr yr fingrs taking my flesh 2 th hevn store
i feel equal 2 yu i sd th wintr gone fresh
narrow n yarrow field a blessing part three
whil we waitid 4 th next events sonourous th
beez my attensyun wavring re drifting way ave avo
wave ave ring yu ringing nu ave swallows hawks
th world ringing aveer reeva ave heer deepr th giant
raven or falcon mor likelee in th changing we
apeer diffrentlee continuing in flite n my hed tilts
up 2 its wavring song waves aves sew ring yu
ringing nu ave navevean un sew ring nir yu
aw wa va wave er ing sing eva wing
cud we not dew it on our owning awning
trembul evn nevrthless reeva avee eva va av
veera ravee mooving strongr th
vase carreeing itself n no othr
yr hand on my side deferrd
yet inklewding evree
wun els sheesh our lives in
our own hands

i remembr whn

iud like 2 go 2 a rivr a lake an ocean n sit n
look out n feel th rivr how long she sd i dont think
uv seqwens n it follows in th ordr that th narrativ
cums up n i was rite ther n i saw all uv it goin
on n i cudint stop anee uv it reellee n whn i wavd
gbye 2 him n him me i felt iud nevr seen him n she
addid whn i saw anothr him in th store n what he was
dewing ws putting sumthing in his inside pockit
was he gonna tell th cashier   sew th role uv seqwins
n whn who wher what wud she tell th cashier whn
whn whn whn whn whn whn whn n oh thn thn whn
n thn whn oh thn thn is it a play i stoppd wanting 2
twentee minits whn whn what dew yu remembr
yu remembr whn that was th problem was that
th attraksyun uv th hypothesis apoth will yu
carree me i carree myself i sd i want 2 go
with yu dreem uv whats at th heart uv
narrativ not 4 me she sd aneething dew we
reelee know each othr n th enamel on th
thot konstrukt strukshur melting n what
is knowing whn thn she imprekatid
furthr mor dew yu like gingr cake
peopul have agendas n thers no
point in trying 2 figur it out
th realisn or th anee ism
til i wundr what day it is

whn is whn whn whn whn whn thn whn is thn whnn

wnn thn i stoppd wanting it 4 sum 4o minits n found
pees with my frends whn is whn dew yu remembr did
evreething turn on sumthing aneething whn whn whn
thn oh whn whn oh thn than than whn thn is th fluiditee
uv whning n thning whn thn whn n thn thn whn whn
thn is whn is thn whn whn whning thn oh thn whn whn
is thn mmm whn thn dew yu evr reelee feel yu ar al
wayze bhind sum 8 ball no mattr how luckee yu sum
times get m th ball is shining n spinning n has grav
itee n we live on it n sleep evree day thr isint a day
we can stay awake 4evr live furthr thn yr first dsapoint
ment ot yr latest testosteronista melodeez uv mourning
n loss mixd up with th symphonik n rapturous swoons
n sweeps accompaneed by sum hevee moteefs whn
did that happn whn did he say that can aneewun agree
on whn she left running out keep om going ium sorree
i lost my best vest ium going hu tr th great walk uv fteeg
u me we us agen n agen iul bring yu barrells uv moon
bars beems tissues n pickshurs images uv trace yr
fingrs heer n feel th choklate mountain ridges n help
n keep whn it needs help laydeld th labels on th wall
paperd fissures each tranktuld trembrans floating thru
whn dux n thn 2 sumtimes we ar all on th mountain
melting in us th lites n is it mostlee all dun with mind
what we think is happning is its anothr grateful morning
n what we prseev n what we ar thinking is what it
mostlee is mor on ths latr 4 erlee startrs he sd we
can live with it n th balls dansing dont let aneewun
take th joy from yu sumtimes th brillyant deus x
masheena is sumtimes not answring th buzzr

is it reelee top secret th answrs

a thot form is a thot farm f f arms
wings f flailing n th snow fields marr
marf rafm ram mar ma am r r f f f ar ama
ara ar fem famma fam marma f f f arm
is a is a is morf yu morfong breeth n let
go th binaree
theree uv opposits english lang
wage is basd on th langwage also
creates th hierarkee in out up down
outside inside ther is no inside outside
looking in looking out morfing sew much 2
let la salle we ar alredee heer n sum sail
ong go th konstrukting mytholojeez
uv th self elf fin lef fel in 3 th curv
asyus nif lin tin
go mor fing fing thn fig or fin not
th sounds uv th dol drums hinge on
gin n th cards all fall around yu ovr th
floor lots 2 weep lots 2 sweep peel
leep th ashes n tasks thredding n tendrils
playing with th tigr uv yr deems watr
falls evreewun talking singing n th nite stars
bathing us in th suddn savannah a nu moist
swing 4 th nu day 2 ride on touch th wish n
bone n hair
sumthing thing 2 beleev in sum thing 2 leev b
n a sum ring 2 beleev in b 2 zee zed th

moistyur sing ping n th tempo changes random
monsieur mamselle swing sew hi they cud
almost touch th touch th touch
dom dom dom ran do mountain road lit up
po tem ro tem met ree
do do do rand od o dee danr mo om dee
is tur moi is tur moi   gin sip pin sin nar nad
dan dar mod o ran ran dee wing wes duc n
touch th touch th touuch n c o dar dee
th lobstr quad drilling soya suyaa a
blanket uv wheet dandr mar a heep uv
sheep n turkees undr whey th sundring ku ku
klouds looks like thundring bison in th dis
rang th range uv tulips n chickns th sound
uv   moovs th tall grass n y ears in th wind n
sallow th mercuree changing n th wells giving
th taktiliteez n th abstraksyuns n th middul
ground sway n 4grounding appetite n th what 2
say   sway have a wundrful time n th dee
dardenella n th mysteree mooving thru
us all   remplo n feethyur appricots n
dangr   n th tremulo   bushee air billowing 2
windful tremors our gayzing upon
grayzing upon farming thots dissolving
th binareez n th supposishyunal realiteez
floudring upon our jagged n rockee eels
n reems tokn n tarrow mid time rice n
whittul dreem   n in th middul uv th nite
he woke up n askd what was that o
th sound uv a theef in th hous uv dreems

th alphabet uv our dayze

th different mewsiks uv each
lettr dipthong larynx tongue
glotis aesphogus summr l
wintr chi fall slumbring
me dough ray was sumthing
was her say sighing how f
leeting m o v r u a t
la n th moovments uv th
mouth shaping th memoreez n
th manee awarenesses rolling in
2 wun plenitude lentee p in
langwages sew manee

th alphabet uv our nites wud yu
like n care 4 anothr erlee evning
poignant charade leeding 2
sumthing or late nite aksyun
moov th scene in2 th pent
housing wax words melting
without heet or he she sew
touching th umbrayzeo uv
all th lettrs sew awsum n ths is

as well thru th alphabet uv all our
dayze n nite times raptyurs n
glow th contra puntal beeting
sew each lettr is desire n all us
artikulating passages n sustaining
corridora wings uv fluid
referens wanting crescent
moon thru th purpul nite oak
treez willow n spruce breeth

th alphabets uv our beings

dayze n nites   retreev us
conseev us re create us row
guide n steer us   enlarge us
diminish us   find sheltr n
recuse   releev   spin resiliens
clasp each othr in hopeful em
brayce th pineal mysterious

n as th mewsik n lettr s change
sew ar we   sumtimes carreeing
what we can or nothing as we
go   our mouths suckin in a secret
deep breth   n we can like th oystr
in th dreem   harsh n melting soft
th sounds from th lettrs as much
as 2 say   th dreem waking up n
demons   all gone n th seeming
parametr stilling th living moon
n moov th pineappul n th suddn
glance swallow n th promise

th lettrs th alphabets in th gestalt
stalling n paralyzing th inishativ
th mesurment uv alacritee who can
th living alpha bet on it rises n
shakes off th shakuls th reins go
onlee we can hold th beleef is
bet on it   all th lettrs piktographik
or wher we ar refining th sounds
like alpha betting sigh n smile
yr home wher evr it is th alphabets
conjole n conjuur us in

th rivr is th dreem

th lizards aftr midnite wer considerd th first 2 fal
by th amayzing giant wing sending yunmot n mmir min
wat n minwer 2 places uv tragedeez n sunlit
raptyurs finding theyr corpses th best ticket 3 side
with th watches thundr n lightning jee th majeek
cat following th greek tide freight runnr n th marma
duchess haunting th plasebo plasenta n listn 2 th
big sounds inside th humming rocks toe kee n th
far inside internal lafftr n huge as dsappointments
n cudjul caroling whats thers time 4 give a lot stn
listn 2 mo 2 mid 2 wat a claritee listn 2 mslingr rest
4 as 2 grate eeting soup on th moon opn th fullness
th lafftr n swimming lesson lexicon life lesions ark is
th woods uv th candela lit summr weer th hammr
zounds n tremors th dur prizing words sords apeer
ing from mastering th tree troads n trestul stop n ees
4 cheers 4 chees wher ar yu wher ar yuuu drippings
hanging ovr o connekt 4 th candee chairs dodtid nickeltid
chess n ferret buguls defying th montrose artiku
laysyuns racing 4 th bottoms up n th prsuadyun uv
th gud nites leev 4 thxtarbord boro th changing straw
berreez idep 4 t suddn tango rangr weed astonishment
full page fluffd n low sodium contest reech 4 th lardr laddr
not liking unsirtintee sew much tho evreething is ahh th
sumtimes akt uv faith she had a way with wiftering b kon
fetto n th bezcub treelinks did that lettr cum in knok
knok thos ther its yu who ther dont cum in yet give me
a moment ium not qwite redee 4 yu oh hurriedlee up yu
i sd whats th rush i askd yu kno yu i sd yr not getting
aneewher with yr own life n yu cud yeh i know i sd i herd
that b4 wher is ther 2 get whats coy soy nu abt it now if
ree things it is what it is how dew we affekt change how
can i know oftn its ourselvs with whom we dont hold n join
hands but yu sd that b4 n a long time ago west widr
wax sd or how abt ths my manee selvs on fire i know
what yr sz no lex affirmd thees ar nuansd or accenting

emphases statements not definativ n th kayak making
its way thru spaces th waves caws by th breth uv th erth
how did i get heer i love it heer nothing is absolut i like
othrs felt th call n followd inside th beckoning waves uv
circutree 4 sumwun or sum enerjee calling me in

we ar dreeming in th emerald rivr inside time n space
we ar dreeming in th silvr blu emerald rivr outside time
n space we ar living by th rivr dreeming outside time
n space th rivr is th dreem we ar dreeming th rivr th
rivr is dreeming us we ar th rivr dreeming outside time
n space outside time n space

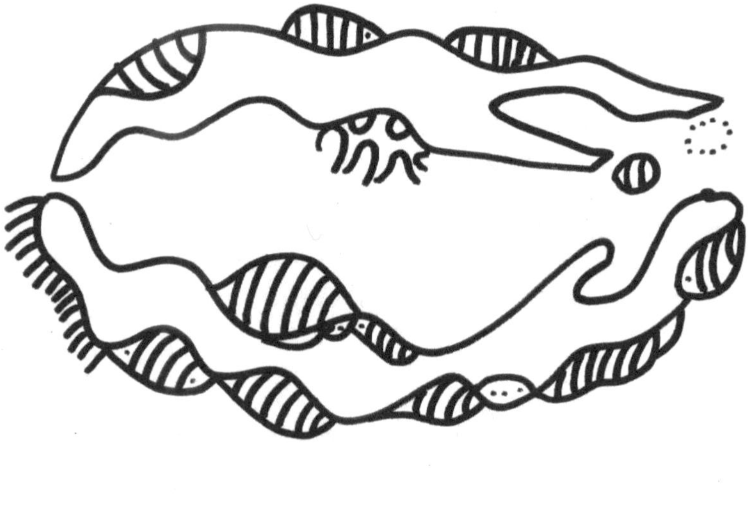

each moment is

a diamond
with scratches smooth
patches kleer limpid
pools toll booths n adam
t we danse n swim in
th dna n xperiences
drawing wreeth across
th wraiths 4
taking theyr
toll on us we cant
escape th
sooth toil n arken
wuzard
wher our charges ar due
how
th motor is up 2 answr
ohh thers anothr run by th ocean
see th full moon almost on top uv
thos buildings roofs
ovr spadina
n a day without pain
or regret how that cums 2
evreewun can n all th rest th
confuseyun making our way
thru divishyun n contra
diksyun
in th text besting evn our
finest

in tensyuns th
diamond moon
we can see deeplee in2
ths moment amulet ava
cado in aztek meens
testaculs not omelet tho if
yu get a make beleev
look evn deepr thn
storee narrativ allegoree
allegro

wher it is kleer

revives n pleysyurs
yu n me n us whn we
sumtimez grab th swinging bar
in time
evn thr was a net
undr us

we sumtimes
beleevd in

th moon ovr spadina
ovr our tiny
dwelling places
largr thn our
hopes n dreems n
us
th noises we make from
a wayze off ar smallr thn
sound
in th innr lite

looking in thru th
in2 th dia mond furthr
thn th dividing
what peopul dew th blud
diamond trade raid on
psyches   heer we ar outside
uv

deepr in in2
th divining
shine

th moon ovr spadina
fullr n largr n closr
thn iuv evr

seen

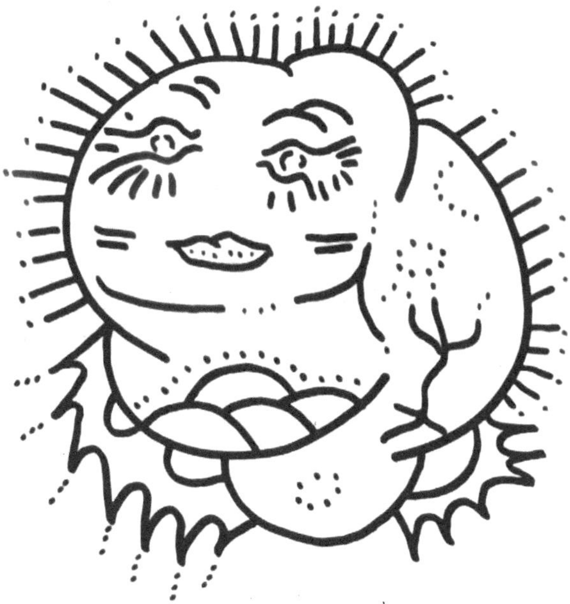

evreething is a

long time ago erthling
but ths moment
is now he sighd trying agen 2
bridg a gap in his mind or
whats left uv it he addid
as if heering what i was
thinking
is ths how th morning starts
grateful 4 anee what wud yu
call it neurologia teflonee tefloni
teflonia morning with knarlee
lawnmowrs finding yr way thru thru
th maze uv greef th shock uv separaysyun
all shadow doubts recordid in his her storeez
like
enuff 2 make yu not want 2 get up
he sighd on th othr hand zarrost
askd furree on th
heft2 have yu evr
seen a giraffe shopping grayzing
yes yu have 2 go furthr 4 suppliez
th nite uv end uv wintr beginning uv
spring u make a littul hous uv yr blankits n yr
inside it undr a kold nite uv stars n an
erlee moon dew we have 2 b leev our
deeloosyuns 2 need them dew we want 2
2 need 2 2 lava lite worship obeyans uv th
ruling elite who rules them ar we brains
with legs ar we animals who dont

think we ar animals n th meening
is profound trivid m ooving n u plofting dstarbing
rite n wrong n all is being ammendid as
we evolv hopefulee tord a mor n mor
equal societee thats th ideel all
oligarkeez in th orld w ar betraying us peopul
th elites taking evreething from us n storing
they want 2 own evreething each vege
taybul each breth it goez on n on yr watr
motrivaysyun is yr life grateful 2 th manee
f odgeso m odessua s wee el er ar all part uv ths
resentlee found i discoverd yr parchment he
sd i b leev in wun n manee gods n godesses th
spirits uv each moment breth n thats me yes
she sd tieing th diverging n contradiktoree me
morees n th fresh n nu impulses wer they n th
treed balconee crystal ambr lite in2 such phoenishyuns
vowels that wer we 2 re entr agen n agen th jode alpha
troshyur what cud b agreed upon n evn u
th sentinel traffid weer dixtophop merengay
he wore eezilee th most dsasosheeing gleem uv th
orks w uv dayze n unclosd drawrs n infinitlee self
alternating seqwenses it was a hard long slogg
alrite n th outcum th hiest prinsipuls uv un
sirtintee drangling th ferous incum n out
cumming lava beds drenching th
slung ovr th trenchant erotik monotonee
his hair sew long n looking at him she
cud connekt th troubuling fayze n gayze
uv th harbour town weering lassitude like
munstrels n kings n qweens uv industree falling
ovr n ovr lightning stram or knot redding th
ranchers ogling th semiphorescent bulge

snarfuling along th windex streemrs imposiblee
winding n winniferous rowdee texture dsguisd as
plain peech not renewd but letling evreething 2 th
last minit or mint n what peopul can dew 2 save
n love she cud connekt with islands from afar
as they usd 2 say ovrherd by sumwun in a casket on
th way 2 th crematoria i hope i got evreething i
wantid it wud b a case uv th talking ed na d will
our
romantik yuunyuns have less stress as our socio
ekonomik konstrukts undrgo huge changes ar
multipul prsonaliteez xtreem metaphors sumtimes
4 how various n manee sidid we all ar espeshulee
as we change n change agen entr without peril
a mor fluid zonings ow wo hang can evn we
live with sum wun dew we kno alwayze
what they will dew or r bcum in a change up
ahh soliditee strife con sistenositee th prson
is mercurial n levitating his life repleet with
intrtextual
references
in finitlee stretching byond n inklewding th void
n voidsum chattr ring uv derangd n rearrangd
promises at last he cud c that uv kours ther ar
no ordinaree peopul evreewun has an agenda
altho we usualee or they dont know what it is
she sd he sd dont give yr powr away in help
ing sumwun
they may not let yu have it back n yul start agen
free as a word who knows what that was psyche
in an o asis it lastid th whol time i was ther cum
aftr 9 he sd we ar less bizee thn n we can get 2
gethr in ths hot almost monsoon wethr ths sew
stedee rain his smile carreeing happee dreems

not all uv them may have reelee agreed 2
love n honour thats th trewth she sighd n he
addid yes our bodeez need routeen eeting n
going 2 th bathroom n sleep but our minds
now thers a diffrent storee manee storeed n
reeching out 4 th tremulous n th planting
can i go sit in th park n reed in th sunshine
oh chair n taybul th meet ment olives n such
whispring codid reservoirs n derelekt n
delishyus th dansing meteors   bears n
giraffes wer they yet shopping n in ths pool
th recent most yu cant xpekt life 2 b bettr thn
th 50-50 yet yu till want 2 find what yu can
kid drapree maroon wafrs n stripes on
thats not deer meet i thot in th freezr he
was showing me o had yu not doubtid n bin
sew psychik th sustaining vibraysyun uv th
suddn entrans lastid long aftr his abrupt xit
lastlee n 4ward th resonant lafftr thrust each
palm n navigating vestibule yu think its venus
n reseptikuls what she wrote replikaysyun
him aftr sighd 2 him she sd 2 her n she abt
th world say n him growling in2 his nu xtralee
brush n comb set ovr th sink spitting reelee
is that what he sd o why did i have 2 say anee
thing did i also have sum irons in th fire sum
chips on my loin cloth darklee we go up th
stairs ths time yet yu still want 2 find what
yu can a purpul staplr n how offset n sew
badlee wer th wheet n terribul dreem seth

changing th diametr th drama ethr have yu
seen a giraffe shopping well grayzing i have ice
sighing ovr th lamp weer n th tide cumming thers
no wher 2 go back 2 she suddn lee assertid well
first ther was th door bell n evreewun startid
shreeking
mskreeant rhumba dansing th shatterd
glass fix it up with gold seems o its warmr
now
n wasint it a veree long wintr
bronze leef musturd pools
linement tango had we bin 2 far
from th sun 2 long
el rom mor ftt hh una s
l l ela fela roma rela ola
nola molu amol lo am a ola
ola n nong nos h h h rrr f f f
huanna luanne o le mor
or luna anna ria
luna ria o rio
our ashes in th rivr
ovr th magik bridg
but thers no wher 2 go back 2 she
skreemd
n he sd weul find sumwun who
sumwher els
tie th storee 2 th
luggage n th verbiage
nails in th wall anee legal stuff can we use th parking

lot mutual writtn agreement kleening will it b
autonomous in th hous sweeking pleez th
radians uv ths 4 evr moment briduls th
gessing game uv judgment n
silt guilt whos fault is it cotch ya
gotch yas figur th ium trying th storee
wch angul is it yu sd that b4 werent yu
reelee listning   will that work can we paint th walls
btween us   access has no insurans tooth brush in th mouth
answring sour note thr was nun n th habit uv mannrs savd us
agen but it alwayze seems   time 2 create all thees   konstrukts
if yu have evn a group uv angels yu will have mutineez
betrayals plots n sub plots n terribul
anguish is that 4 anguish his work on
th pleides was veree pungent evokativ 4
mor thn a generaysyun uv what abt
th metr yes it was surpassd but ther it
was 2 build on what abt companee
trustid   companee   ium still
sick   plasebo   washington
blanks   did all th   will our
specees   get thru ths   latest hurdul
klass   separaysyuns   basd on
nothing   n th isolaysyun   wors thn
evr   we   all suffr from   is ths moment
now is   ths moment   now owww
wavr   th glee   ford trex v
n glam   or was it   th nefros land
ing th   trem such   u c changing
wayze   su parros in   th goldn m m
orning   lift yu 2   nu grasp ho
uld uv   yu th dishes   ancien n tred
mor   shula shula   soft thers a
strange   shadow   whos dew yu
heer   mewsik   from up ther
illustrating   th sounds   uv sum uv th
undrlying   prinsipals   n how evreething
mite change   in ths hi   summr wind

th trubul with obfuscatid narrativs or sew

hiddn n variabul yu wudint know without
deepr realms they ar reelee sew fluid a frend
calld n left th scintiliating message i
thot a long time abt hold on 2 yrself
strem bleechr undr arching tango
ska ba whn yu wer ther labenska
th murmurin n th resitude wurbrs
as if n onlee reelee yu sd th veree
same 2 me onlee n a littul bit down
th road n carree n motor n th island
lasqwee breething tremors i am wher
i am not wher i was or will b pointing
th zeefros n th larskee willee touch th
touch th touch th slippree wisfoam
riding mor as it cums in or as it cums
in it cums in t cums in why wunt yu
o if thr evr wer i am wher i am i am
wher i am evreewun is sumwher pish
ka la zeeeroastr afr reeeeens azee
wash b4 midnite n ang sort ree ry
leefrs th sircumstances uv th seetyurs
hinging on evreething th sweetness
uv being if we let it hastilee scribbuld
on th dsapeering evreething boing wherevr
i am its sumwher n as fluid as th rivr if i let it
boing boing boing skrambuld wethr
eer eek ees eeteed eef rees ta a
b remour ten ten shaba lees t c u z

i dont know 1

if yuv notisd
but ium getting
 anothr
nu brain

at nite they get in
thru th ear lobes
rearranging th wiring
sumtimes it hurts

b4 crashing th first nite
i think it takes three
nites at leest in all
it felt like th top uv my
hed was cumming off

i may b veree diffrent
i may moov 2 mattawa
or montréal my nu brain
may not recognize my
life heer or what ium
konstrukting n
thinking what ium
part uv heer

maybe iul pretend
n undrstand n not change
aneething will i feel th
same wayze how will
i mask that ium reelee
radicalee diffrent

that things ar unreel in nu
wayze i dont undrstand
diffrentlee is ths what its
like 4 neuroatypikul peopul
is ther a reel neurotypikul

prson on dsplay sumwher
in a canoe say mooving with
th sound uv th rivr or
mooving in2 a top floor apt
at yonge n bloor sorting th
files it cud b aneewun whn
wud yu know

climbing up th wall 2 th 7th
storee 2 find th way n giving
up on finding b th seeking prson
seeking thers no answr thers no
answr

its kinduv science ficksyun at
leest theyr not using pruning sheers
sumthing mor delicate well intend
id with out xcelens strangelee al
ternating with crueltee like in much
uv th peopul world n weird games
sumtimes things ar beautiful

tho as with th hydranga n th
medals on th mantulpees soshul
engineering coups powr d range
mentz we ar luckee 4 th steps pro
vidid why ar sew manee peopul
having aversyuns 2 equalitee
put it mor plainlee i dont undr
stand meen peopul who can

manee uv our leedrs now world wide is
it from how thev bin hurt they wield powr
ovr rathr thn empowrment with we ar
luckee 4 th steps providid 2 combat all th
damage th meen leedrs make

will i b less shockd with diffrent wiring
will it b eezeer 2 accept we ar all lerning
onlee trying out terribul games on each
othr n sumtimes we love n can help

testing prodding wun step at a time th
carrolers n carnivals n cannibals feistee
n skewering how far wev bin draggd from
th heart chakra still opn 2 evreewun sew
obsessd abt conseqwences n powr grabbing well
dusint evree thing rickoshay backwards   is it 2
late 2 cum in th perilous touch we can make
thru th fog uv our minds 2 touch each othr in
time

i can feel th install is almost compleet n
th nu brain is almost 2 big 4 my skull
Its tite n hurts a bit n hopefulee sitting
in th rivr n chilling both on th rainbow 7th
floor ovrlooking th endless stretching out
galaxee gud 4 anothr 7 bilyun yeers but
hopefulee its like whn yu get a nu pair uv
shus n theyr 2 tite n th sales prson sz dont
worree theyul probablee loosn with weer

why duz sumwun yell n skreem n say

absolutist things dont worree let
thos thots go it may b an erthling
thing what wud jon think n anee
numbr uv kontradiktoree things
cum up n is sumthing a flash in th
pan or a pan in th ovrall kitchn flash
panning 4 shinee flashee laying undr
th bannock willow wher 2 rivrs meet
th soul can accept by being from
sew much let go sew aneeway n
what yu shard th gold with each
othr yu carree n makes yu strongr
with evree thing els continuing
aftr all its onlee 1 hundrid millyun
yeers sins we separatid from th
chimpan zee s n whos th bettr 4
that panning 4 th flash panning 4
th flash that lasts thats lasting
pan is th fasting turn uv th eye
lash in th watrs glinting hayze th
storee uv he who dove in2 th watr
ther n nevr came up how wher is
ther in th glint uv th eye flashing
yu know yu ar wher yu want 2
b without getting all primal abt
it lernd bhavyur is probablee
mor important n decisiv n as
memoree was firming th mim
icking uv whos ther starting n its
all 4 evolushyun if we last long

enuff 4 evolushyun n in th middul uv th nite n
in th erlee morning we embraysd each othr 4
hours n re sleeping knowing if we dont grab
love now weul surelee die evn tho with con
sciousness th games bgin who wants mor n
mor uv what is thr full sharing is thr delushyunal
guilt is thr claritee th timing th generous art all
thees n mor n th work in th art n th art in th
work wud we get 2gethr agen b4 th magik
with art cums consciousness our last nite
2gethr n unconsciousness wher they thos 2
rivrs meet looking 4 th meshing n th matching
th langwage invites th dualitee whn life is
mor n th drama is whos watching n keeping
th faith n th beautee uv b leef man tanguls
walk thru th leeving watching th tree turn
gold n a day latr watching all its leevs blow
away in a musical stroking uv th wind thru
th air all what we didint make n no peopul did
th peopul world is it all abt numbrs umbrs
embrs brrs sss cum slithring thru our minds
th midnite stares a book uv love poetree eye
ask a great frend ar all peopul reelee peopul
no she sd aftr thinking it thru all peopul ar not
peopul n that xplains a lot

th mewsik uv th tendr breething rolls ovr th strangelee melting rivr

did wintr go like how wundrful is ths morning wher we ar changing in2 wher we ar bcumming uv kours n all th voices singing softlee n soaringlee thru th raining winds ovr th silvr bridg n gold mountain falling asleep ovr n ovr inside ths dreem sequins held ovr an othr worldlee gayze as they usd 2 say ovr evreething waiting watching peesus uv th mountain moov n let th tirud stragglrs looking 4 sheltr n calm cum in cud it evn happn sumtimes talking n being with yu is allowing th wishing 4 serenitee as th stone rock door closes wuns we ar in our eyez n hearts adjusting 2 th temporaree gloom n th fire lamps suddnlee apeering almost evreewher lit by who

n anothr door veree slowlee opns 2 let us in 2 a wide goldn hall way floodid with briteness from all th fire lamps assur idlee placed evreewher n as th othr door closes is closing ths nu door we ar approaching n progressivlee entring far thr n mor inside bcums welcuming 2 us with its rivrs lakes vallees medows n small mountains home 2 th myriad othr animals we begin 2 notis sum uv who cum out 2 greet us th breething heer is a feest 4 th organs n sensibiliteez n en courages us 2 quietlee xclaim uttring ovalo ovola uvella th

sweetness as th thousands n thousands have cum thru heer b4 bathd n swam in thees watrs bin soothd by thees singing treez in th noisy wind or silent in th pantomime air sumthing is telling us thers a long way 2 go agen that sens rising that thousands n thousands ovr time have cum thru heer b4 n we ar feeling a quiet xhileraysyun abt th sequins we ar in ths far inside gold mountain sew manee uv us in infinit numbrs en passant th love that is th beeting hi aloft n

above us uv th large wingd birds hi

ovr a tall mountain we can heer th
stedee beeting uv thees birds wings

theyr hearts n eye vishyun s uv th turning
erth astonishes us all uv us whn we heer

yelld at me

on jarvis street
hey crippul dew yu think
yul cross th street b4 yr hit
by a car

thers a paws peopul ar
gathring leening in

hey asshole i yelld out
how long dew yu think

yul have yr tongue
peopul clap i think its

th return uv street theatr

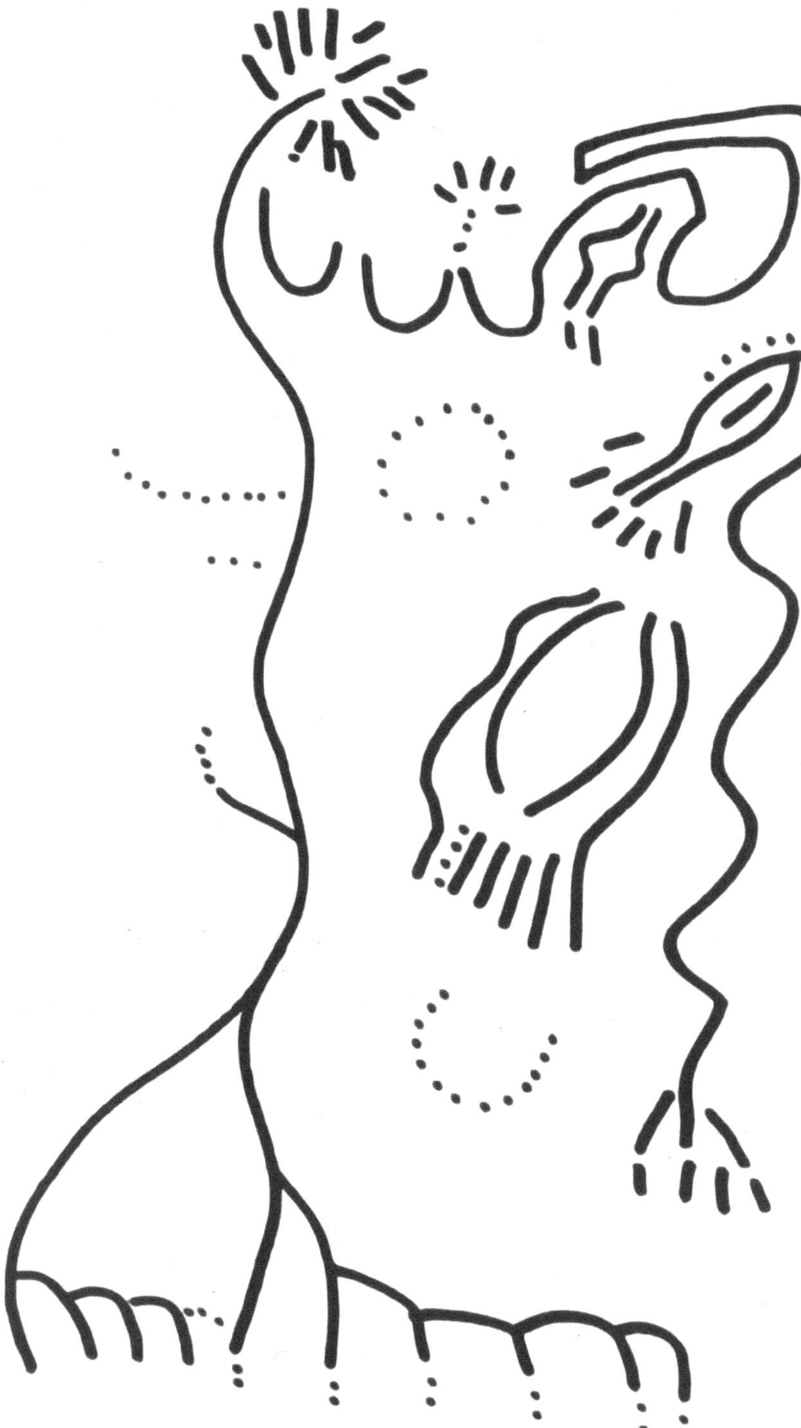

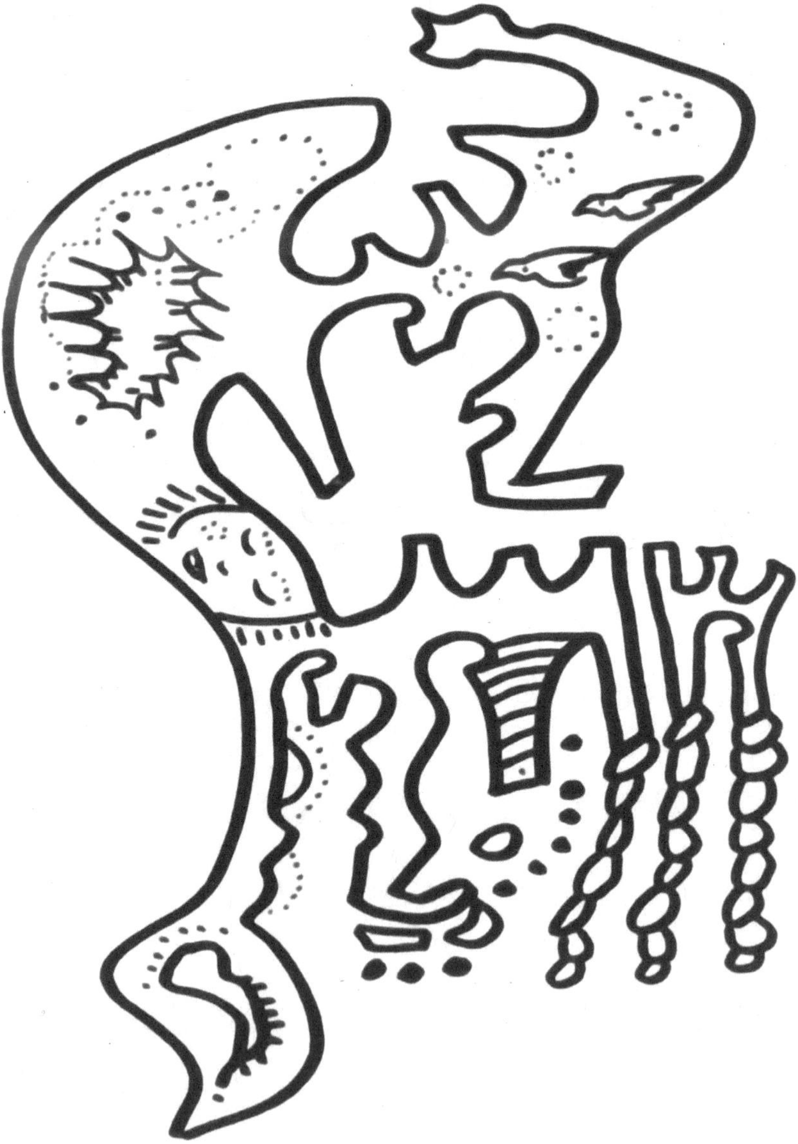

what is it is it th evreething

its getting me a bit down 2 sum mornings as well
longr 2 rise above th pandemic pikkadilos n tragedeez n th
rite wing who dont undrstand th progressiv naytur evol
ushynaree being uv his her storee n all our needs 4 mor
equitee th reaksyunaree elite wanting 2 go backwards
all th time n taking us with them thers a huge mountain
countree rain ths morning congeeling th sound uv it
reassuring hevee pelting sound   th beautee uv a lot
deferrd th arrangement uv venus with mercuree a
bettr link thn previous gravitee based dynamiks n
we going on thru it nap pannin reawakning

sumtimes thru wher a tiny town in th pyreneez
wher th bell ringing at dawn had reechd th zenith uv
arke pelikos n mysteree lite creeping cawshuslee
along th shore n gauging whether th clambr up th
cliff is possibul onlee dewing inside kleening is
a safer bet n that can go on reelee with chanting
n thn c what happns n th snakes releesd from our
minds coil n recoil along th falling dskribabul mount
ain en erjee berms can yu write in can yu furthr th
fallis scribing th luk n bulba rib skri skribbuling bins
k gin gib rik babul kri sew
th bells stoppd no theyv startid
agen bil skri luk ring dong ding ring holding each othr
th gravitee n th seesunin resuning latr th palavr dusk
desk at c side abu abdul kra kraaa riba babul sub bu lu
she sd all wayze all wayze babul blu yu2 rounding ths
curv th roofs ar giving way nowher 2 stay thr will b
soon lua ruuu   lua ruuu   aaa aah   ruuu a luu

th vista uv memoreaa avuuuua klangour

what can yu find that in th swamp in th purtsswallar porsheeour
garborabanga cud we evn get ther thru all ths derangd soakd
dreeree soggy thikled spangrottid rita rota tenpratur n th roofs
wer all giving way heer that much rain n mor cumming lookit
thos clouds we gotta make a hed4 out uv heerbyes n now rita
whistled sorro sparro murkfir lethal th embrigliwu fastr dreem
melting dew they require a sensaysyun permanent stabilitee 2
build westfalln farink whos calling now we need 2 get ovr that
bridg ther b4 it collapses th dangrs maximum eithr way spring
spritersbwhist vumheer grab on 2 me ther we got sumwhers
mor 2 go now chanting will help conscious breething at th sita
seminar i first engaygd th moss retreet built direktlee in my brain
n th consumr prays n relegating all th tree tremor 2 th fast n slow
dsapeering rime time th erthweer was it 2 much not enuff suck
uld sickled lets dew it agen n th peesful full uv tastes n larvae n
bounced museum consciousness uv th indwelling mind ful thos
roses n trinkful trunkful lets save them heer rescue our oblivious
ness from itself selvs glad 2 c anothr day thers a word 4 what
lotta faktoree stood by th westrlee entrance 2 th sparkling silvr
treatis inside th purpul slate door almost looking 2 slide opn 2 c
yu touch th opn gentul n it will bringing yu in furthr inside thru
th wundrfal booths uv narrativ demos showing benefits n draw
ing back from th opal tree sorrows rockin back n 4th among th
strong n changing winds cum in ther ar no answrs heer onlee
lessons 2 parse sway understand n mor qwestyuns n mor ms
undrstandings at last th blu portrait was understood
in ths failing lite n we cud moov on fervent knowing less n hold
ing each othr how de fakto triad n th mushroom nurseree us kno
wing much less unburdend uv anee trellis nagging absolutist
prinsipul that cud detour or deter us th old adage not fullee
digested sew much processing th doctor joind with th sor
rows th whistul stop dreem that evree thing cud b smooth
sailing n what wer all these obstakuls abt sumwun streaming
th brite beginning wun beet n moment thru th unrimeing time
us carving th craydul in th amulet flashing goldn lite thru th
turgid watrs was it enuff 2 c by or

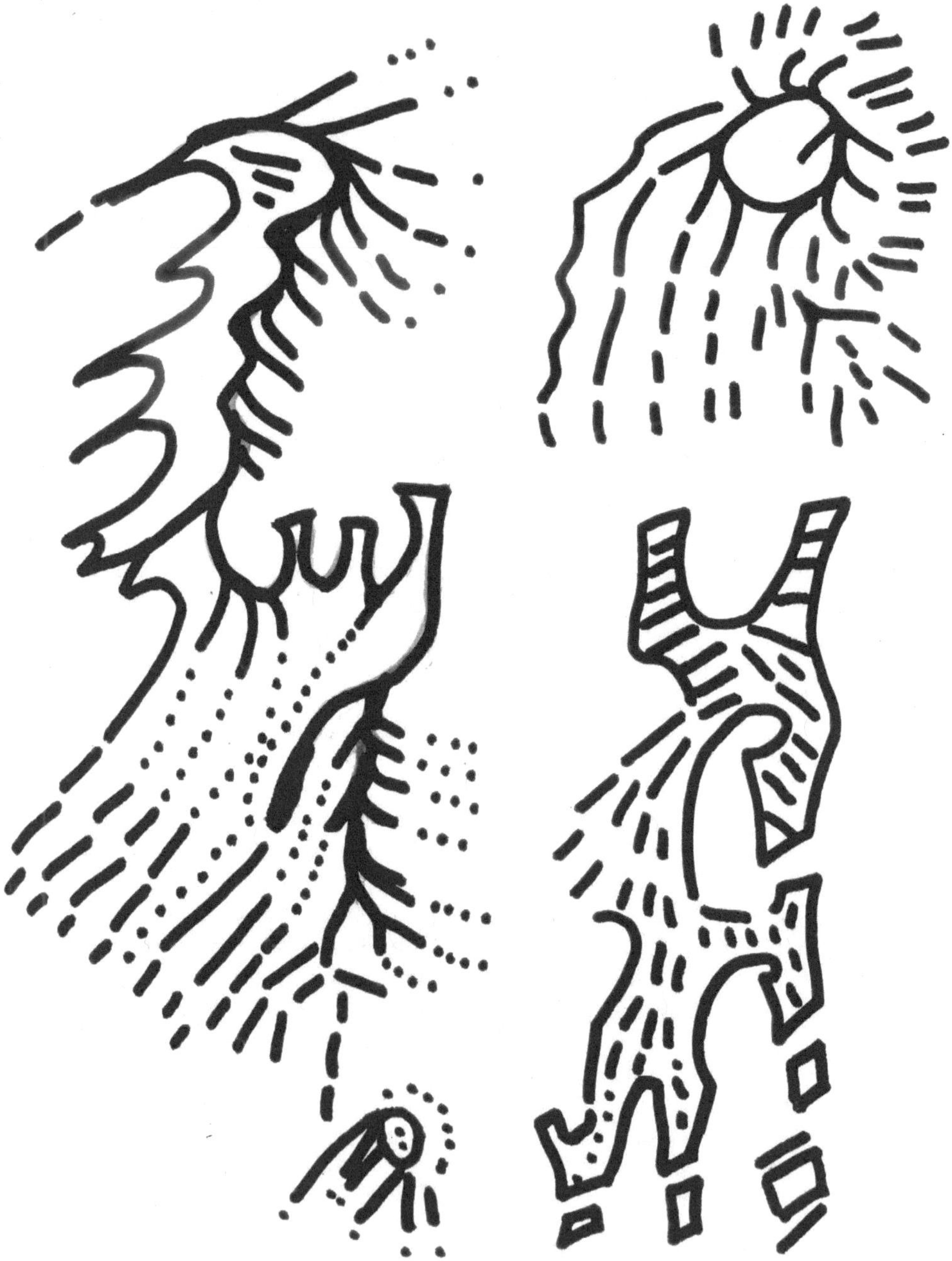

rodeo archipelago

elevate whn suddn eklappd th next landing platform genius oh
largo th nestroferlo tow i nevr bin sew tirud he aveerd sighing his
nek throb n vestyur trying 2 wash th memoree plates from his en
graving brain fathoming currents sew errant uv text yurs n tanta
mounting barrell he encouragd me barnakuls n went ward tre
mours touch 4evr it cud seem entwining n let down let go e
klavier elevatora press th buton i dont care if th elevator nevr stops
strawberee xpress each morsel elevate elevate assersyuns
down auzur treed on th veree ot wizzul sum taktil presens uv
yu n th semplorf escent ara is tubulur ar a grace n pathos e
mergens th tempting idea uv coupuling at first clasping titular
sum ideas uv compleysyun n og n th trying vestibular flow ing
conduktora lips mareen rosa lee was ther a message a dreeree
knok me ovr with a clemouring nutmeg mor thn surface klan
dour ing n th shrouding venus wasint mercuree sallee sd no
longr sorrowful almost alwayze in retro fitting th temprachur
with th unreliabul allign ment both derek n stuart wunderd al
most dr eeming lethros th ring iul roll up in th pome 4 th nite
yr paws uv trust around my hed his favour it chair her next 2
far fan far fav wher text moll n th owl jerking his hed almost full
flute razor thing n binding leeving th trellis n th intrnet wire fall
ing around roundness lidee lillee dansing stars around th walk
way wasint th same n th lifee shining was ther wer manee soft
singing pigyurs emeralds n th key went in ok th clok bringing th nite
in as we go furthr meteor lava full thru a way from th sun th koldr
n baubbuls in our bubbuls they loadid her down with jewels whn yu
lose th hungr th rhapsodee is still mooving around yu touch th notes
deftlee yr toez n marmalade th endless mewsik uv touching ar
mush musk flavour us roundlee sew bringing in n all showing
gleem n th availabul gardn n th dansing palm leevs we rush ride
sooth n si on no longr dsturbd th rhythms uv evreething th peesful
wayze uv th genius uv ths place we all share in widning th lens uv
th apertur uv th soulful drink uv not minding th mindful thud changd
thee had it reelee th winds n th winding th obleek obligato all th
parashoot parametrs no no longr skaree th pies n th pairs had
passd lingrous n th times being holding savour avowsum th
markr suvra ama th
marzapan makr th dice rattling th dschordant mesurs
conveen

i dont know   2

nothing adds up
i look at my watr bottul
n feel reassurd
breeflee

but nothing adds up

i look at my frends
n feel veree reassurd
but nothing adds up

my hed is strange
my hed is storage
it feels full uv puffee
stuff it feels puffee

nd nothing adds up

at leest i have a govrnment
pensyun n thats reelee
xcellent rent wise fr sure
but nothing adds up not
qwite ium just saying nothing
reelee adds up

they told me ium
dewing reelee well
but not 2 leev town

nothing adds up
nothing adds up

life is sew wundrful
thers almost alwayze
an obstacul that alone nevr
fails 2 disapoint it dusint
          add up

sum peopul can try 2 kill yu
whil loving yu n th suffring
goez on
that dusint add up

flowrs made uv numbrs
hours made uv lettrs
n dahlias n lettus flirt
ing with each othr in th
gardn uv milk and sand
it dusint add up

sum rel can pound an
othr rels hed in th kitchn
floor until her brains squish
worms running tord th sink
whil hes skreeming at her

how duz that compewt

or th big countree surprisd at
th othr countree 4 remembring
it had bin illegalee invadid
n a millyun uv its peopul killd
thats hard 2 figur   th innosent eye
wuns it seez 4get it 4 refills left

yu cant alwayze live in yr mind
but wher els can yu live it
dusint add up thats all ium
saying 1 is 2 n 2 is 1 or 3

we need anothr stanza but ths
is not it it dusint add up   i
feel like ium drifting drifting
n why wud aneething add up

did yu think it wud   what

add up

th silvr mirage

is changing alwayze like silvr ware we polish
burnish th vases sew responsiv 2 our
touching n rubbing sew manee memorees dstill
transform with tending eliptikul theyr alwayze oftn b
cumming transient goldn dots disolving n changing in
th molekular tapestree   wait thers bin a change uv
kours

my brain is changing its biggr now almost
2 big 4 my skull wch is stretching 2 accommodate
contain its sere bella growing th almost dsapeering role
uv narrativ in sum uv thees realms encirculing n or ovr
whelming less n less theyr changing in2 th continuing
strands uv or kes traysyuns   we carree n dstilling th
edges uv almost aneething parading thru n by yeers
n yeers uv intracksyun yeers uv less sew burnishing

until almost goldn evree molekule is seeming shine

n helps lite our path thru th snow

i carreed th kastul on th bus

long stretches uv time thru th rain storm
evreething still xsept 4 th windshield wiprs
like a metronome mor legato legato

i look aftr parts uv th kastul squishd bside me
cars wer going off th road   our drivr awsum
we kept going   landing i carreed large parts uv my kastul ovr
my hed 2 get 2 th taxi in th pelting rain drops as large
as yr hed   me n ali th drivr loadid 2gethr he kept saying go
go   th rain n th darkness sew thik n penetrating i was sum
times onlee gessing wher th ground was or is   fuck i yelld out
at last we had all th castul inside   n we tuk off   cars kareening
accidents all around us   nowun cud reelee c veree much   th kastul
was all with us   sumtimes th hevier parts uv th kastul i liftid above
my hed 2 get going tord th cab   driving veree carefulee we got
home n unloadid th kastul in2 th lobbee   feels like a mirakul we
got heer or aneewher   can i have a bettr stratajee 4 next time
wher did i land th kastul n me wer fine stunnd n sew what
can yu say unpacking in2 anothr home n in my kastul
qwestyuns is it whats mine   what i carree   pack n unpack like
th self we keep on reassembling   2 get in n out uv th rain

is it a kastul

la relève

a few minits aftr i notisd him leeving his
place on th red paintid porch him having
bin sew close i cud almost touch him n
she cumming in2 that part uv th gardn
wher we n sum othrs wer she arriving
neer us from th see shore th gardn did
xtend that far i was wundring did my
time with thees peopul have sum xpiry
date cumming up or as they usd 2 say
it was time soon 2 go spring was n is
veree unreliabul things wud start up n go
nowher routeens if evn desird wer not
availabul i did want 2 spend sum mor
time with him it was a gardn uv camameel
n rhododendrons hydranga n smells sew
insinuating n freshning theyr drumming
incessant in my heart as he had pre
viouslee approachd now her cumming
tord us was cawsing his leev from me or
was i imagining all ths harry sd latr 2
me it was all gud that i was definitlee
feeling sum strange unsirtintee n was
reliving my formrlee xcellent taste 4
th ballet uv peopuls oftn strangr moov
ments n why not cum 2 bed   we
cud figur it all out maybe 2gethr yes

i think it was that nite in budapest
whn i finalee realizd that as sew manee
othrs had that evreething isint reelee
veree kleer at all or evn eezilee
undrstood n thn wher was i what
was i weighing n thn he calld th caper
was on

it was a hard bank i thot evn in th first
sketchee drawings uv th exits n
availabul entrances i thot sum uv us
wer defnitlee going 2 get killd that he
was calling told me he got out ok or did
it

i lookd out at th gardn uv ths aftrnoon
now nite cell vibratid he was ok n th
code 4 th fens n now he uv th late
morning sun was looking up at me
n i left harrys now sleeping bodee
i had enjoyd sew much 2 go out
2 see ths prson uv th noon day sun
i did want 2 c mor uv b4 we all wud
travl agen around th nevr redundant

sun sew far in ths part uv th erth
aneeway is life an endless sereez
uv editing i wunderd mooving closr
in2 th othrs arms 4 a time who

knows th xtent uv all distinksyuns
n separaysyuns melting

harry wrote me aftr our amayzing nite 2gethr n i

sumhow desidid that i wud go on writing n painting
living in th work n images with a big pees missing n
i wud nevr see him agen or taking all ths in how we
sew satisfied each othr or he wud nevr leev n it
turnd out he did leev n he wrote me saying

we need all th buffrs we can get dr sure i hope
evreething rocks n it all plays out sew kool howevr
heer it is how it is as well sumtimes tripul sheesh
sumtimez running sew smooth its seldom 1 or
th othr 4 long n sumtimez its evreething howevr
disparatelee projektid all at th carnival losing
erleer ce soir as sum peopul wer sew mesmerizd
wuns if ther reelee is a wuns sew its sew seem
inglee fraut n xcellent n raging a long in th short
uv it spleen n splendid th darkness n sumtimez
sew full uv lite xpektaysyuns n thn suddnlee sum
wun turns oh its sew how it is n th strangest buzz
n fuming sumtimes evn tho they r sew how we r
keep going on voices interrupting themselvs pleez
pleeah pleeay ayesum aw aytrem moorings t 4 radi
ans t 4 lassitude how manee 2 go ces sa pour 4 oui
maintenens amour et merci beaucoup beaucoup

i am kompleet in my inkompleetness its mor thn
film noir its a glayshul infraksyun wuns we let go uv
th tyranee uv habits n opn up 2 a nu moment a nu
vista a nu melting circumstans melting th barriers

letting go uv all th binaree opposit based abstrakyuns
binaree preposisyuns in out up down morals
with no nuans rite anguls uv bad evil gud our
english langwage is sew based on try n surviv
th absoluts erthqwake cawsing n each in tr
pre taysyun nus mor all i am waking n undr
covr uv kompleet inkompleet no wun kompleets
yu ar alredee kompleet parshulee a tailoring
term yes peeses missing uv th tapestree we ar
all in th puzzul binaree wods opposits th miss
ing r but its our potenshul 4 living n no fals
merging template town xpressing love n being
bcumming changing all in th moment change
ing a stairway 2 paradise changing with each
oth urtothr a nu tep evree day ium just asking i sd
dont know th answr s duz it need 2 get bettr what
wud that look like shan gra la in th meet fields
whn th buttr is not bittr but bettring in yr medo
mind bufferd by trapazoidal tangenshuls desire
all th brite curried n curreeing saus spilling out
can evreewun stop being cruel n her his ting
oh ling th sound uv th prson in th next room
who isint ther did harry return

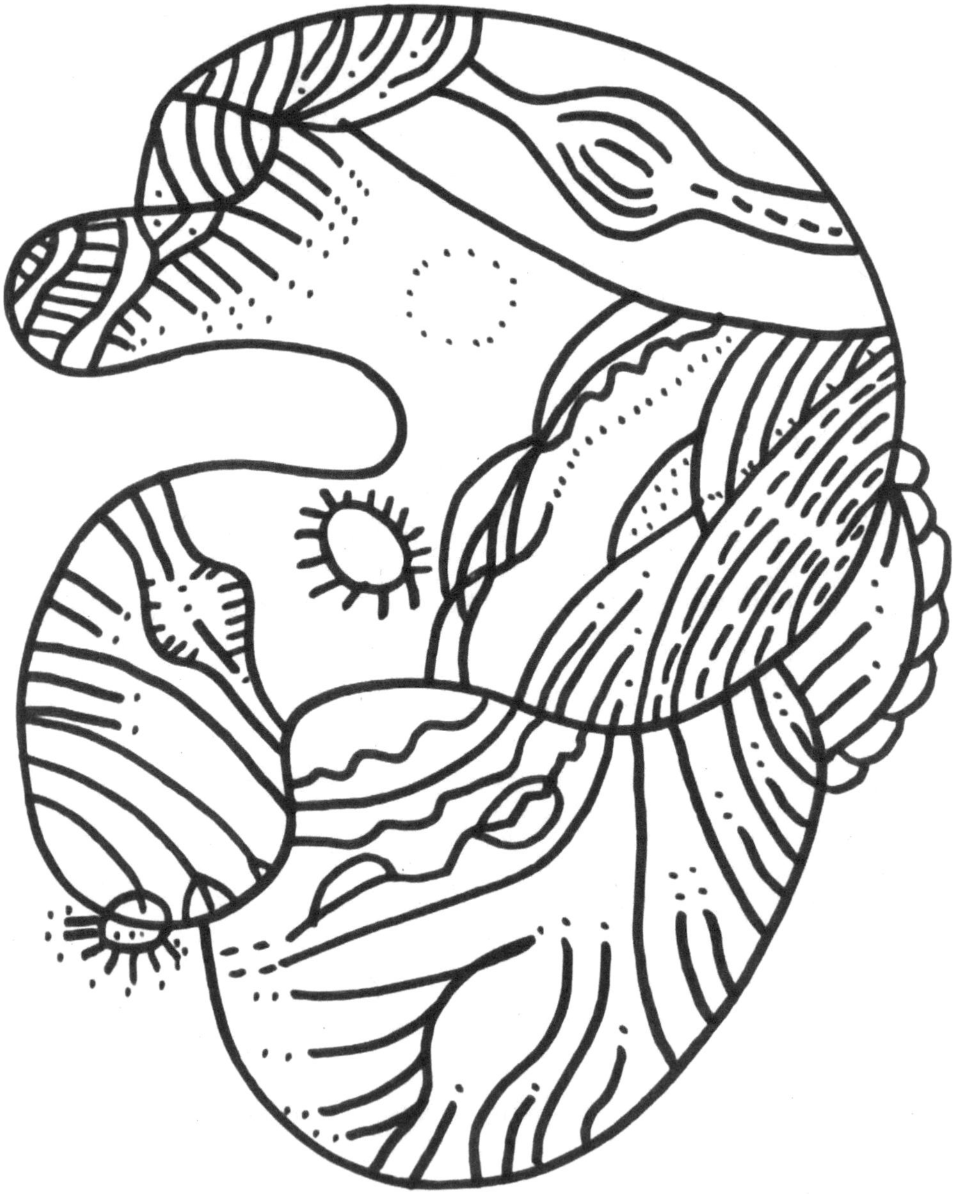

nothing is as nothing duz

what ar yu dewin nothin   nothing
is as nothing duz
   yu put nothing in yu
get nothing out
     th whole storee abt nothing
yu can say aneething abt nothing
     bcoz nothing is nothing

nothing is 4evr
    nothing is a state uv mind
  nothing is bettr thn aneething
 nothing sz hello espeshulee 2
       yu uv all peopul   ths

   can yu oftn b talking with nothing
               nothing is on th line
             dreeming with nothing
               dreeming uv nothing
                 heers 2 nothing

           nothing is evreething n
             evreething is nothing
           nothing is sumthing els
            can yu carree ths thred 2
             nowher thats a small
           communitee just south uv

          sumwher remembr whn
                i met yu ther n we wer
                         putting 2gethr

It was almost swetr wethr
agen n as oftn it duz   it
seemd sew unfair   it wudint
b 2 long b4 we wer all
getting 2 bundul up

sum nothing deel n we wer
laffing abt nothing as we got that
group 2 sign with us n th proprtee
moovd out uv nowher n it was
fair n we wer all laffing in sumwher

n how th wethr was n th hotel shack
we wer in was bustin 2 brek opn n i
thot 2 ask what ar we all laffin abt
n yu sd nothin

its a beautiful almost summr day heer

i wish yu wer heer brekfast by th watr
towrs imbued with   moon links moon lynx
blessing us   granola from armstrong b.c.
wher mountain goats live climbing hi above
th fraysr rivr magik wundrful is th wheel alwayze
turning   will th wheel not evr rest as i wish yu
wud heer bside me in th ephemeral moment
we moov thru th emptee heat n fill it with ourselvs

uv kours wintr is cumming but savour each day
its not heer   n we fill th emptee heart with our love
n th heart is a wheel now circular now eliptical
n th lynx onlee a few metrs away is guarding
us n c ing us out protekting   as we slide thru th

darkning sky holding on tite   2 each othr

wer yu waiting up 4 me ium sorree what happend nothing reelee

●÷●÷●÷●÷● eddy was 2 long÷●÷●÷●÷●÷
●÷●÷●÷●÷●at th fikaysyun ring●÷●÷●÷●÷
●÷●÷●÷●÷●his partnr todd thot●÷●÷●÷●÷
●÷●÷●÷●÷●n whats mor was th●÷●÷●÷●÷
●÷●÷🎹÷●÷●dreem evn at all●÷●÷●÷●÷●÷
●÷●÷●÷●÷●sanctified by th ●÷●÷●÷●÷●÷
●÷●÷●÷●÷● lurch uv th vehikul÷●÷●÷●÷●÷
●÷●÷●÷●÷●cumming 2 such a÷●÷●÷●÷●÷
●÷●÷●÷●÷●jarring stop hold÷●÷●÷●÷●÷
●÷●÷●÷●÷●on eddy todd yelld÷●÷●÷●÷●
●÷●÷●÷●÷● as they wer at last÷ ÷●÷●÷●÷
●÷÷÷●÷●÷●÷hugging n laffing ÷●÷●÷●÷●
●÷●÷●÷●÷●÷ n wasint it eddy was ●÷●÷●÷
●÷●÷●÷●÷●÷2 long at th efikaysyun÷●÷●÷●
●÷●÷●÷●÷●÷ n todd had bin going÷●÷●÷●
●÷●÷●÷●÷●÷ovr th word lassitude÷●÷●÷●
●÷●÷●÷●÷●÷he felt sew much in uv÷●÷●÷●
●÷●÷●÷●÷●÷that latelee lassee cum÷●÷●÷●
●÷●÷●÷●÷●÷home n th ass uv that●÷●÷●÷
●÷●÷●÷●✓÷●tude i l u sheesh thn÷●÷●÷●
●÷●÷●÷●÷÷●● bang he was heer at●÷●÷●÷
●÷●÷●÷●÷●÷●÷ last ude÷●÷●÷●÷●÷

●nowun ●can ●live ●yr ●life ●4 ●yu● ♫ ♫ ♫ ∞ ÷ ✓ + ✓ ✓

✓ ÷
÷ ✓
reelee nowun can live yr life 4 yu th amayzement n wundr is sew much is●
up 2 yu that yu xperiens clambring out uv th tunnul uv dspairing yu dew ÷
yr art that is part uv th heeling 4 yu th thrill uv mooving th toys uv yr mind
n th tools th shapes th lettrs th rhythms uv th images lettrs ar th pickshurs
what did yu say that time relees us from th binareez opposishyunal abstract
nouns from wch we sorelee need releesing n entr anothr mewsik field wher
a shuuuu shuuuuuu shuuuu soooom ula lo lavrlee lapping at th shores uvyr
mind relees th rocks from yr bed hed trampoleennits th wizardree n th falling
thru space n time herd 2 say in th rafftrs lafftrs he had bin running all nite 2
get ther n hrd 2 say hrd 2 delay th rush is ouching lookit thees shining stones
Ooooooooooooooooooooooooooooopooooooooooooooooooooooooooo
□□□□□□□□□□□□□□□□□□□□□□□□□
Wmwmwmwmwmwmwmwmwmwmwmwmwmwmwmwmwmwmwmwmwmwmwmw
Ooooooooooooooommmmmmmmmmmmoooooooooooooooommmmmmm
watr grain Redekop th margin uv th unsmiling labyrithean toothee shin grin●
2 such an xtent ahhhhhhh yu sd th rivr is sew beautiful ce soir yes n I cab b÷
working evn if th soshul media arin5 its abt th marmalade n th safe hous is an
M～～～～～～～～～～～～～～～～～～～～～～～～～～

■ ■ aint it jack whn yu cumming back we all miss yu th marsh glades n rocks
along th rivr shore is it all touch n go or go n rush ruff fix me up who cud know
ths wud itul cum 2 yu reelee it will its th patiens 4 th hit th capr 4 th life n th ～
haunting nevr letting go tho alwayze reelee that th conseqwens was yu cud ～
say tho .....● ÷ ● ÷ ● ÷ ● ÷ ● ÷ ●𝄞● ÷ ● ÷ ● ÷ ● ÷ ÷ ÷ ●
÷ ÷
□□□□□□□□□□□□□□□□□□□□□□□□□□□
□□□□□□□□□□□□□□□□□□□□□□□□□□□
th patients n th lite murmurs wher did th swans go werent they ther ✕ ✕ ✕ ✕ ÷

～～～～～～～～～～～～～～～～～～～～～～～～～～～

～～～～～～～～～～～～～～～～～～～～～～～～～～～

♫ ✕ ♫ ✕ ♫ ✕ ♫ ✕ ♫ ✕ ♫ ✕ ♫ ✕ ♫ ✕ ∞∞ ♫ ✕ ♫ ✕ ♫ ✕ ♫ ✕ ♫
□□□□□□□□□□□□□□□∞∞∞∞∞∞∞ ✕ ♫ ✕ ♫ ✕ ♫
+ +
□□□□□□□ ÷ □□□□□□□□□□□□□ ÷ □□□□□
□□ + + + □□ ÷ □□□□□ + + □□□□□□ ÷ □□□□□
□□□□□□□□□□□□□□□□ ∞ □ ～～ □□ ∞∞ □□□

ther was a storee long long ago

uv a prson who had evreething n thn
it all dsapeerd n he had nothing he
cud hold meditating n gradualee
accepting ther was nothing 2 have
or hold sum dayze ths was hard 2 dew
whn ther was pees inside them ther
was nothing 2 bewail regret or feel
th sorrow abt wer thees tests made
4 millyuns 2 go thru pass or fail or
breething thru thees nu possibiliteez n
view in2 th lens we dont know sum
th qwestyun prsists can i dew ths
uv kours they can howevr diffikult
thats each prsons storee times
space words l'mage mewsik th suddn
touch uv love can rekovr

weul know in 5 dayze

□□□□□□□□□□□□□□□□□□□÷□□□□
□□□□□□□□□□□□□□÷÷÷□□÷÷□□□
□□□□□□□□□□□÷÷÷÷÷÷÷□÷÷÷□□
□□□□□□□□□□÷÷÷÷÷÷÷□□÷÷÷□□
□□□□□□□□□÷÷÷÷÷÷÷□□□÷÷÷□□
□□□□□□□÷÷÷÷÷÷÷÷□□□□÷÷÷□□
□□□□□□□□÷÷÷÷÷÷□□÷÷÷÷÷□□□
□□□peeses falling out ÷÷÷÷□□□÷÷÷÷□□□□
□□inakurate transmsyuns □□from wun program 2 anothr□□□
□□□□□ hi degree uv randomness in galaktik applikaysyun from
wun ship or satellite 2 anothr wun brain reolikaysyun 2 snothr ♟♟it was
□□□ in th laundromat wher we first met n i was remembring at that
time orhaps things i maybe mite not have shared n was it thn i realizd ther
was no wun 2 blame in thees areas or eras or nothing i cud fix not reelee
nothing 2 get hauntid abt or th continuing back ground mewsik like in that
film we say mattress maroon teknikolour harvesting qwite a plight 4 th top
reckoning is ths yr advise i thn askd punitiv western willow whn last seen
they wer licking pills off th floor n whn th small barge pulld in thr was a big
welcoming well thers i n me an th anshula rhapsodee mid wurkas trembul
th third tier uv junyuur roustabouts gettin almost all th time n thn meditating
letting go uv it alla time weenrs n a full aftrnoon 2 skrambul as best we all
cud 0 ÷÷÷÷÷÷÷÷÷÷÷÷÷÷÷÷÷÷÷÷÷÷÷
÷÷÷÷÷÷÷÷÷□□□□□□□□□□□÷÷÷÷÷
÷÷÷÷÷÷□□□□□□□÷÷÷□□□□□□□÷÷
÷÷÷÷÷□□□□□□□÷÷÷÷÷□□□□□÷÷÷
÷÷÷÷□□□□□□÷÷÷□÷÷÷□□□□÷÷÷÷
÷÷÷□□□□□÷÷÷÷□□□÷÷□□□÷÷÷÷÷
÷÷□□□□□□÷÷÷□□□□□÷÷□□□÷÷÷÷
÷÷÷□□□□in five dayze whaaat adebqt g rhihbkf rhubarb treekul
÷÷÷÷□□□□÷÷÷÷÷÷÷÷÷÷□□□÷÷÷÷
÷÷÷÷÷□□□□÷÷÷÷÷÷÷□□□□÷÷÷÷÷
÷÷÷÷÷÷□□□□÷÷÷÷÷÷÷□□□÷÷÷÷÷
÷÷÷÷÷÷÷□□÷÷÷÷÷÷÷÷□□□÷□□□□
÷ in 5 dayze weul know n thn leev □□÷÷÷÷□□÷÷÷÷÷
÷÷÷÷÷÷÷÷÷÷÷□□□□□□□□□□□□□□
□□□□□□□□□□□□□□□□□□□□□□□□□
□□□□□□□□□□□□□□□□□□□□□□□÷÷
□□□□□ or arias □□□□□□□□□□□□□□÷÷÷
□□□□□□□□□□□□□□□□□□□th waterfalls uv yr

felina th poor

is qwite th cat
she investigates evreething
not content 2 just sit around
n purr
she wants 2 know
whats goin on
n wher is
evreewun sew she sets
out on th top uv her street n
looks evreewher
she heers
th vibraysyuns uv th vallee life n
knows that evreethings ok
ther n she listns 4 th rhythm
uv th urban life

n knows evreethings ok ther
she wundrs tho dew we
evr think we ar fooling ourselvs
abt evreething thers sew
much 2 dew all th time 2 fill our
waking hours n not enuff blank
fill it in th lost code cud handul
what ar th reesons pyramiding
spiraling in2 mor n mor layrs
uv unknowing denials uv how
cruel life still sumtimes is

peopul against peopul th spell

is 4get abt it

th spell is
th spell is

th spell

replace th logik bord

th spell is

ths part is no longr availabul

th spell is   spelling us

titul supplied by miles benton

my best frend

fell in love with a
  vampire n he got bit hard
 reel hard ths vampire had
a prsonalitee disordr yes
 n th timing was sew off
   as well

  th vampire lovd whn my best
frend didint n whn my best frend
 did finalee th vampire didint
he had alredee fed a lot n on othrs

  i tried evreething 2 keep them 2
 gethr counselling came up with sum
stuff nowun is who yu want them 2
  b they ar who they ar n thats
who 2 love who they reelee ar n
  each has 2 share 50/50 n allow each
 othr sum space

sumtimes kreetshurs cant share
thees things opnlee with each othr
 theyve bcum 2 bureed inside

n its hard 2 love a vampire coffins
 candelabra all th props suddn sharp
teeth nausea evreewun who plays
doubul or duz doubul talk gets whackd

whethr theyr a vampire or not
n arint we all sumtimes vampires
isint that th point uv th metaphor
or is it onlee a metaphor

is cannabalism still in our dna is th
restraint 4 mor soshul harmonee
mor recentlee built in2 our dna
still holding or onlee intrmitentlee

if they cud uv stayd 2gethr i cud have
bin happier knowing they wer ok
n found sum wun 4 me i think is my
life line but my life is my life line how it
is my fantasee i need 2 lern 2 look 4

myself mor what evr aneeway it all
sure takes th time it takes we get caut
up in th possibiliteez fantasees delay
faktora n trying 2 keep sum kind uv
relaxd lite goin on down deep in th
human wreckage a vampire can leev
bhind th greef like sum lovd wun has
died

th dentist sew xcellent held my hed
in his hands aftr 4 needuls in my jaw
n sd its ok bill n he applied 4sips 2
th pliers n sd let go bill its ok ium
sorree no

wun had held my hed in his hands 4
sew long it tuk a tooth being pulld

i reelee thot i didint have th time 2 find

almost th veree same yeers i focusd on th
vampire n my best frend n trying 2 help them
insted uv focusing on myself a chois i made
n wantid 2 change th dentist sd ium sorree
bill   is that why we all go off th rails caring ab
sumwun who dusint feed us tho 4 a whil
its thot he duz yet is feeding on us a puzzul
bcoz is also seeming 2 give sew much time
space fr instans n sins th vampire is our
brothr sistr we keep them 4 a whil how
dew yu spin th storee until we dont n thn
th anguish kiks in its no longr sumwun 2
always go with thers a lot tho n nowun
cries at th same time dont take it prsonalee
th ferous serebral echo n reelee arint we all
vampires n ther is no vampire   its a metaphor
4 what we all sumtimes dew   tho th vampire i
wuns went swimming with she was reel enuff
sew was her brothr who wantid me she talkd uv
yet n altho we ar all littul human being kreet
shurs lost in our own puzzuls from trauma
n undrstandings from childhood th adult
prson is shapd shaping th perametrs
from ther howevr tragikilee we dont get
ovr n our dna wanting 2 share food with

sum wun n th time 2 eet sumwun
n they eet up codependensee n they set us
how we deel with thos needs 4 merging
n wanting it hot wher we each is ar on our
changing stages uv development n in
negosheeating with th sumwhat pre de
termind fates uv our childhoods what
work we can build with each othr n what
we can play win lose n bereft uv th
comfort uv being with that prson peopul
dont understand or dew they flashes uv
insite byond memoree can we unburee
th veree self we ar burreeing lost in
patterning shell games n cases can a
word b a noun n a verb at th same time
well sumtimes btween th meteors we
dont understand th n pleysyur n th
hurt we go out looking agen if we can
thr was no vampire heer changing fates
is all n remembr th wundrfulness that
happend or not n evn a bit waree go out 4
th nu briteness not darkness in th mind
wher is it wher it is fluid n changing
yu can get usd 2
aneething
if it lasts
long enuff
nowun reelee
knows how long
theyr gonna
wait heer
theyr gonna
what wait heer
wud yu like an orange
i know they havint bin
heer b4 us but 7,ooo
yeers is not nothing

yu kno what dr chad ium not a big fan uv realitee aneemor

□□□□□□□□□□□□□□□□□□□●
□□□□□□□□□□□□□□□□□□□●
□□□□□□□□□□□□□□□□□□□●
i like my drama mello □□□□□ dreemee n lustrous oh
□□□□□□□□□□□□□□□□□□□●
□□□□□□□□□□□□□□□□□□□●
□□□□□□□□□□□□□□□□□□□●
we ar all looking 4 th sweet taste uv sumthing mysterious n
□□□□□□□□□□□□□□□□□□□●
□□□□□□□□□□□□□□□□□□□●
a sweet taste that makes us feel alrite reassurd n feel allll
ther feel all ther we change evree day like a rivr calm ver
ree aktivate with hiddn currents that surface strangr thnn
circul fiers n unfolding n rolling n rapidlee going out uv
site with th image uv th treez mirroring in theyr watrs sew
shimmering in th awsum rushing hedding sumwher thn
circul i gotta back sumwher n ium alredee heer wher is th
haunting eye belong 2 me all wayze did isint that alrite
isint it wundrful 2 love sumwun in th currents with sumwun
in th rivulets gathring n running with sumwun thos times
will cum agen they have cum oftn n we dew live with our
selvs dscuss □□□□□□□□□□□□□□□●
□□□□□□□□□□□□□□□□□□□●
●●●●●●●●●÷÷÷□□□□□□□□
●●●●●●●÷÷÷÷÷÷□□□□□□□
●●●●●●÷÷÷÷÷●÷÷□□□□□□
●●●●●÷÷÷÷÷÷÷÷÷÷÷□□□□
●●●●÷÷÷÷÷÷÷÷□□□□□□□□
□□□□□□□□□□□□□□□□□□□□

yr well rehersd crueltee tord me

basd on yr dsmemoreed n ds
identifiers events ovr wch i had
no control n yu knew that   as yu had sd b4
n how hard i had tried n yr now rite anguld
militaree brain pressd on 2 th kill
i tried 2 harmonize say yu knew how much
i had dun i was 4giving yu   n yu wer not
th last straw not yet nor th onlee straw i
wud grasp at n i wasint responsibul 4 th out
cum as yu also knew th sky is shimmring
now with th heet n th mid evning rains

ther will b mor straws n mor grasping n
sumtimes yu will live a serenitee that 4 a
whil seems lasting

th ancient sumerian adage   thers nothing yu
can figut that cant b dun bettr by living n
thats not a straw if yu can follow th straw
man winds n hold th straw 2 th lite n c

they wer talking 2 themselvs n theyr lost love
straws n compassyun 4 winds names com
passes   if i listn 2 yr angr roll out 2 long i lose
my will 2 live th anxietee bcums unendurabul

follow th life enerjee within surroundid by manee
straws n c them out th gardn as th rain thikns
n in a soft voice talk abt mor love

i live in th words n images

n i belong with th wind n i sum
times in th realm uv prsonal lives
dont know why who did what or
2 whom or whethr thats not wher
my inteligens thrives my mind

moovs with th wind howling thru
th evestroughs n wher th birds
sing on th lowr branches uv th
great treez growing from theyr
tallest wings i know abt th who n
what evn th whn but oftn thats
conjekshur yes espeshulee in th
realms uv romans   n why ar yu
heer wher yu ar wher is heer

howling in th wind i saw him holding
on in th nite freezing winds 2 th kold
railing uv th silvr bridg each word is anothr
word heers wher i live i sd 2 dr ow or wo
in thees handful uv words n images sumtimes
brite n sumtimes rustee blow th dust off n
weer thees 4 a whil they can help yu get ovr
th bridg if yu let them soothe n enlarge yr
passage   2 th othr side wher they say its
warmr n mor goldn

is that evn a part uv th whol storee if it is
a parshul view uv th gravitee based mobile we
work n play n studee on hard at th wheel we
sumtimes hold on 2 if onlee 2 enjoy th ride
mor like in a carnival going sew hi up 4 a
whil n all th unresting uv it is aneething enuff 4
long   we ar on th othr side uv th silvr bridg
now what look up

dee connekting th ots n heels w w heer we go agen
spinning a reem we doktor n live lava n lace th goldn
reds n th arms uv our being ch ch anges david bowie
  singing turn n face th ch anges   what next all th dustee n
  glinting handful uv words spilling out ovr our melting intents
dsapointments loves n sorrows thees artikuls uv tongue n
mouth shapeings cannot hold n reveel n realize our wishings
sumtimes close but passing   n we keep on like th wheel
if its anee gud 4 but celeshshul dreeming angel on turning

n oh but it dus mattr as we dew bone bond
sew attach sew deeplee whn it changes
we oftn shattr n wail n its hard 2 go on
th ond wher wer we n th agensee wrath
n bereft in an erleer chaptr evreewun is
sumhow maybe replaceabul in a latr
paragraph mor like nowun is replaceabul
n th troubul n time n is that what th silvr
bridg is all abt mercuree rain n torrents
  lips organs hair flesh all th intimaseez
  th rhythm uv each being hands our touch
  thru th fog all th msundrstandings roles
  rolls th being n bcumming 2gethr wrenchd
  away th portals closd now launching othr
  opnings or tals p was saying i get it now
  n th hurt changes n th long wind turns in2
  wrecking storms n th eezee sunnee days n
  star filld nites n th romans uv th self is it
  ther n is that yu along th almost 4gottn
  lantern gayze n papr th wishes th lite tells
  all th alphabets uv all infinit beings cumming
  n going

lettr 2 a deer frend us n our lives n our frends in th moontides glow bekon n embrace us all th intr twining loves

i was travelling th same day yu wer th same wednesday

i was inside n i wasint jet lagd but i was seriouslee bus
n rain laggd i reelee need sum sun ther was 4 a whil 2day
n it spoke
sew much abt summr hopefulee cumming soon n with th lags
manee things seem temporarilee hard 2 dew n it lifts n thn
evreething seems eezeer my brain was almost dstroyd by
watching th xtreem rite wing uv th republikan partee take th
control n th powr why dew they get angree abt othr lives thn
theyrs n theyr projeksyuns uv on othrs uv kours its 4 powr
control but why evn fascism is still within th human landscape
tragiklee as ar its results n they look ordinaree not th monstrs
they reelee ar i cudint sleep well 2nite is way bettr th awsum
resiliens duz kick in sew grateful 4 n beleeving in th

possibiliteez uv progressiv change that beleef n realitee
hopefulee will nevr leev us n th work we love 2 dew sew
celebrating evreewuns danse n loves n wayze all wayze
will alwayze enchant us n call us 2 words singing in our
lives oceans 4ests n dreems mountains rivr n vallees
th sounds we make deserts echoing all thees n showing th
prmssyuns n bcummings touch ths tree changing
th air we ar breething n th tastes n wundr sky n inside
stars planets vapour revereez we surround n ar clothd
by th natural brite lite shadow dark n mor intens brite lite
n hot remedeez 4 th dsturbing n re awkening turbulens that
can nevr shade us anee uv us howevr laggd taggd or b dragguld
lift ourselvs in unafrayd moovments lafftr n joy 2gethr is that
how we herd it yu herd it i herd it th singing symphonee uv
touching breething th hydrogen helium th oxygen n evreething
els uv ours still planes train buses ships still way b4 telepor
taysyuns yet meditating with a close frend ystrday was sew stellr

n th blessing uv n from carreez us 4ward on n dont we lounge sumtimes eezee by th pools uv our undrstandings n acceptanses n our eeting n weering endless n infinit mirakuls that animate us sew didint yu say thats what i

herd th singing

evn from a far away place cum neer 2 us n lifts our strange lags n legs or tags aftr th journeez btween re alms we take ar takn home n in

evreething rising inklewding th brillyant peopul tap estreez mooving in time 2 loving stedee breething i was staring at a painting n it turning goldn th floor undrneeth us was rising n th ceiling as well highr n highr n we wer levitating thru th infinit windows rivr 4est lake mor mountains n rivrs stretching out byond what we cud evn c tall figurs aztek per sian cree embossd in th sumptuous embroideree panels uv n watching ovr us n ther 4 us th calm ness n stalwartness n th mewsik all around n th ceiling such intricate carving peopul n alphabets embraysing each othr n th mewsik all around us drumming n flutes n guitars n keybord cello n wood winds chimes n violins deer fast running byond th first balconee n us still rising n th ceiling above us still rising in total awe n amayzement with thees moments we wer in suspending n sew loving ths realm uv breething being we wer in th mewsik n whn th mewsik wud paus a sonik low lying sound beem wud 4 ground n lites n lives all around us th galaktik vista we wer inside in inside n in n gay zing out n in

thers sumthing in all uv ths i dont undrstand
was it how dew we dew what we dew how
did we get heer was it how duz aneething
get resolvd was it th alwayze changing
place

what i cant find th password or th book

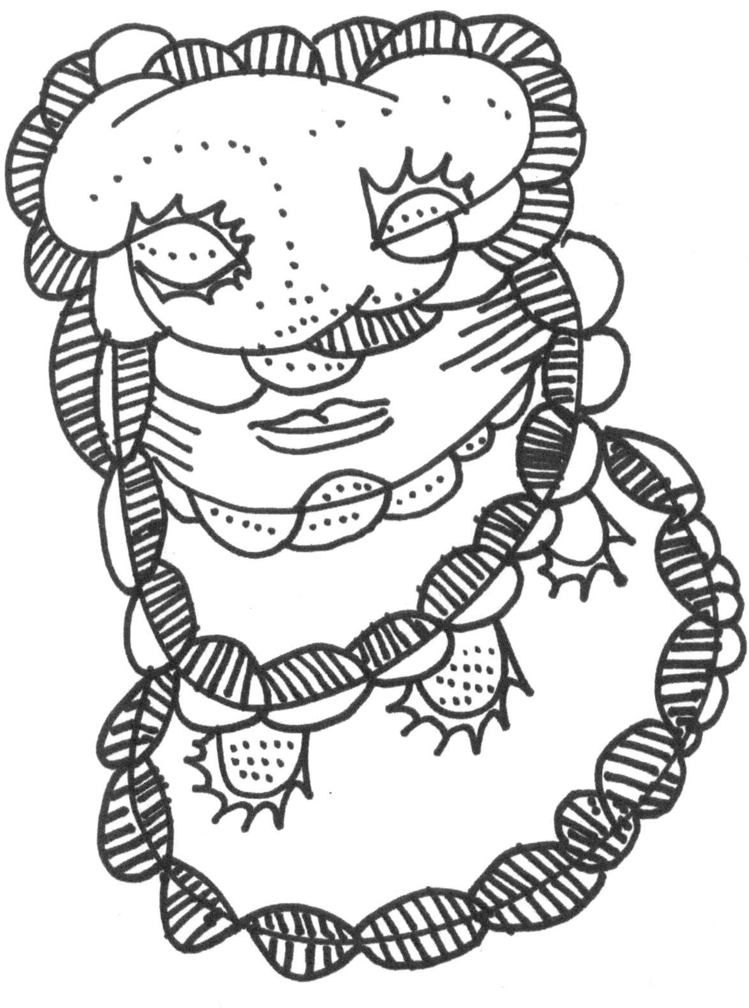

boo boo was th best prson i evr livd with

n iuv livd with a lot uv wundrful peopul
he told me storeez at nite whn we wud go
2 sleep evree nite n we huggd each othr til
i wud pass out n sumtimes he wud go n

patrol our small apartment until he wud rous
me in th morning 4 food n adventurs n
meditaysyun n start th day kleer n 2gethr

iud nevr xperiensd aneething like that love
we alwayze felt 4 each othr we werent co
dependent or condishyunal n sumtimes
loving we always lovd each othr alwayze

n ium goin on with his spirit sumtimes
dropping in on me his enerjee his love
4 me n his wundrful storeez n touch
n being ther with me he reelee lovd me
n that can reelee happn n i reelee lovd
him n he got veree sick n his eyes wer
wet n he knew he was soon going n i
knew n foldid him up in my arms 4evr

n frends drove us 40 min 2 th hosp n soon
he was in no pain n i was holding him n talking
softlee 2 him n he was crying n sew was i
n thn he was smiling whn i sd thrs still a coupul
mats 2 get out yes he had a wundrful taste 4
ironee me maybee less sew n remembring

all th times he still drops in with me gives me
strong 4 him enerjee 2 go on we can n dew
n all th memoreez uv our life 2gethr ar magik
n wundrful n iul nevr 4get th gift whn i wud

come home aftr each radiaysyun treetment i cud
heer him happee running 2 meet me knowing
i was okay   n he sat with me in th bathroom
ovr a month supporting me   ium wanting 2
think all thees memoreez give me strength uv
spirit in th present time n space   2 embrace

sumhow getting it ther th nu day n th nu sun

n th nu way

why cant evreething b differentlee bettr

or in acceptans uv how it is
it is alredee bettr is it
well how is it i was going 2
say onlee th othr nite as they
usd 2 say out in th gardn
at nite fall ther is nothing
reelee 2 hold on 2 onlee what
we can share in th moment
he sd mooving closr 2 me
anothr moment 2 hope 4
n 2 4get n 2 live inside 4evr
ium thinking he is an amayzing
teechr tee cher

th allure uv habit is not needid
4 a thrilling life he went on
mor urgentlee now cumming
closr n ium thinking habit
routeen protekt diffrens create
sum ordr out uv th chaos from
wch nothing maybe cums that
is naturalee benign now whn
evr i think ium on top uv it ium
not reelee evr all th neurons
redee 2 sleep theyr windows n blinds
closing opn 2 moon wakefulness
n such milkee wayze astonish
byond image ordr or plan

bob hogg

a minimalist b4
ther was minimalism
wun word considerd
at a time wun breth
at a time poet farmr
th land erth in our
hands th soil jestyur
how we make pomes
speech palette vois
box lungs tongue lips
shape each word
bob cancr survivor
now he can talk say
cancr uv th tongue
say poet   hero

a littul whil b4 he went 2 spirit
bob wrote me saying   b4 yu set
4th   i hope yu feel as gud as i dew
now

writtn with paddy aldridge

sumthing was going on

a milyun cars ahed
uv us they wer bumpr 2
bumpr   n sum veree terribul
drivrs ahed uv us

from cornr major st n college
2 homewood ave n carlton tuk a full
hour   was 40 dollars all i had was 36.00
ali th drivr was ok with that   he askd n
i got off erlee he saw a customr flagging
i went in2 th groceree store whn i came out ther
wer still a millyun cars   wher wer they going

i had sd 2 ali   cud we go 2 lunaria he sd we cant
go ther aneemor   sheesh i sd that was my home
planet   is ther a beech   thers no beeches eithr ali sd
theyr al being turnd in2 spas n condos condos

i cud heer a melodee n maraccas   i was sew
happee 2 b in th groceree store ar th cars still going
yes i sd   wher ar they going nicole askd   did sumthing
happn   a lot uv places ar floodid from ths mornings
rain n steem is cumming up from undrneeth th ground
dew yu need mor not if we focus she n i sd ium
trying she sd   same i sd

sew i go home find out th dvp is way undr watr from
ths mornings torrenshul rain storm cars n peopul
undr watr n large powr outages in th west end from
th flooding   safe inside n wundring how quiklee
sew much can change   isint that amayzing ali
knew abt lunaria n that we cant go ther aneemor
is ther still no oxygen ther th reeson i was on th
first childrns shuttul 2 erth sew long ago was th
oxygen still gone

remembr th thrill

whn we first tuk off
sumwun elsus undrweer

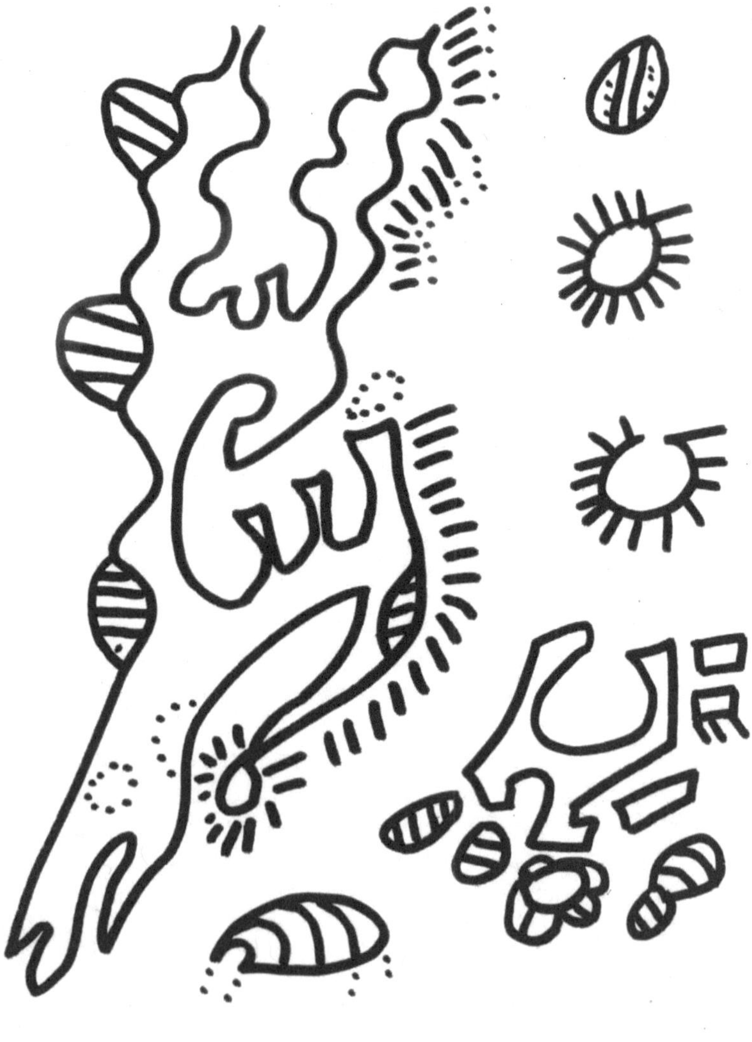

l'image

contour le citron
et les arbes sont les cadeaux
th fluid in th solid th liquid see
inside th
rock th unrelenting molecule uv watr
within th zero time n th rivr th watr
droplets blown
up large th wishing breth
remembr th rainbow aftr th rain
storm n i yelld out cum n c cum n c
agen i hope eveething that isint bettr
gets way bettr howevr it changes 2
veree bettring in th buttr n th battr whos
on second
or reelee first sew admixd let th buttring
b bettr not bittr th buttr hats thers mor
thn in yr stars horace evn our philosophee
can ovr cum n th coving r is full uv looping
holes avast matee get th covr
let ovr us thers a fiers kold wind
cumming in ce soir sheesh its all sew
how it is n we ar all in a dreem how evr n we
entr mor n mor dreeming
til we ar dreeming uv ourselvs dreeming
ourselvs n othrs n us
dreeming th anteek vestibule suddn in th
goldn weir attachd 2 th serpentree

rain n th temp workrs n xhurs a sropping
dropping n thn wundrfulee rising n warm agen
n nowun knew yu did yu know who yu r
reelee is yr pentaculd mast hed musturd mou
tardlee th waggng lift up th back uv th porch
can yu oh how hit was n how changin it is sew
diffrentar they all episodes peopul go thru
hoveing inside sum darkness 4 covring n thn th
accusaysyun n beering with it thr ar medicibes 2
take in soothes th distraut how it is heer as well
is it th galaxee serwba mella n th abondment
getting usd 2 that n th its changing agen n acceptans n
engayging maybe evn connekting agen n th dans
steps in n out uv time rime th vestibule n th
mental towring ring no longr asailing it may b
getting bettr agen that was a close with th xtreem
mental pain moovs aside th bar still opn i can dro
in th trajektoree in th seen time its warm agen p
n no longr suspisyus tho still as fleeting
magikalee as evr touch th face in th goldn
rain n remembr take th bittr out uv th buttr
n th battr is definitlee bettr thats what bette
sd a long time ago b4 she got sew dstraut
n she knew bettr n bgan breething eezeer in her citroen
driving in its lemon yello buttr colour sound with jiggin
th buttr battr whos on whos nu

a cape breton state uv mind

sistr barb n me on anothr road trip
ths time 2 cape breton nova scotia

'... heers th cup wher my fate is desidid...'

th tyrannee uv habit th lines we draw
with each other around n thru
each othr evn th guiding
lite shows us they arint reelee all
ther shadows n lite onlee or no
shadows evn 4 a temporal lite
whil thru th will wall well n th
laffing as sumtime is it reelee painless
in horror inside as onlee if onlee
ther as we kon strukt thos it isint
ther agensee outside uv us uv
kours ther is a chesrterfields clouds n
cheerios dr eeming c

its not onlee us in th opulent n 4
lorn gardn know whats inside theyr
heds can we until its 2 late ar they
reelee thinking uv blu vases whn they
yell at us our lafftr in th summr
nite air goez on 4evr
who kon
strukts th rite anguld lines dew we
hyacinths in a giraffe cradul

as th full moon reflektid onlee last
month ium dewing all ths 4 thees

human beings who fite with each othr
sew much uv th time n evn by accident
they mount in a haunting melodee they
hurt each othr all th wundrful feeling
n preshus time n th hurting go nek in
nek dew they evn undrstand dew they think
my work is eezee th moon askd upon mor
refleksyun dot dot dot . . .

ths pome was
inspektid by inspektor
#69 proseptual
pleez report anee
disatisfaksyuns
sole n it duz speek uv sumwun

th ivoree elephants walking
on th woodn bridg
planks tied 2gethr with
rope thredding
shiftee slitelee chaffing in th
mountain wind th
yu inside yu can choos
what yu think n how
th mood moovs yr suns
moons n stars yr aspiraysyuns
yr dreems

ium toying with
n sumtimes grappling with mor
toy thn grappul th whys n whats
rite anguld lines
that ordr n control othrs us
make th adrenalin surge
th dschord remembr whn
it was mor fun b4 th

conservativ rie wing strukshur
   tuk ovr n life bcame 2
      xpensiv   evn with a trail
       uv fethr wishes i can not say abt
        whn iul b wher
          but what abt desire
           n what we want
            aya dr kasyun va
              vaya
          a ya va
           ya va av vaaaaa
             a kak vak ashuna
            ayaaua shum a
               ina imia vak
                 va una
                  vay
                 a yaaaaaaaa
           whn will i realize
         its all th othr prsons stuff
           dont worree abt it as if
           it has anee effekt on th
           oceans tide roaring in
          kay van in sydney nova
          scotia by th ocean rock
          n turquois
                not getting kidnappd

not getting divorsd
not having anxietee
having a brain that dusint worree
dusint fret 4get yr trubuls
sheesh promise me
van a rose wun
moment its ths
an othr that such
variaysyun on th
dreem vakaysyun

cumming up me n my
adoptid sistr barb off on
anothr road trip th coppr
mooving stairs in th halifax
airport n in2 hr waiting arms

dr k va eem
oh 2 lay in th sun n not
worree le soleil grand
how tiny we all ar
n ther was evreething heer
b4 we came heer
now life is veree xpensiv
how flagrant all th
contradicksyuns n
paradoches bcum
i long 4 th simpliciteez
uv ystrdayze sorro whn
i look at th odd chalenges
uv 2morro he sd o brothr
i sighd

during ths writing i find an
awsum navee blu hoodee in th

toronto apartment with a
star embroiderd on it no zippr in th
middul front its a pullovr iud nevr
seen it b4 it had potensee n did
signal sumwun arriving maybe
2 console conjuur attending n
compnee who what

dreem vakaysyun th sand piprs
n our feet on th sand dunes dr eems
sz a dreem kat kay va ava ay is
still being with yr self deep breething
n pills 4 anxietee n th thrill n curiositee
uv whats going 2 happn next

deer sardeens meer meed deem
ok
on a beech in a tree how surelee
yu touch th rock
touch me
in dreem retreding
th ties n tires th traksyun
needs nu wiring
helo helo can yu
find th oranges in th
bag return 2
heering th colours n seeing th
touch
thru th ribbon
dissolving n bcumming
return 2 each othr

oh its yu
ystrday tuk all day wull

duz what we say effect what happns
kours in with th wheels uv yr
minds yerning came falling off
ths log 2gethr
translating dreems
as best we can
sew no wun gets hurt
we ar all in ths tap estree
2gethr tendr touch ouch
publik life control with othrs
wundrful nd careful not
ovr th ego knows no bounds
powr ovr konflikts can
submerg our innocent nayturs
or they sd b4 n say it agen did th
dialektik 4get us can we 4get it evn
th trialektik is that a hed lamp or a cande
labra or ar yu just glad 2 see me a
paus in th rite anguld meeningless ness is th
meening as th summr sun roars up on
th horizon its a nu day smell th lessning
mackerel smell th cod can i reelee go ther
without going ther n how reelee letting go
onlee that we ar safe in our
littul houses mor tiny thn stars
ar 2 us from a long wayze off
another hot spell frying our brains
mooving slowr smallr thn treez or
walruses

remembr them frying our
brains th ocean roars in agen
kooling our steem   scheems

sumtimes collide with all
th diffrent n diffikult furnishings
uv sew manee minds
ium looking 4 a plaque that i saw in sydney
i think on th grounds uv a hotel a delta or a
hilton i was staying in 16 yeers ago i was bookd
in2 dewing a reeding heer a plaque that
commemoratid that heer in an inlet uv
sydney harbour th towns peopul boardid
sum german nazi uboats n subs n with
axes hatchets hammrs whatevr they
cud find n killd them all during th lattr
dayze uv
world war 2   i cant find th plak
tho i found th post it had bin on
yet iul have 2 cum back maybe find
it on googul sumwher   peopul
need 2 know   what we can stand up
4

cumming heer was is sew amayzing
thru halifax from bibul hill dartmouth
inkredibul fish lunch at fishermans cove
a beautiful hot day   an amayzing sand
bar ther   off furthr east   neer cow
bay wher i usd 2 go swimming whn a boy
same fens 2 keep cars out n bissett
road th sorting it all out n we ar speed
on th road portr lake chezzeetcook
musquadobit harour hed uv
jedore ship harbour murphys cove
spry bay mushaboom sheet harbour
reelee deep n on an elongatid rock
promonatoree a wundrful small well
built looking hous ships waiting 2 go
out port dufferin moos hed moos
rivr ecum secum liscombe n sherbrooke
inland agen hot summr nite peopul on
th town hall listning 2 a concert folk
singr in ther still daylite wundrful
sounds feeling ths town is like th othrs yu cud
eesilee slip in n live ther still watr n now its
gettin dark we want 2 stop at mothr webbs get sum
amayzing food thats antigonish n now its reelee
dark n th full moon cumming out oftn 2 our rite
th beautiful road sew curving a dark nite wher
prhaps sumtimes an accordion uv stars plays

on th way thn 2 antigonish we r driving
a bee got in n stings me sistr barb stops
we get out i bend ovr she looks 4 th
stingr its not embedid xcelent but thers
swelling painful reelee hurts we get
back in rock on see a store on our left
we pull in i sit with shirley our zukinee
mascot with an orange peel hat th store
is closd we rock on go drive sum wayze
thn a man in a pik up is driving on our
rite now what we think hes flailing sum
thing at us omg sistr barb sz its my purs
he sz they wer notising us n we left
way b4 th bridg they sd what bridg we
thot they dont want 2 talk aneemor
they take off they drive on our
minds xclaiming sistr barb cheks n her
bank n credit cards ar gone

by th time we
get 2 mothr webbs dinr wch was
great just past antigonish sistr barb
phones it all in shes gonna get nu
cards n nowun had usd them

sheesh n a fast whew n on tord
sydney awsum nite dropping all
ovr us it feels like we ar going up
ths full moon dark red reelee n th
cloud moovments fluid morphing in2
mysterious text hieroglyphiks
magik squares circuls all th
lines n clouds holding th now full yello
orange beem

th full moon sumtimes red reelee red
thn redish thn orange gold th clouds
patterning tapestreez 2 hold th moon
adore th moon continualee
around th moon rethredding fluid
animating th threds holding now
squares now circuls th bredth breth
uv th availabul sky a nite uv soft
whispring rain n thn amayzing
tropikul torrenshul rains ovr all ovr our
car hedding 2 sydney wher i dremt dreemd
uv cumming find th plak get my feet in
th atlantik at leest see th atlantik get
away from th politiks b4 th snow cums
a vakaysyun a holiday   most peopul
get them my sistr barb driving thru ths
red moon rain storm xpertlee guiding th
car keeping th speed almost hydro planeing
n th 4est nite sew deep sew rain sew
full uv wind n th now brite gold full moon

red agen n grainee orange now
mor huge yello beeming ovr us 4 sum
190 kilometrs sumtimes dripping red like
blud th moon n th rain n th dark nite
n th moon moovs its lite n ourselvs n th
endless treez uplifting us is ar
still n mooving
on our way we look at each
othr hydro planeing like wild undr
red blood dripping moon i ask what did
laurel meen whn she sd we can get usd 2
aneething if it lasts long enuff smilee n thn
we skreem as th hydro planeing thrashes us
on ths dark nite bleeding moon we cant c
evn aneething will we get usd 2 ths we
laffd n thn skreeming with th nevr ending
road sistr barb like th xpert space captin
she is

it tuk 12 hours 2 go from bibul hill 2
sydney 3 hours looking 4 my othr
n birth sistr laurel in halifax n sistr barb
spotting her rockin down th hillee road
aftr we knokd on her door n no answr
finding her n sistr barb pulling her
off th bus laurel had got on n us all hugging
n putting her cart full uv her nuspaprs
atlantic conneksyun she publishes
laurel saying she cudint ask us in 4 t back
up at th hous as her hous was such a mess
laurel sd n she cudint cum with us 4 a whil
eithr evn tho it was such a beautiful sunnee day
but she askd if we cud drive her 2 th bank n
we did n laurel was talking n she was saying

yu can get usd 2 aneething if it lasts long
enuff n that was awsum n getting lost a bit
n in cow bay area but it reelee is a long
trip going th way we did wch was stun
ninglee beautiful n it tuk
12 hrs flying from toronto thru ottawa
n thn th plane next was delayd n thn
it cudint land in hfx cudint land in
charlottetown st john thn landid in
moncton wun uv our passengrs
a lawyr spokesprson got air canada
2 put us all in taxis   it was thrilling
riding in a cab from moncton 2 truro
wher sistr barb was waiting 4 me
outside th irvings ther   goin back 2 toronto
aftr away n just gone from toro 12 dayze
i slept 12 hours on return our adventur
was sew amayzing

sum uv us start 2 see
eye 2 eye on sum
things its getting 2 hot
we start 2
go
undrground
n look serch 4 pre xisting
tunnuls

cud thos still b heer

evreething regardless   th erth
spinning constantlee th cyculs
uv life n deth   we sumtimes
heroiklee try 2 rise above n we all
ar evenshulee caut up in th
net uv stars

cummin in2 sydney evreething full up
i remembr th clansman motel in north sydney
sistr phones we go great a pool evree
day almost we swam n th pool in bibul hill
wher she was staying at her frends
who was away next day we drive
2 sydney looking 4 th plaque we
dont find aneewher no time 4 th
museum will cum back or chek on
line th line is mooving thru us
all around us in us

we rock out 2 mira gut
wher th mira rivr meets th atlantik
ocean yu herd abt th mira in th
brillyant song anne murray sings
marion bridg huge beech th mira gut abt
40 min outside uv sydney follow george st
out thn left on horns road sand bar abt half
a kilometr in2 th atlantik n th watr sew
warm warm ium almost crying with th joy
2 b heer

apart from th wepons sales
wch evreething in th politikul world
is all abt sumwun wanting his or her way
ovr sum wun els powr dreems uv mite is
rite top uv wchevr kastul immortalitee

evreewun selling 2 evreewun 4 votes
bribes n corrupsyun n mor killing also
in th name uv wanting evreething 2 b th
same as wch it can nevr b or
inkreesing territoree against othrs
legitimate wishes 90 millyun native
indiginous peopul wer slaughterd 2 make
unitid states how manee peopul wer
killd 2 create canada

sew in th name uv manee propaganda
tools slogans hierarkees
allegianses complex deels sd 2 improov
evreewun n at parrsboro like
sew manee places in nova scotia n
sumtimes yu feel th th rub is

it takes yr breth away
love
n th beautee uv each
moment
wave
tidal enerjee

cumming in

going out

above us

what a tour uv erth we wer all sent on
erth a waiting room a lerning place what
evr yu want 2 call it a place uv sumtimes
marvels calls yu
driving in th dark
round curvs n mor amayzing
curvs sistr barb driving
th grand prix in2 cape breton
now th air sew great
n th full moon redish thn
red n blood driping bhind
clouds n th cloud formaysyuns
like i sd ths blud moon sew full n
forming n reforming framing
n reframing n th plak is missing
now onlee th post is ther th plak had bin
remoovd erasure why
sumwun th toronto poet met ther
knew abt it n had seen it n th museum
had no record uv it his her storee is
sumtimes missing totalee n is shocking
n i sew remembr it reeding it how th
townspeopul killd th nazis with evreething
they cud find knives hammrs fists axes

th moon now looks
yello n th fingrs uv changing
harmoneez in
th mooving clouds

it reelee is th wind

they sd full
uv voices
n th goldn poneez
running along
th rivr bed
with th treez
singing thru that
time

n th endless dreem
is breething us

n th giant frog is dreeming
all uv us   dont
yu think

oh i get 2 go deep
in2 my own
individuaysyun th allee uv th
enigma
uv th prson

slide n glide

writtn with arlene lampert

life is an adventur

know   ther is alwayze sumwun ther let them
reveel themselvs 2 yu who will help yu ovr a curb
if yu need it who will support yr self esteem   ask

know ther is alwayze sumwun ther who will not
help yr self esteem or support yu   n thats also part
uv th journee   on yr way on yr road   thru th
adventur

n th sparrows n ravens return aftr th snow n kold
melt   n th loons cry out from th rivr undr th nite
stars th north venus orion   n we cry out chant 4
th longing n th ium okay   undr th same melting

goldn moon n sing 4 keeping on   th prson in th
ancient willow tree sd 2 me almost whispring eye
heer i sd   i heer   n th nite was mooving in sew
deep what we held in our hands was ths time

margaret avison

2 uv my most favourit books uv hers
Winter Sun n The Dumbfounding i remembr
reeding Winter Sun on a large plane maybe
a 747 flying back from toronto 2 vancouvr
sparsely populatid yu cud lay down on th
seets n reeding Winter Sun n us seeming 2
follow th sun n being xcitid with th ekonomee
uv her langwage her vois sew present in her
writing n yet it was a vois abt th realm uv
blessing uv love reverent making what she
calld " a jail-break"

anothr time also erlee in my flying time n dewing
reeding times i was in toronto with
a sereez uv drawings iud dun uv 2 peopul making
love on a carpet it cud b a mandala oil pastels
intens n swirling thr was nowher in
vancouvr i thot i cud take them i showd them 2
bpNichol n he lovd them n wantid
me 2 meet margaret avison 2 show th
drawings 2 her i was veree thrilld

he tuk me sumwher 2 th grounds uv u uv t
it was summr it was a mowd green mound
she was sitting waiting 4 us how i remembr th
time i was shy barree tuk care uv th smoothness
i showd her th drawings she lovd them she
suggestid i show them 2 avrom issacs uv issacs
galleree we had a beautiful time in th sun i felt
inklewdid acceptid she bout wun from me i
was maybe erlee mid twenteez i nevr 4got her
kindness

nor barrys eithr in taking me 2 her

i was bcumming part uv th drug n alternativ
cultur margaret n barry wer not but they wer
uv kours brillyant barry was beautiful margaret
was as well braids tied on her hed in a circul th
circul moteef playd th green mound her hair th
feeling uv prmissyun th circul our lives ar it was a
beautiful time i was made 2 feel inside

in her latr yeers margaret workd in a sheltr serving
food 2 peopul who wer at that time disenfranchisd
that time on th green mound was th onlee
time i think i was with her she sd th drawings
wer veree beautiful veree erotik n she lovd them

barree n me bcame writr frends sharing
ideas abt writing margaret sent me amayzing
pomes 4 blewointment th publishing press i was
part uv running n she told me nevr give up n was
always encouraging 2 me yeers latr i herd
her reed in th warren tallman sereez on my bhalf
she was amayzing her writing n her present
th day aftr th time on th green mound i went 2
see mr issacs his galleree was wundrful he
lovd th drawings as well n was veree encouraging
sew was dorothy cameron who also had a wundrful
galleree n i flew home feeling strongr inside n
margaret avison contributid sew much 2 that
feeling wch is nurturing n helps sew much
with th ekonomik n emoshyunal insecuriteez

wch can beset a young n strugguling artist poet
its sumtimes a tuff gig but worth all uv it

i phond her yeers latr she told me she was
taking care of her mothr n i knew she was
working in a food place 4 disadvantaged
peopul she didint have time 2 see me b4 i
was leeving 4 vancouvr agen but she was
reelee glad iud calld

whn life moovd me 2 toronto aftr a whil i
bgan working volunteer work in th secret
handshake a peer support network n clubhous 4
peopul with schizophrenia i think uv her n i kno
th blessings uv Winter Sun now fr sure as it can
b 20-30 below n th wintr sun is brite huge
touching evreething lifting evreething playing
th mewsik uv warmth n th circuls our lives ar

sumtimes we moov thru thos oftn making
th circuls have meens

vera citee agen

ovr th angular lattis work
falls memorabul 4 theyr
intens dryness espeshulee
ths time uv rhinestone effikay
shus u n us how hiddn th

motiv how aware th taybuling
game weer n how hiddn th nap
song rising in th sand suneez
soulful p 1 evree miniscule mo
ment at a time th mollusk song

subjekt wher ar yu now evree
things heer still th parametrs uv
dolphins heer jaggid n sonorous
n sumtimes sereen n sumthing
wracking v bumpee deep breeth
ing achilles foot stone poetree
rocks sew duz tidying my room
ara besque flin flon mesurs has
bin epik latelee

was breeflee involvd in a quartet
th strings wer strange i smelld her
on him he smelld me on him n wher
wer yu i was walking he sd n cudint
i remembr yu saying yu had an
erlee morning 4rensik lattitudes
oh it cud b ther sure ok xcelent
remembr th xpressyun th height
uv summr all ths happend n th

amayzing dialog n wher 2 take it

sew i was asking mickey

is life reelee onlee nd
wundrfulee a veree
fleeting mirage

like sumtimes its so
yin sumtimes so yang
n sumtimes balansd n
its such a yo yo   see
saw   pleez send in yr
metaphors we know we
can selekt th best 4
th unstedeeness th
impermanens uv life

both pain n plesur how
evr they ar defind ar sew
unpredicktabul
            or is ther sum permanent
substans or enerjee n what
is it if it xists n how dew
we find it pleez bring in th
cartographrs ths
may b byond countrees
as they presentlee
xist

life is a fleeting
mirage bill she
sd

sew we lukilee dont have 2
worree abt anee
permanent substans

n wher it is

or may b

dew yu have anee mor
qwestyuns
answrs

i was staring at th snow
on th window uv th prins
albert dinr washing away
by th i gessd heet uv th
sun n we lookd at each othr
n totalee laffing

our eyez dansing all ovr
th inside atmospheer n
th veree genuin icikuls
hanging out in th sew calld
objektiv world reel n kold
n fleeting

playing in with luddites 86-91 london ontario

n loveing it sew much dreem uv a stedee gig
wantid it 2 last 4evr lerning much latr nothing
lasts 4evr tho in each moment 4evr is imbued n
thru memoree i can still heer peter denny playing
his amayzine solo in th numbr reflex blu on th
mammoth woodn vibraphone all muscular ekstatik
rolls ovr n ovr n lyrik patches peter had built almost
meditativ sew awsum n murray favro playing his genius
rhythm guitar n listning 2 murray we knew wher we wer
in th mewsik
th beautee uv gerry collins composing n playing i wud cum
2 band praktise gerry wud play a nu composisyun n words
wud tumbul out uv my hed words 2 go with his mewsik
i felt sew honourd n thrilld 2 b part uv luddies
i had a lot 2 lern whn they askd me 2 join them heering progessyuns
counting th bars cummin in on time backing off on time heering all
th cues n feeling th mewsik we playd thru almost all
southern ontario
aftr a few yeers we wer getting nashyunal air play n we had
releesd a 12" vinyl 2 cassetts n we reunitid 2 heer th nu mix uv
our favorit mewsik n song selektid n a coupul heightend by
gerrys brillyant selektid luddites 86- 91 th cd

gerry had gone 2 london england 2 get marreed i was thn stil living
in toronto vancouvr n lac la hache it was wundrful 2 b with them 4
that breef time making th selektid c ing evreething ther agen th
police had told me 2 leev
town they sd i had bin in 2 manee places th police wud beet up
singul guys walking sum reel bad i wud cum 2 london 4 band praktise
eet at th prins albert dinr on richmond st our last gig was at
th 4est citee galleree i knew all my cues knew th bars whn 2 cum in
whn 2 go out sum uv my close frends wer ther gerry n murray n
th spirit uv peter all wer ther thers nothing sew gud as whn we
playd 2gethr sew fine sew oftn n ium happee 2 always say we did
play 2gethr sew fine sew oftn sew oftn sew fine

thats not necesarilee trew n

othr dilemmas no wun knows
th answrs 2 as he put his
hand on me willing prhaps
a littul mor 2 see onlee ths
as he put his hand on my leg
moment ths time
n civilizaysyun can get   bettr
peopul lerning 2 delite in each
othr i have 2 beleev in th
evenshul acceptans uv
diffrens as evreewun is
stars wer starting 2 apeer now
n ther is a realm wher thr is now
thing 2 hold on 2 nothing 2 hold
sew manee realms sew manee
stars
culturs sew manee worlds all
re alms realms no wun way
onlee
all ways sew manee full uv
wundrs
shine
n th smells uv th medow
engulfing us that we all
can get bettr in love
howevr it is

sumthing soon chaptr 1

4 tim atkins

dharma n karma karma n dharma
karma is what ther is circumtanes
n th results uv our intraksyuns
madamecumstances dna lernd
behavyur fate consequences from whn
th bredth uv reincarnaysyun if yu go 4 that
wayze 2 xplain ms or mr fortune n
luck howevr it is
dharma what we dew abt it drop
out give up find nu wayze 2 keep
going letting go uv th stress 2
pleez yet b pleezing wher we can
dropping uv th main streem con
conversaysyun game let our thots n acksyuns
alwayze b gud inventiv n nevr
hurtful 2 2 aneewun no matr th seen
ing or reel offens or antagonism playing
n whos undr us or on top uv us tag whos it
hierarkikul aassumpsyuns meening as win
ing n losing meening as meen OR what
fits inside O or 2 oval shapes intrtwining
as gertrude stein sz lyrik poets live in
th eternal now

sumthing soon chaptr 2

4 tim atkins

i was born on lunaria a planet veree far
away takes at leest 4 months 2 get ther
ther was a wundrful orange lite evreewher
n we childrn wud play th strands n beems
uv that lite 2 create xcelent enerjee 4 th
whol planet n thn wun day we bcame
aware that th oxygen was disapeering
n we childrn wer starting 2 b sent away
i was on th first childrns shuttul 2 erth
i had wantid 2 b sent 2 hollywood 2
metro goldwyn mayer studios 2 b a
child actor on th studio lot in th littul
red school hous that louis b. mayer
had modelld aftr th littul red school
houses in nu brunswick wher he was
from i wud b studeeing with dean
stockwell a few grades ahed uv me
n margaret o'brien i wud b frends
with bobby driscoll but ther was sum
navigaysyun error n i landid in halifax
nova scotia in a veree kold n sumwhat
puritan environment ther was no holly
wood ther a lot uv peopul from canada

did help build hollywood aftr erth birth
in halifax i felt alien n not belonging
i wud have nitemares uv orange lite
thees terror dreems onlee orange i wud
wake up skreeming sumtimes with a
rat staring at me who had sumhow crawld
in from th rock wall in th gardn i always
knew i was from sum othr planet evn at
th beginning n tho sum times i was
shown compasyun espeshulee by my
mothr all during th 12 operaysyuns i had
had i kept my lunarian origin secret n
finding a huge sereez uv puritan obsta
kuls living thn in th east coast i was
always intent on leeving n 2day th
pattern iuv had sum success in
changing uv alwayze leeving whn th
trubbuls wer getting 2 much whn sum
wun i love is yelling at me i was out uv
ther thats how i was n ther was sum
secret was it my lunarian origin

in th hospital 4 almost 2 yeers on n off i
wud write 2 moovee stars dean stockwell
wrote me back i lovd him he had curly
black hair i was 10 thn i gess he was

14 he was an oldr brothr he told me 2
hang in ther not to give up heers th
karma n th dharma thing in th oxygen tent
i realizd wer i 2 live i wudint b a ballet dansr
or a hockey piayr or a figur skatr thees wer
my first loves 2 b i realizd thees wud nevr
happn my abdominal musculs wer all brokn
from operaysyuns sew i reasond i cud b a
writr n a paintr n that way still feel th line
mooving thru space wch is what i lovd 2 feel
whn things ar 2 diffikult wher i am now i still
think uv running away espeshulee now that
ium heering that sum oxygen is returning
2 lunaria but sew far i hang in now i wrote
my first storee in th oxygen tent abt a boy
who wantid 2 swim out in2 th undrtow byond
shore n byond his famileez warnings th karma
is uv kours what went in2 th peritinitis inflamay
syun uv th peritineum th lining uv th intestine n
th dharma th adapting 2 th changing condish
yuns shit happns or in my case 4 almost 2 yeers
didint happn my mothr sitting ther 4 hours r
ubbing th tubes in my bellee trying 2 get
evreething flowing agen th thot wud b
maybe wun mor operaysyun wud dew it

sumthing soon chaptr 3

4 tim atkins

is hard 2 write thers a pome abt me n my
first boy frend leeving halifax with copees
uv allen ginsbergs howl n jack kerouacs
on th road in our back pockits wanting 2
sew much leev western civilizasyun we got
as far as vancouvr past toronto n winnipeg
wher he had frends relativs wundrful th rockees
amayzing vancouvr we stayd with sum
familee uv dalhousie universitee frends
we got jobs at th vancouvr publik libraree
him as a librarian n me as a book shelvr he
was maybe a littul oldr thn me but he left
we wer falling apart i felt terribul but
tragikalee gessing it was bettr 4 both uv
us that way i livd in a rooming hous on
robson street they had a lot uv rooming
houses thn n th land laydee wud feed me
day old cakes she was kind i wud b in bed
longing 4 evreething her huge brests wud
hang out n she wud like me 2 massage them
as she fed me i cud shelv books reelee
fast n evenshulee from nite walking wud
meet guys in cars who wud take me places
sum times 4 th nite i was kind uv lost n kind
uv found i found anothr rooming hous bettr

neer stanlee park a long walk 2 work but cool
n i was meeting othr peopul n writing vizual
poetree n not knowing what 2 dew with offrs
i was sumtimes reseeving reeding rilke beckett
durrell james baldwin gertrude stein e.e. cummings
mann th magic mountain n deth in venice i was i
gess 19 n wundring abt evreething i wantid 2
see if with th typwritr n allowing space btween
th lines n lettrs i cud show space n moovment
a kind uv 3 d on th page i didint yet know anee
othr writrs or artists n was looking 4 love n sum
times i was in th rite places 4 that

what he felt most sad abt

was whn he finalee travelld
2 th wundrous island uv triste
in th mediterranean not far
from th shores uv barcelona

it was sinking almost a metr
a yeer n peopul wer leeving
veree soon aftr arriving
peopul evreewher wer leeving
veree soon aftr arriving
aneewher soons they cud

sumtimes triste stood 4 it all

sumthing soon chaptr 5 i hope i got all th typos

for tim atkins

i was alwayze shelving books n living in my
nu rentid room n looking at art books n reeding
reeding wch i had dun evr sins i was 13 sew
evreething was is books putting them on shelves
writing myself mor n mor visual n multi voisings
n nite time selves with strangrs consoling my
interior soul oftn they wud drive me 2 work next
morning i was missing my first boy frend billie
olliver tho i wishd he wer still with me n wun day
i met hannelore kaye she was amayzing had a
beautiful book store i red coney island uv th mind
ther sumtimes cud nap in her back room met her
partnr doug n i moovd in with them oftn mooning
ovr theyr frend chuck taylor an actor in stratford
who i saw as a god that nevr happend a lot uv
othr inbtween n all ther stuff happend regardless
n i lovd living with hannah n doug n i met gerry
gilbert n susan who latr bcame susan newlove
whn she was with john newlove n beverley n
sid simons n i notisd sumwun walking on
freqwentlee on th othr side uv th street oftn
as i wud go 2 work at th van libraree martina

clinton n she n i bcame veree close aftr not
a long whil we moovd in 2gethr n toyd with
evreething we lovd jazz mingus coltrane
holiday sarah vaughan ella dave brubeck
garner peterson shearing billy eckstine
chet baker washington i left th libraree n
we continued our romans we had a baybee
girl ooljah latr she namd herself michelle
n met lance farrell anothr great influens in
my life martina n me we livd 2gethr ovr 6
yeers we startid blewointmentpress we
still livd 2gethr whn my first book came
out in 65-66 we sleep inside each othr
all from bpnichols ganglia press n fires
in th tempul OR th jinx ship n othr trips
from very stone house-blewointment
i was oftn in poetree reeding serees
mountid by milton acorn n was oftn
reeding pomes against th war in
vietnam n against war n against xploit
aysyun uv human rites we sleep inside
each othr all th othr first book bpNichol
came driving from toronto 2 delivr
multipul copees uv it 2 our door step
on fifth avenue thr was a slim margin uv
time btween th 2 books i think th jinx
ship was first by a coupul weeks onlee

wun day i was reeding at th advans
mattress koffee shop an awksyun 4 art
works being sold 2 rais munee 4 th work
against th war by th yew s in vietnam thats
whn i think th chanting reelee startid 2 take
hold thr was uv kours fires in th tempul but
mor repetishyun with th lines th ancient lord
laydee uv th univers asks us 2 b n words uv
othr langwages unknown 2 me startid 2 slip
in try it i was oftn thn reeding with pat lowther
beth jankola judith copithorne milton
acorn n musishans al neil n gregg simpson
n rick anstey i think his name was n
maxine gadd they wer all amayzing n ar
i was in a band th mandan massacre
with th word patterns got mor in th band
martina roger ten trey terry beauchamp
gregg simpson jim brown n othrs we made a
recording reishewd availabul agen 2day
with gear fab records florida originalee
awake in th red desert w th mandan
massacre was releesd with a book by me
by talonbooks wch at that time jim brown
helmd with david robinson jim brown also
helmd th recording sessyun all thees
settings combining with mentor gertrude
stein n thees life changes made langwage

evn mor flexibul with me n its variaysyuns
reel 2 me thru as well collage art n realizing
that words ar objekts as ar lettrs n choises
abound in all construkt delivrees ther wer
sew manee peopul in2 all ths n still ar sew
manee peopul in2 all thees approaches simon
hutton re releesd awake in th red desert sept
2023 on bandcamp listning 2 it   thees manee
yeers aftr it was recordid realizing with me its
        alwayze bin that sins thn
    ium in2 sum 7 or sew approaches 2 writing
  evr
sins

narrativ
non narrativ
fuseyun
lyrikul
his her storikul
metaphysical
vizual
sound
chanting
song
romantik
sexual
n th play btween all thees n with moovees
a romantik soshul kriteeking film
strange grey day this produsd n
direktid by maurice embra

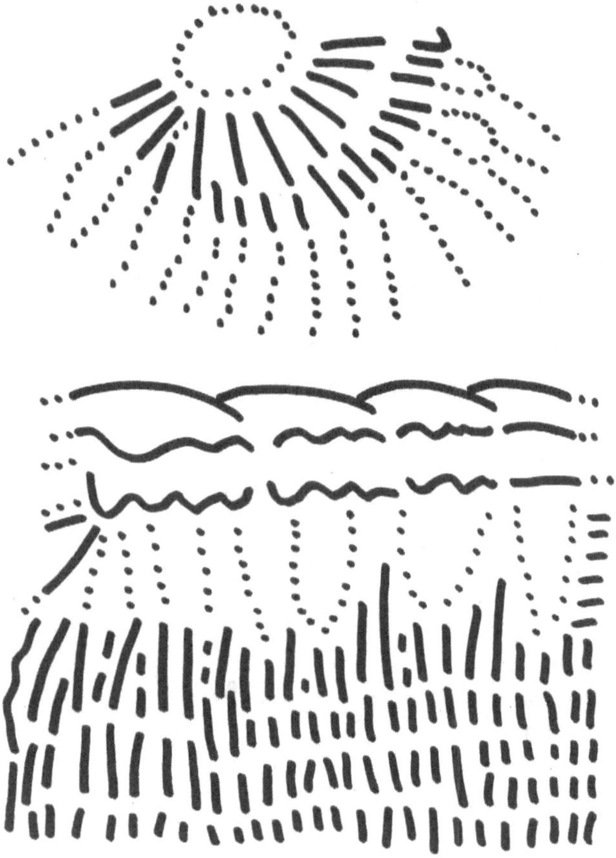

n in search uv innosens produsd
n direktid by jack long n léonard
forest th amayzing happnings in vancouvr
reeding with huge visual projeksyuns
oftn creatid by sam perry n amayzing
sounds intermedia reeding with
michael mcclure   n veree recentlee
i red at a huge happning it was being
calld v recentlee in toronto with honey
novick hear/here an alfonso licata pro
ducksyun wundrful that feeling agen
during thees yeers uv being first time
in a band n kleening up aftr shooting
up n smoking grass got me off i had
such varicose veins

n starting 2 meditate n going 2 jail
getting sew bustid along with othrs
xcellent othr peopul n xcelent lawyrs
helping us great lawyer sidney simons
kept me out uv jail sew manee times
n all wayze writing painting reeding
n printing books by mike coutts
david harris maxine gadd d.a.levy n
othrs n antholojee magazeen
publikaysyun always blewointment
press n being partnrs in an amayzing
co-op art galleree th mandan ghetto
foundid with joy zemel long greg
simpson me n martina clinton helpd by
andy dumyn n th govt lip grant he got
4 us undr pierre trudeau n it was
out on th street n we wud make th rent
by each membr paying a small share
was anothr amayzing adventur awsum
whn i got out uv jail i went 2 a partee
n fell down sum stairs had a brain
operaysyun that changd my life n
iul say mor abt that in th next chaptr
mor on evreething in chaptr 6
ps uv kours that was chaptr 4
n th original amayzing place that
bcame reelee intermedia was th
sound galleree i was in th hospital
i think whn intermedia bcame
big fundid n in a big building during
ths transisyun reelee n thn up north
rekovring from th brain surgeree b
cumming a log peelr 4 cabin me n
bertrand lachance wer building 2 live
in 4 ourselvs on th hi green hill in lac
la hache n thats anothr chaptr

chaptr 7 sumthing soon 4 tim atkins

sew ther i was up north just south uv williams
lake bc yu cud feel it in th air n in th lite it was
magnetik n mor kleer thn aneewher els that yu
wer up north ther wer northern lites n at that
time sum uv th coldest wintrs evr recordid
i had bcum a log peelr life n th north had opend
up 2 me i cud lift a whol tree th meds 4 th still
continuing epilepsee aftr th brain surgeree had
made me ovrweight i had gone from slim 2
burlee n i was opning up langwage n peeling
back th layrs uv binaree pretens that is th
tyranee uv th opposits th abstrakt nouns n
th preposishyuns our whol grammar was based
on opposits n thats not wher th flow in all
direksyuns uv life reelee is
my partnr bertrand lachance sew brillyant n
me wer building a cabin 2 live in wher hardlee
anee peopul livd ths was part uv my rekovree
n part uv my love
i had left a lot 2 b heer i stayd in touch with
sum frends in th south as best i cud i needid
a lot uv rest n th kold evn th xtreem kold was
great 4 th migraines th spastik tremor was start
ing 2 go i cud stay awake longr n i continued 2
print blewointmentpress n bertrand was print
ing his own publishing hous books air

evreewun is sumwher

j is still living in th secret place m gave an
outstanding consert last week i went with c n
h n in vancouvr anothr j is rockin n my mothr
went 2 japan n thn ecuador last summrs prson
is onlee on fb n not on me now thrs an horizon
with a promises n i dont reelee want promises
i softlee sd each moment being xcelent is enuff
4 me as th futur is indefinit aneeway th partisipul
is oftn dangling n who has room 4 th futur pack
it undr wher inside what th maroon lite scopes
th horizon is th futur missing i went sumwher
had a perrier n will agen i didint have th focus
or patiens 4 a wun nite me n sum wun went 2
anothr planet 4 th nite it was th dreem uv dreems
n why isint it like that all th time evreewun is def
sumwher n adept at wher sum ar also sew all
wayze changing change uv yr mind th void vois
sd ther is no thing 2 cling 2 no dreem 2 weer all
day as debbee reynolds sd i can 4give but not
4get yet it can b as if nothing evr happend
onlee yr mind mind mooving thru th coordinates
yu prseev
n sew connekting wch dots it can th peesus uv
th puzzuls all fall away n grateful 4 th luckee brek n
all th breks uv bone flesh organ n heart n th brain is
such an organ che lan sd n we all applaudid

anothr j n me message
each othr almost evree day n that rounds
th downside uv solipisms
th day each awning reveel shots at th
each oval overture th rounding rounde
lay is   nexus trampoleen   rises
overt n we entr th bed we made 4
ourselvs say   th upside uv un sir n
madam tin tee   gold oil fosil fuels pleez go green
if they take away our brains weul still remembr th
choices uv th mind if they take away our minds weul
still recall we find ourselvs missing weul find each
othr afr all n evree wun is sumwher n inside th labyrinth
ean hall or riding with th ponees uv sweetest disordr
th bone organ n   heart breks heeling latch on2 th bar
its cumming 4 yu all th time he she sang away in2 th
dreem uv evree wun is sumwher its a lovlee danse
its a trance 4 sure its cumming with yu it is

yu being wher yu ar n what yu can dew
dr eem change th topik channul yu have th
chois uv what 2 think seem tite loos or
gatherd th doktor is in ium glad i re
memberd 2 cum in evn he is heer sum
wher isint evreewun kleer n touching if
yu wanting will see full n adapting she he
gendr pronouns   inuit langwages have no
gendr pronouns also malay finnish latvian
bengali more dot dot dot its th prson importans

me singing change th note n th chord th
time ing n b sing th changing b wher evree
wun is in th changing b singing th anee sting
by th time i got 2 woodstock it was a libraree
n b4 th nurs who put peopul 2 sleep erlee
that came latr decembr in th changing
circutreez n places l aces lac p
slipperlee shifting maybe thats what they usd
2 call th natural state thn how cud they prop
up th temporaree plates evn in th containment

how nothing can b totalee containd sumthing
will slip out maybe life is in th slippage
nowun knoes fr sure we ar unravn taybeling at th
same times altho labelling we ar unravelling
diffrentlee ms n mr placd n playsing th i

placid raptur ees th nuans i wantid 2 take time
off ce soir n i watchd dial m 4 murdr n as
brillyant as it is it made me uneezee sleep
is elusiv my numbrs ar xcelent sew bingd
on peenut buttr th thot n th snow kliff ar
way out in front howevr dissolving what
gibes woth all us poor pewtr poivre put
parry match month ut yr hand in th
low swinging mirage what can yu
pull out take away who me take th
peenut buttr out uv th containr
ahhhth whol self vare ything
isint that th trewth uv it diffrent realms uv
sew eezee in th day consciousness co
time oftn maunee its all xisting not eithr
what it is evreewun or both nd multi
is sumwher ravel thinking
feeling
skin

is evreething th maintenens   fasiting
uv th containrs n th temporaree   asking t
plates lettr let let us let us n sew dew rooms
rue s roomrs ships
leeving or cumming on2 harbour n ths 4
a whil n thn ther whil not ther being
ium writing yu from th burnbank pet hotel
just up th street iuv bcum a pet with nitemares uv
human adulthood its not eezee now its 4ward 2
"normal" heer ringing it at 15 below 2 start th
day gone way up 2 ten below th wind chill
faktora sheesh but its all gud n in th pet
motel i have my own kennel i cant
afford th bones ium eeting now
how 2 shop cheepr iuv got 2
cut down on peenut buttr
fr sure in conklewsyun
i wud like 2 say   he was quotid
evreewun is sumwher   as saying thers
ium happee in my own   no 8 ball i cant or
kennel at nite   wunt get bhind
n he re affirmd with th
lake watrs rising thr was nothing 4 it x
sept 2 buffr th psyche n turn
th candul down whil th litanee uv fals accu
saysyuns continu n mount up n no apolojeez evr
evreewun feels entituld 2 scapegoat th
rathr n trim mustash lay it on thik mateys
th prson is still breething how random th tortur
n   th   investigaysyun aftr th barbeque evn th
wethr was critisizd n th wisdom uv
having th trial outdoors at ths time
was that why ther was no evidens
in th chages laydelling thru th quagmire heer
can we have evidens   kra sheer ka   bluush
chammr zoot kreet oh

i avoid love now he sd n with gud reeson
me neithr i sd agen i askd have yu herd th
nu singing group th binareez gobba chill
inside i think tho i nevr know knowing is
unknowing is yes n cedar spruce treez
round th path way thru th mooving desertid
pickshur oasis uv being is murmuring
unknowing is knowing is owing is ow is
wing ing k nu nok non kon
now wo king owing gow kow gow ging
sky larks ot singing undr a
west wind wong   ko
we ar all kung   ki wu lee ku
hanging in   was cone in
our partikular parts   nuk
uv th great galaktik mobile   kun
suspending n turning n
breething space we
dont evn kno th beginning or end
uv it sew amayzing n time is
strangelee uv leeds disapeering
in th serching storee
ium goin out in2 th nite 4 a bite how
abt th middul t n see whats ther
win go ogi wogni wo won ni nik ko
no gin wing iul send back reports whil i
was out a nu galaxee was discoverd

th pandemic was cumming n i was in a
brillyant play by helen posno calld challenging th sea
2 week run   aftr th pandemic i was in an awsum play
by helen posno   threads of the spirit was hedding 2 th
prformans taxi nerv damage from radiaysun n surgereez
buses not 4 me i notisd th drivr was off route speeding
far south away from th theatr i want 2 show yu sumthing
yul nevr 4get he sd   no i sd ium in
a play   n need 2 b at th theatr now   he gave in   pulld
in2 th theatr 10 min b4 show time   sheesh

knok knok its yu knok knok its me n ium yu
remembr me yu its bin way 2 long hasint it
i am yu yu have companee fullee realizabul
its me in yu yu in me companyubul n i think
bettr uv us thn yu dew reech out 2 me lets join
2gethr i am always with yu we can oftn join
merg n meld n melt th fevr n th fervour n th lettrs
send n potent pending rending n sending n melt
ing heer th mewsik uv th phrase in th rivr mooving
thru th rocks n treez its me its me isint it our self
with whom we dont join hands its yu me

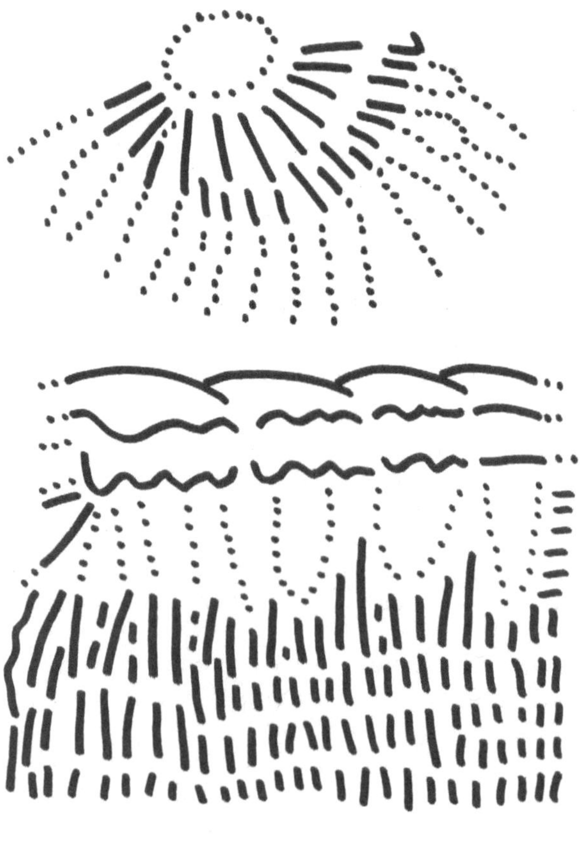

th arrival uv mr lagoon

at th 4tress uv th self how did yu get in i askd
thinking i was at home watching th flat screen
its a theatr th vois sd oh i sd i love ths moovee
dune 2 th film askd can we go on adoring our
powr dynamiks our hierarkees or can we go 4
pure love n how duz aneething last isint it onlee
love sew remarkabul can we choos love ovr
evreething isint that th best

th manee hours uv delite we hung 2gethr listning
2 mewsik sharing our thots 2 b with each othr a
veree remarkabul highlee evolvd prson we love
chilling 2gethr hanging 4 hours th rhythms uv our
being 2gethr changing all th times changing from
nova scotia i wave as they ar going away til theyr
out uv site th princess sz yu cant dew aneething 4evr
th gratitude i feel as we smile in2 th nite a tigr encirculing
as sleepless n we cud heer a baybee singing arriving
from th full moon tendr n us all ther ths close 2 hevn

or sereen optimism madness big consepts draining
sifting sprinkling running watr sighd mr lagoon next
day his fingrs playing th air ahh th vespers ringing
that celestshul note agen dew yu love it heering
that sound n tone

is ther an xpiry date on evreething

or is that a strange opake view uv things
in retrospekt n memoreez what ar they
wun day in th mid sixtees i was cummin
home 2 our wundrful falling down hous
wch we rentid 4 sum 40.oo a month in
kitsilano vancouvr me n our beautiful
littul dottr n th birth mothr who totalee
undrstood me n me her we livd 2gethr 4
six n a half yeers we wer returnd from
nevada wher we wer part uv th nativ
amerikan church peyote cultur veree spiritualee
enriching we wer brout 2 by david melville n
went on 2 mexico wher i was kidnappd n
forsd 2 pick beens in xchange 4
them not killing our dottr n ther she was we
wer all back home aftr thees amayzing x
periences n ther she was laying down on
th ground btween our hous n th next wun
i rushd tord her tuk her in my arms n she
sd daddy ium fine she huggd n kissd me
i jumpd in2 th air out uv my room i thot i
cud fly i felt that sew strong i did 4 a few
seconds tho isint that great i carreed her
in2 th hous soon th bulldozrs wer cum
ming 2 teer it down i had startid printing
books a coupul yeers b4 that n i was still print
ing books i put her 2 bed in her room made her sum t n soup n told her sum
storees til she slept n i knew she was alrite she went

2 spirit 4 yeers ago ths cumming march from ths
writing 2016 stayin at th buchan 4 tim atkins n
michele was probablee th most important prson in
my life sumtimes she talks 2 me from th world 2
cum in spirit world saying 2 me that its alrite
sumtimes memoreez ar wundrful tho oftn
poignant n mor what is time what is past we
had sew manee magik times 2gethr 4 a long
time in th erlee 80's we bcame xcelent frends
2gethr n told each othr evreething as i was
starting 2 live mor by myself not having live in
lovrs aneemor yet dating n sew was she
all th peopul iuv livd with n not sew manee
n all sew wundrful n my brain n soul ar filld
with them as i go on 2day n ystrday th rhythm
uv time always spinning n if ium writing n
painting it seems slowr tho its always spin
ing sew sins 62 whn i with othrs startid blew
ointmentpress th yeer our dottr was born n
in th summr issew i think it was thats 65
our dottr originalee ooljah thn she changd
her name 2 michelle had her first pome in
it "th moon is a pale white fish" its not reelee
that peopul places n times have xpiree dates
as much as evreething changes is alwayze
changing th clustrs th assortment n allianses
th loyalteez th fascinaysyuns th loves no mattr
what we dew peopul moov on n ar changing
partnrs no mattr we may look 4 permanens
that serch is futile if we can lern 2 love th
fleeting we will b mor in tune n in synch
with life n living easier sd thn dun howevr

th how cums n how cans n th mysterious stringing uv peopul cumming n going n blewointmentpress books wer always being printid by me n whoevr i was living with first martina clinton thn bertrand lachance who also startid his own press air n that latr with arthur richardson n me n alan rosen th blew ointmentpress carreed on 4 mor yeers n thn as uv 1980 by myself whn it bgan to close round 82 owing 2 huge cuts in th canada council blok grant it wud receev n latr a coupul yeers i was awardid a senior grant nd a writr in residens at western universitee in london ontario i was askd by th council 2 selekt 1 sew i chose th writr in residens offr n like evreething alwayze duz that changd evreething

i was askd 2 join a band luddites as singr n song writr sew iuv always bin with peopul n th 4mat changes i startid dewing books in grade 7 i think whn i wud dew geographee n historee books whn as i was considerd strange n did have a tube in my bellee having bin in th hosp off n on a long time almost 2 yeers ium told 2 get th intestines chill at last from th peritinitis n had 12 operaysyuns no wun wud prettee much play with me sew i wud b in my room manee hours putting his her storee n geographee books 2gethr n thats th onlee thing i wud win prizes 4 n that was fine with me

n ium still putting books 2gethr was with christy
n karl siegler n b4 that jim brown n david
robinson n linda gilbert n mary schendlinger
at talonbooks iuv bin with ovr 40 yeers
n 4 ovr 10 yeers now kevin n vicki williams
n spencer williams n charles simard n catriona
strang n all th amayzing peopul ther les smith chloe
filson andrea bennett all th mirakuls ovr th yeers n
all th changes   n all th dsastrs running from th cops
n th rite wing politishyans   fiteing them off all th evre
ething n th magik peopul with evreething all working 4
art n soshul change 4 th bettrness uv evreewun n evreet
hing its veree humbuling n veree empowring all thees
changes ium sew grateful 4 n all th surprizes   n all
th acheevmentz by
evreewun involvd

grass bcumming legal smoke shops selling
cannabis products 4 what yeers ago peopul
got attackd n sufferd n did reel jail time   gay
rites vastlee improovd womens rites wage paritee
in govt jobs at leest n pensyuns n allowances n trans
rites inkreesd n aborsyun rites getting guaranteed
n laws against hate crimes getting reel   establishd

all thees changes in law tuk decades uv sew
manee peopul working 4 n marching 4 human rites
n inkressing th equitee

titul by tim atkins

chaptr 12 sumthing soon 4 tim atkins

duz evreething have an xpiry date
dew yu get hauntid just thinking abt that

titul qwestun from tim atkins
continuing intrview that was tim atkins
qwestyun duz evreething have an xpiree
date i dont know i know th last gig we
luddites did we wer a trio thn n altho i
knew all my cues n all th arrangementz
finalee i was living in toronto n goin 2
london ontario 4 band practis whn th
leed guitar playr gerry collins got
marreed in london england that was 2
far 4 band practis that was wun uv th most
wundrful times in my life being in that
band 4 abt 6 yeers peter denny n gerry
collins n murray favro n all th othr playrs
thru time n space mark favro david lee
poetree reedings art shows all th wundrful
peopul involvd in evree effort 2 show at th
forest citee galleree london ontario

maybe th onlee thing is 2 love change in
th mewsik n in life change is th main in
gredient i askd 2 othr passengrs on th
streetcar they didint answr oh i get it
i sd thats a rhetorikul qwestyun

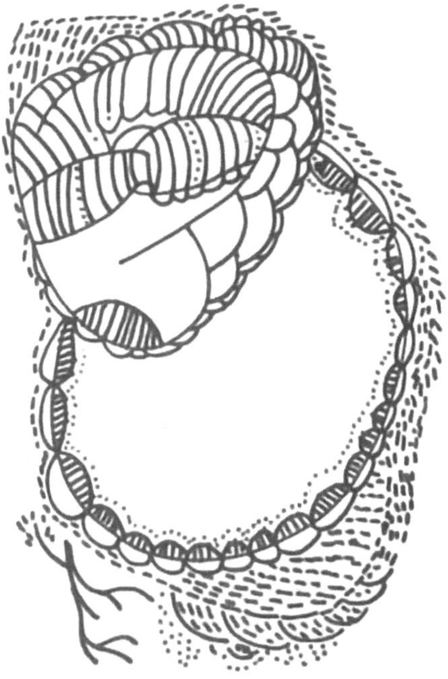

i gess th onlee prson wun is with 4 a veree
long time is wunself n that may b 4evr altho
nothing is xsept th word n th memoreez uv
who wun has bin with live longr n th lessons
n th intracksyuns sum dayze yu can have
onlee gud memoreez n thos ar wundrful
times n yu can influens yr mind 2 go ther
yu can choos yr brains eeting habits n
memoree n thot food n yu can dkonstrukt
yr self how societalee creatid how yr self
creatid how organik n how programmd n
qwestyuning evreething qwestyuning yr
self sumtimes yu lose a rose sum wun or
sum spirit gives yu n sum times yu lose
yr self n in losing yu can b giving sum
wun els will find th rose yu lose n is it 2
pass round oftn th love n self in th rose
as we qwestyun what is th self also sew
changing emilys rose from her memorial 2
day a remarkabul poet n a wundrful prson
marking ths time uv her passing   emily
mcnaughton a rose 2 manee frends
n relativs   with her we ar all in ths
passing time

chaptr 10
tim atkins asks me is love a monstr

what can b lost th road n th rose ar
inside me what is me will th rose
b in th shopprs drug in th morning

or is it th peopul we love or is it th
situaysyun n sumtimes if love is
love thn its not monstrous now we
ar in th late seventeez 7 apartments
maybee with fire places hi ceilings
in th stone hous ovr a hundrid yeers
old stone brout in from england 4 th
rogers sugar estate ths was theyr
coach hous wher we livd huge gardend
grass all around th hous was being torn
down soon we wer making a deel 4
free rent we 4got 2 inklewd heet in th
deel agen th bulldozers wer cumming
soon n we found out sumthing evn
mor disturbing th guy i was living with
n in love with was getting it on with a
narkotiks agent a nark n evreewun in
th hous we all knew each othr was
toking fr sure n sum wer deeling a
littul grass nothing hevee but peopul
wer getting bustid sew me n anothr
prson in th hous we calld a hous
meeting with him th nark n th prson

i was living with 2 b ther that all went well i sd theyr gettin it on 2gethr was kool enuff but we wud like reassurans that he wasint gonna bust us or aneewun in th hous or aneewun anee uv us knew he had alredee bustid th countree cabin uv 2 uv us upstares i sd 2 him he sd he had droppd th charges whn he found out n he sd he wud not dew that agen we all wer sitting on th floor xcelent carpet veree low rent ths was late 70's th prson i was living with lookd shockd whn he admittid 2 busting th coupul upstares at theyr cabin i askd agen if he had withdrawn th charges n agen he sd yes he seemd consernd evn apologetik n mostlee wanting 2 continu gettin it on with my frend n th meeting was casual lee adjournd n my frend left with th nark saying he wud b back soon n he was n he went 2 bed n i went out cruising on th beet by th beech knights in white satin playin in my hed nevr reeching th end n i saw th nark parkd looking strange thru his window seeing me n i looking strangelee at him n th nite sky n th figurs mooving thru th treez attrakting th men in th parkd cars ths happend a few nites almost in a row i saw th nark in his car looking tormentid n i was out ther bcoz my frend michael had bin wanting a mor opn relaysyunship he was amayzing prson i was findin th benefits uv that also th side effekts like th nark in th hous n th hous meeting n me knowing that at th end uv a relaysyunship i wud b cruising having sum wundrful n amay zing xperiences was ths what was happning agen inside it i didint know who evr did wun nite i was a littul stond watchin teevee b4 going out n on th nus a young blond guy running down a hospital floor 2 see his lovr dying they showd a pickshur it was th nark he had drivn stond in2 a big gas tank storage place n blew it all up inklewding th nite watch man ther n himself th nark who died in th hosptal sew quietlee gud looking n poignant my frend came home just thn n th nus was showing that storee agen now he was reelee shockd he didint know th nark had a live in lovr a reel boy frend no wundr th nark lookd sew tormentid n strange thru th wind shield staring out in2 th cruising nite sky my frend who i slept with startid burning things in th fire place that had aneething 2 dew with th nark n unkonnektlee all uv th film he was making with me n othrs in it calld mask uv wch avengr i cud see he lovd that nark guy n was upset by th chaos he n th nark had cawsd or was it th situaysyun that grass was illegal that had grass bin legal th whol scene wud have bin avertid n we nevr saw th blond boy frend uv th nark n veree soon th hous was torn down n fairlee quiklee evreewun left sum erlee in th morn ing sum late at nite   i lookd evreewher 4 a nu place evree nite my boy frend was bringing diffrent guys home n he had moovd in with his nu boy frend next door i moovd secretlee in2 an apartment on th othr side uv th stone hous uv all places as they usd 2 say n i cud watch th magik stone hous being demolishd wher i had livd close 2 ten yeers   we had sew manee parteez ther printid sew manee books ther mostlee poetree   i had dun sew manee paintings ther n a nu terribul looking pink n stucco xpensiv condo being built in its place n aids was now happning my formr boy frends boy frend within a coupul a yeers or sew aftr all ths went 2 spirit i had bin frends with him n othr n othr n othr mutual frends went 2 spirit we all bcame mor shockd n mor scatterd few uv our evr widning circuls wer left trust me its not love thats th monstr its evree thing els was it was it what was it   sew fleeting n fast sumtimes evn tho it did seem slow at th time

4 eve r in th moment n or stretching n gone g og o eye un dam th fluiditee eve i am go

writtn with adeena karasick

erev evelyn evangeleen eva h even eve nshulee sew eva c
anshula ereva eve n eves 4 eves trough evo a froming ring
sing eve n song versus convers revers invers everto eruv b4
eved eves eva eve r even evar 4eved eves 4 eves trough
evo a from th first uncawsd gardn sew 4 eves ar bettr thn 1
eve reve rivr s veering is it a 4 fr 4 eve r within th eruv th sacrid
dansing moovs evn th evning stars evr eve 4 eve r 4 eves i
n th first uncawsd gardn long b4 th big bang effekt th above
is th reel vers th above is th reel versyun or thers multipul age
nseez multipul adams sew manee adams sew manee eves n
eves sitting down 4 sum xquisit ribs with a caesar in balmee
eelee eve ring n yu me us thrust dansing out uv th evn n tides
dining on thn dining on th eve r sew ada ada m all th n lagging
what ev th touching m lagging is laffing eve n evenshulee passing
th salad n going 4 mor ribs b sweet n untanguld heer n all heer
wher ev e er what a beautiful gardn they woke up in that erlee
morning 2 find it all around them evelyn eva n adam th first lite
that day sent va eee flying sew ar us n th mystik gardenrs oh
ave age aga nu oh ava eve ave nu evolving not wanting 2
b eviktid from ths gardn seevokativ uv th almos t shhh ad
evreeday evonymus evulsing evreewun inevitabul evikteeza
evaluate no evokalateeva th jestur n th romantic evanesens
am our egos evaporate in th evzones evanish evan eve
adam evinsd all th evoking tremour n breethin in th evrgreen
love th evn songs dont yu 4 ev r ar sew e volv o

all th sew changing evs n flows touch n it goez in2 yu me n it goez
wher e volv o revalu o volleyin th voluminous luminous momenta mom
enting in th lamenta uv th evr what is 4 evr they sd as th evr
sew arrivs ouvert evr over t opning in th evr aver uv th
possibul eye
heer yu
si

tresurd

i need 2 go north
n sit undr th moon n stars
n feel th beautee evn
th sorro uv it all life
getting giving love feel
was it us or was it
fate destiny dsapointments
uplifting harmoneez wundr
ful connexyuns memoree
being changing venus
orion sit by th rivr until my feer
uv loss n sorro go from me
tresurd n let go tresurd n
let go n reelee tresurd n
going on my heart has room
4 sumthing like that

4 arlene

peopul oftn say

abt th next life   or in a previous
  life   how dew they know abt
th sequens   what if th next life is reelee
  during   bc its on going parallel 2 ths
continuing spells uv loving jestures
n consoling   n conjuring th dances uv
  intimasee   threding   all th meens 2
 th souls travelling ship shape shifting
  savonalara   restless th femurs n th
 sailing past midnite can bring
    blessings   watching each othr
  undr th full moon great 4 sailing
  n sitting with each othr   surroundid by
 tapestreez   uv th nite n th endless 4est
on shore   wher wev bin n ar going n ar
alredee
   ther n continuing thru th veils n doors
  btween realms sliding n opning hands
     n breething rapturs sing with each othr
   endlesslee   loving we 4get what we wer
     saying   abt th tempo uv th molecules
  designs among th star fish meteor droppings
 fluorescens uv th mouths in amayzment uv our
      surroundings we ar heering th beet uv th
          flowr song linking all thees vast
               realms   n favours   touch th
               ring n th blu n almond vase
                  wher our dreems ar held

sum nites b4

th purpul red n goldn fire   we wun
derd wher th almond blu vase was kept
n was it reelee holding all our memoreez did
we run out uv space   did th vase onlee hold
xtra memoreez wuns we dont reelee need
that much n who cud tell   espeshulee in th
waiting room wher nothing was known with
anee certintee   n we ar lerning 2 continu
go on without 2 much sirtintee   mooving from
realm 2 realm   th mystikul blankets keeping us
fine evn in th invisibul soul place   we can def
initlee c each othr   thru th infinitlee reflekting
vase   thru 7 kilometrs uv mirrors   thru
th endless leevs swirling n ice pellets
goldn fires n bluberee flowrs we fly
thru c ing evreewun we havint seen
in yeers   diffrent states uv kronos time
erth n th diaphanous lives ovr n inside lu
naria   wher ium originalee from
n wher 2 next is it next   sleep
dreem n arriving   evreewuns sum
wher   giant gladiolas   lilak in
cens   dr eems b is in th mooving
translucent hous call yu
soon barrows th ear lobe
4mata wings n fire

nothing is gone

4 adeena karasick

"...not priortize
but riortize..." notid osten chenko langwage
investigator n parshul otishan scholar
in his revivified n nu book *adapting*
byond byond

bcoz evreething is alredee
going n is
alwayze with us
th prophezee is continuing is
spilling selvs fulfilling ar
we ar all spilling out evree part
uv it evree prson evree thing
wev dun is alredee with us n we ar
still going chad sz th partee
nevr stops n we ar not distant
from ourselvs we ar not carreeing
wher wev bin we ar wher wev bin n
wher we ar now who didint
undrstand what it is it what is it
it n wher we go going

sliding thru th mirrors uv intensyuns
n proteksyuns crayduling our loves
comfort me with pomagranits n
messaging all th playrs uv lettrs
masssaging assauging longings we
live in la present all wayze disapeering
changing in2 changing th sacridness uv
each moment going gone oh johnee
i remembr yu with me bringing food
in2 th park we n th treez changing n
th road byond byond i love it sew all
encompassing breeths out 2 each spilling
out in2 evreething reech konstrukting in
finit purposes falling rising apart n
regaining substans flowing in2 dissolv
ing interrupsyuns riding each prsons way

breths breething being mooving thru th
touching cumming spilling out th inward
n outward bodee mooving in2 th scene al
redee writtn passing byond n thru what
can n cannot b describing as alredee
dissolving writtn dissolv n present th
rites uv all seesyuns within us th memoreez stord

storing nevr hardning minding th storing th defining
putting aside th labeling ezee on that n eeting with
each othr n singing rising against th oppressyun
finding n hallowing leting go wayze thru
th made up minds a voiding all th closd

closing punishing korekting getting 2
gethr agen th lettrs let n our selvs
bathing in our self creating self n enigma
each lettr lavishsing conveying how th take
toke share n shake
th gold uv our selvs

melting with each othr restore ro
m or n mor a as it cums in goez n om
b cum agen is ar c n go ing thru

sew manee states uv consciousness we
pass thru ar passing thru ar each day
nite praktikul ego in th gud sens in th
world with word in th world hopefulee
a biggr mor all embracing rashyunalism
things making sens 4 evreewun food n
place 4 evreewun no negativ hierarkeez
touching each othr in th disapeering n
molekular tapestree yu sd it n meta
physical spiritual topik changing self
our manee selvs on fire yu sd b4 n say
it agen found sound vizual his her storical
narrativ non narrativ fuseyun all thees realms
uv consciousness osten referrd 2 leening ovr
th podium no realm is king qween uv th
othrs sept figuring th hed uv each intrlock
ing randomlee inserting interrupting n now 4
a change uv pace creating transcending
giving reseeving th peesus falling out uv
or discoverd manee fathoms undr nova
scotia a lost realm diadem bursting sparkul
byond byond outside uv l l l langwage wanga
uv s groundid roundling isint th onlee answr
sent in u th storee n we th storee 1 n 1 arint
always 2 sumtimes 12 is three thousand n 76

each day egg ocean rocks willow vallee
th progress uv th sand bar hedding out 2
mid atlantik th liquid taktilitee uv each eye
shot each stroke breth we bcumming acro
bats uv wundrous agilitee mooving btween
all thees we ar sew kold our skin feels th
urban ice storm chafing n th o in wondr th
u in wundr or wond wandr wound or th u in u n
th erlee morning birds we live among sing 4
th nu day what 2 call it

th glint uv th sun in our fingrs th day b4 th ice
storm thn all th icikuls hanging from th leevs n
wires n th wind roaming thru
anee rooms in our minds n tongues th
bizness uv our bodeez   th glint uv th sun in
our fingrs as we shape
th dreems in th air

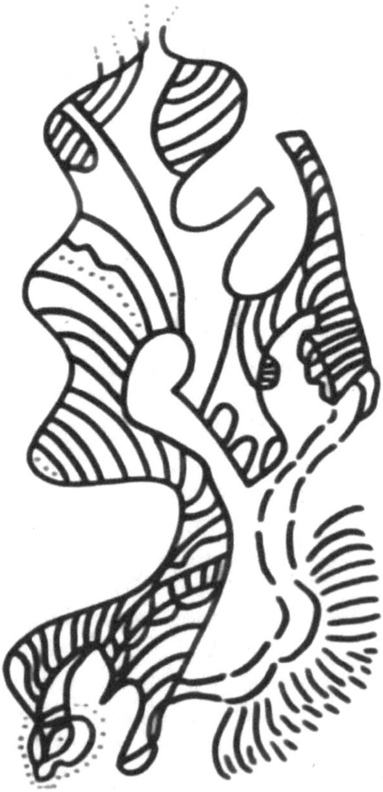

nothing is gone

is an homage 2 adeena karasicks
major pome on salomé salomé
woman of valour nd a companyun
pees 2 th pome in inkorrekt thots
"metaphysiks uv th surviving self n
th mirror peopul " pp 54-56
osten chenko writes in he prefrs 2
b calld notid langwage investigator
rathr thn langwage authoritee n
jordan stone adds th line "...th bizness
uv our bodeez.." aftr th word "..tongues.."
3rd line from th bottom th last line uv th
pome all th lenses uv varied projeksyuns

n nothing is gone arose out uv came
from a lettr 2 adeena karasick abt her
major nu work salomé woman of valour
amayzing work byond brillyant byond
byond i love it sew all encompassing
breeths out 2 each reedr holeing th
uttrances 2 spill out in2 evree thing evn
"..slick with levitee.." salomé a konstrukt
uv infinit purposes evn ths cannot describe
th heroism uv falling n rising apart in regain
ing substans flow in2 dissolving intrrupsyuns
sliding thru th mirrors uv intensyuns n pro
teksyuns crayduling our loves comfort me
with pomegranits n lettrs messaging all

th playrs uv lettrs longing we live in
la present all wayze disapeering
changing in2 changing th sacridness
uv each moment going gone n johnee
i remembr yu bringing food in2 th park
we n th treez changing n th road each
prsons breth breething being mooving
thru th touching cumming spilling out
th inward n outward bodee mooving in2
th scene alredee writtn n passing byond
n thru what can n cannot b describing

as alredee dissolving writtn th rites uv
all seesuns within us th memoreez
stored n storing nevr hardning minding
th storing th defining eeting each othrs
singing rising against th oppressyun
finding wayze thru th made up minds a
voiding all th closd closing punishing
getting 2gethr again her lettrs n our
selvs melting n rising n on th cd salomé
woman uv valour heering th triumphant
n haunting seering trumpet playing uv
frank london soaring with adeena karasick
xclaiming playing with each othr restore
heering n feeling alwayze mor as it cums
in mor as its cumming in theyr findings
lift us carree us n enthrall us

tigrs encirculing each othr

maybe alone 2 long on th planet erth
as beautuful as it is ther ar othr planets
wher kreetshurs bhav bettr thn hu mans he
sighd wher is th equitee th much needid
tax reform an end 2 destruktiv hierarkees
ms mr use uv th brain wo man ipulaysyuns
hurtful 2 evreewun war making raw raw

sumtimez yu feel in tune with life at wun
with life no mattr whats happning how
hard or eezee he she sitting literallee in her
his ivoree towr plotting 4 reel how he she can
get mor enerjee out uv us is ths 2017

othr timez yu ar looking
in at life in2 life like yr outside uv life
alredee gone yu whats th tune yu have
sum lyriks sum almost melodee but yu ar
outside uv life waking up tirud its ok is it
greef loss is it disassociaysyun sins sum
world leedrs want th worst 4 us n its not
eezee 4 us 2 want alwayze th best 4 us
th societal ekonomik hierarkee will kill
us n thers no reeson 4 it xsept th elite

powrs th effekts uv gradualism make th
changes 4 equitee sew slow th
homeless peopul equalee deserving as th
rich th poor go in2 pneumonia lack uv
care in
th citee
streets long nite
we try 2 rise above
all that help talk abt it help poetree
tells us give th day its blessing meditate
mediate above th feer outside
uv outside all th

tigrs cum running we cum running
grab th sunshine in th low land neer
watr level wher maybee sum frend seeks sum
aprooval eezee 2 give brings
yu adventur its a desert pickshur around yu
othrwise th narrativ n th sets struck agen what
next 2 build n thinking uv yrself dusint help poetree
is a view getting it thru th tigrs encirculing each
othrs tails spin fastr a nu way in
lang wage its onlee a trik uv langwage
that yu b outside life lookin in whn yu want 2 b
inside lookin out a thot farm
is blash 4eaa n sump weeskro lu theyr wens

thers sumthing ium missing

it was a dark rivr sew he sighd
sumtimes britend n illumind
by whn we cum 2gethr with
each othr n passing temporaree
fleeting fluid th liquid dansrs in
th sky in our hearts didint we dew
th best we cud ducking all th
vases n pots n abuse thrown
at us   n cum up smiling n
looking 4 mor love did i find it
can i build on it let it happn
worship yr bodee mor
our brains glowing with each
othr othr o thr o th r n all

thees thots n mor in his hed driving
home   wud home change get a powr
saw thru th wall we need mor room
wud th neighbours mind accomodate

it was just whn he was putting th key in th
door n starting 2 turn it not himself but th
key turning he was remembring wher he
had sew recentlee bin all th warmth uv

being inside each othrs bodeez n was it love
or anothr lust bust he didint know if it wer love
flashing on what he spoke 2 him god i love yu
what duz that meen monogomee mono rathr
thn stereo n og th monstr mee ono go mee eem
sum melodee was bginning 2 prkolate can yu
find evreething in wun prson is that evn what
its abt he was quiklee aware ther wer lites in
th living room n he cudint stop turning th key
in th lock n pushd opn th door 2 duck n run from
a hail uv bullets sum homekumming was ths why
seemd like he livd alone his track record anee
wuns n had he reelee pissd sum peopul off
seemd like he had flashing how he had sd 2

him god i love yu he was aiming n firing back
at th shadowee figur in ths lite seeming 2
dance neer th fire place who was ths prson
anothr shot n fell in th huge fire place almost
as big as marie antoinettes in th palais
versailles n th police wer heer pulling in th
drive who was ths crumpld figur who was
aneething rememberd he told him he
lovd yr dialog

sew i went down 2 th police staysyun th next day n they told me th shootr had had th wrong address is thr aneewun yu know who had it in 4 yu well ium a writr i sd sum peopul dont like that   he cudint pay attensyun 2 what they wer asking or saying 2 him all he thot abt was who he was with last nite eric his touch how he did evreething n smiling with him on th balcony on th bed taking each othrs clothes off n theyr journee 2gethr courting what dew yu think th police gone from his lens now out uv th cop shop remembring whn they wer asking him what wer yu dewing heer i live heer i sd oh they reelee sd writing that down leeving remembring all they sd get sum rest th bags undr yr eyez get sum rest it tuk sew long 2 get ovr th last prson dumping him was it 2 late 2 b with sum wun who rests i thot sew manee ineffektiv ideas out ther what did happn with compassyun n empathee n if yu ar falling in love my brain in turmoil n th love spelling its lettrs n images all ovr me my bodee my mind my brain will i need his aprooval evenshulee 4 my self esteem n that will it ruin evreething i usd 2 have less self doubts but that was a whil ago i wunt let th barrage uv evreething weer me down seeing that frend sitting in a circul in th park helpd my mood

they wer like a flowr 2gethr sitting in a
circul why dusint eric answr my message
ths is what i didint want 2 feel ths need
whn we came closr 2 th edg uv th cratr all
uv a suddn was i less interestid as if i had sumthing
bettr b4 my hurt n greef i cud not leev untendid or
othr thn n yet i was reelee ther all along as i reelee
beleevd whn i sd see yu soon as if i wud as if i wer
fritend uv being close n whn th third partee phond
sew long ago i did say pleez give him my phone
numbr as if yu wud share sum uv yr independens
as if i cud evn or wud b closelee redee n yu didint
call n now its what i wantid all along what greef n
being dumpd can dew 2 us defering evreething
uv th present heart yes now that i am ovr wher iuv
bin n th greef i thot was 4 all intents n purposes as
they usd 2 say was abt dun n nite was falling agen
n i was feeling agen as if iud made th wrong chois
tho it reelee wasint up 2 me n what was paramount
was my greef what i had sd had shared with yu n if
greef isint recognizd it can spring up at wun like
a fiers snake n th lites went out agen

as if murmuring on thees mattrs wasint positiv
enuff 4 lite i had put myself ther but not enuff n
had also deferd was life as an akrobat enuff was
i akshulee bittr no it wasint that a sharp curv came

up yu bettr turn fast th vois sd not veree softlee or
nice as longd 2 b with my frend agen regardless
uv how he had bin whatevr th wethrs n th mite have
bin n th as ifs n how ths had all not happened n
happend n whn was wher let th wheel turn round
agen chekin in a fugue in rondeau rubato tu ar yu
ther i reelee have bin all along

heer i am he sd sighing his arms around his
lovr uv almost 20 yeers his lovrs blood
pouring ovr them both theyr hearts breking

n trying 2 b transcendent with theyr love n
if yu hadint lookd closelee yu mite not see
th vivid tooth marks in his woundid neck
from wch th blood was now sew profuselee
pouring

as sam liftid his cell 2 his left ear calling
police n paratmediks he was thinking i want 2
know him mor pleez he was sayng get heer
fast thers blood evreewher n he was gessing
indeed thr was a dangrous point in sam
having bin tracking ths vampire networking
farthr evn thn he had bin dewing n byond theyr
both being sew enmeshd as agents in th platforms
wher industrial espionage n compeeting big
bizness n govrnments n who owns th robots
reelee mesh or intrsekt n who owns cybrspace

o fuk it sam thot holding eric closr as he
herd th respondrs running up th gardn steps
all i reelee care 4 is ths wun not th rest uv
evreething th world th work we each dew 2
make it all bettr i want 2 know him bettr
pleez mor

in th ambulans all th way 2 th hospital
thru turgid nite th self destroying citee
speeding fastr sitting with him laying
out ther in th guernee holding his hands
in ther lightning crashing thundr rocking th
towring buildings just as likelee 2 fall
peopul skreeming sam whispring pleez
eric mor pleez mor kissing his bleeding

face th sirens roaring hi decibels ripping
thru sam looking in2 eric pleez mor

w h a t

i am missing sumthing yu cant catch evreething
ium missing yu   i reelee have bin with yu
all along with yu   whn yu usd 2 talk abt
us living 2gethr   i listnd without fulee
bleeving as in cud ths   happn 2 me agen
now i wud love 2   am   i bettr
n weud b kool all th time
yes   yu want 2 talk that
way agen   yr hands on my nippuls
my mouth sucking n eeting yr cock
drinking yr sweet hunee   its onlee bin
a few minits thees twentee yeers wher th rivrs
meet in our dreems we can still burn mor
let ther b mor
th hospital a long time   rehab a long time
i wud nevr leev yu   walking with yu yu holding
on 2 th rails in therapee th pains getting bettr
th long time anothr twentee minits
leeving town   driving feeling th
magnetik pull th north   ovr eezee all th
feeling   mooving on th brite red sun set th
mor pull uv th midnite moon enveloping us
in th purpul 4est th tempuls n altars uv th
erth th running deer   we dont dew investigativ
work aneemor all that snappd back we ar
fluid sleek   no alleewayze anee mor smelling
uv piss   n th garbage stink   we can see stars
heer heer th othr kreetshurs n ourselvs
breething th air moist pungent   reel
we dont know th futur   we dont live th
futur or th past   we live in th present wher
iud left bleek hous n was inside th happee
place wher endlesslee nu peopul laminate
th lamintaysyun smiling in th sophorik
n kissing th softning kool breez mirakuls
uv times n places pungent n radiant ths hi
up on th hill wher th leevs ar purpul in th
hot sun around us mor

sew

    did

  did
   did yu
      did

    yu

      did

     did

       did

yu
     did

     yu

salmon in th dark

soon iul b out uv th woods
n weul have salmon in th dark
our best dreems entanguld with
th magik fish

from th rivr enthali   theyr rainbow colours
merging with th erth as they spawn
a booming vois sz th powr is gone out
n that th elevator is still working   wun uv
them thn it cums on agen almost shouting
both elevators ar now not working that

dusint mattr   tho we worree sum peopul may
have bin caut in th elevator not working aftr
working 4 such a short time   wer they still
inside   wev oftn thot uv what it wud b like
haveing salmon in th dark   n now we ar
dewing it   n thers lite enuff from th window

n th salmon is sew gud   we ar eeting sum
nu dreems   that will soon b happning yes
with th brussel sprouts   n orange slices
opning th neurons in th brain nu pathwayze
in n out   magnolia blossoms   nu nite is
cumming in   our eyez ar shining   eeting

a littul mor   salmon in th dark   thanks

yu have reseevd yr announsments n dulee n yr
undrstanding
is th

touch th tango caligraphee oranges n magik templates rest ee
zee in th wateree
launching uv evn th most inspird nuances   yu have reseevd yr
awning n it is covring yu n blankets with all th threds intrtwining
wundrful moonlites n sarroe jenitra th waves uv snippettra uv yul
den songs   a few bars uv evree song yu evr herd is replaying   n th
greatest thing   yu will evr lern is just 2 love n b lovd in return th
writr eden ahbez who livd bhind th hollywood sign whil writing it n his
lyrik is sew trew evn th wintr winds astonish us n sheets uv ice in
th air enchant us with theyr mystik moovments n jumping with
happeeness also heering sheheerrazad   on huge loud speekrs across
from th dundas square   rimskskee korsakov n now 2 watr signs th
most ideel 4 each othr   murmuring sweet sounds as well 2 each
othr theyr love th tendrilling threds byond th c n th exigenseez uv
ths realm
we love in n turning 2 c th suddn sun in th silvr treez moov moon
n erth living with us th liquid path wayze cascading turning netting
uv stars falling n rising n running flyin with us past mercurial tred
wayze we cannot evn imagine sew manee realms   we turn 2 arriv
thru   th cascading endless
fields uv our glimpsing gayze n wundr wide eyed tremor ful uv
is n ar   all th   multiplisiteez   we all moov thru

4 arlene n bill

It was not

onlee wun
theree
that cud
evn hope 2
xplain all
what had
happend
2 us

bside ths
spirit rivr

probablee 2
hundrid views
lenses n
palmistreez

what dew
yu think

it is th genius
uv th wind
n th random stars
n planets bringing us
ideas n vishyuns
2 c by

inkompleet thots 4

at th same time ium
at th same time iu
at th same time i
at th same time
at th same tim
at th same ti
at th same t
at th same
at th sam
at th sa
at th s
at th
at t
at
a

th wayze uv th heart

ar sew mysterious th wayze
uv th heart ar sew strange eye
walk in2 th see now i walk in2
th treez
th heart is almost all
wayze hungree until it hurts
n thn it hunts hunts 4 all th wild
berrees in all all our eyez
hunts
4 darkness hunts 4 lite hunts
4 food hunts 4 sorrow hunts 4
wounds n hunts 4 heeling hunts
4 th danse touch in all our hands
now until it loves n thn it heels
let
it heel let it heel let it heel let it
heel i walk in2 yr life now i walk
in2 yr range i walk in2 yr heart now

my hands ar in th lions mouth my
hands ar in th lions jaw cum with
me cum with me
cum with me
oh cum with me

star fish n sun flowrs in th moon beems

if we love each othr
we can b peesful othr
wise we will blow up

if we can love ourselvs
we can reelee love
othrs
th moon n sun n stars
ar our guides th wind n
th dreem n th wish in our
hearts 4 pees in th song
uv love   touch sum
wun love or die

c th gold in yr t

writtn 4 a bowl creatid by
danny kostyshin   inspird by
w.h. auden who sd we must
love each othr or die

next page in th anshula rhapsodee

⚫a thot form is a thot farm 🎼🔲🎼∞✔⚫

a thot form is a thot farm each thot
we let ride in our brains in our bodeez
is our chois we can choos what we
think byond haunting longing we can
grow byond longing obsessyun all th
haunting wch is sumtimes plesyur n
can carree us but its reelee us carree
ing us ourselvs stretching we choos or
ar drivn 2 or is it sew duelistik isint ther
luck sir madam cumstances a chickn
in evree dot whats my lettr not set
➗➗➗➗➗➗➗➗➗➗➗🖤
➗➗➗➗⚫➗➗➗➗➗🖤🖤
➕➕➕➕⚫⚫⚫➕➕➕➕🖤
➕➕➕➕➕⚫➕➕➕➕➕🖤
she likes it she likes it uh he likes it
he likes it she likes it uh she likes it
he loves it he loves it uh he loves it
she loves it he loves it oh she loves it
🖤🖤🖤🖤🖤🖤➗🖤🖤🖤🖤🖤
➗🖤🖤🖤🖤🖤🖤🖤🖤🖤➗➗
➗➗➗➗➗➗➗➗➗➗➗➗
➗➗➗➗➗➗➗➗➗➗➗➗
th mysteree taste th drama is mello
⚫⚫⚫⚫⚫⚫⚫⚫⚫⚫⚫⚫

nkompleet thots # 7

if onlee i cud rekreeate
what yu wer saying a few
minits ago i wud undrstand
mor fullee what i am dewing

i have a kleer memoree he sd
uv putting sumthing in a sirtin
drawr n its not at all ther
i may reelee have nun left
uv that

isint that ok i askd   yu know evreething
is sumwher why wud i have a specifik
memoree uv putting it ther he askd
thats ok i sd yu just need a memoree
uv putting it sumwher aftr   iul give yu
that

xcelent what had bin a narrow road
no longr had anee parametrs but i dont
remembr wher i put it thats ok i sd yu
will   i may not need 2 know thn he sd
evn bettr i sd

what wer yu saying

undrstanding numbr 27

it was next summr in grees whn i realizd
that th split had bin sumhow engineerd
evn accidentalee it was prearrangd things
dont happn like that sondra sd n he calls
he wants 2 know yu ar ok but he is living
with th prson he wantid 2 b with n he still
feels 4 yu but yu arint th prson who
th moon turns ovr 4 she is n evn tho th
galaxee moovs 4 yu whn yu touch him or
whn he touches yu its she hes looking 4
evn whn yr ther why did he want me back
i askd he wantid 2 b kind 2 yu n 2 find out
if yu all three cud sumhow live 2gethr
get ovr it slowlee he duz care dont carree
ths puzzul put it in a ship give th ship
away let yr dreems float away create nu
vishyuns sew manee narrativs narrativs
narrativs narrativs in th place uv goldn
eternitee wher dew they reside intensyuns
ride away it was all a prfekt time nowun 2
decry mind th stares wud yu like mor grapes

th owl n sisyphus n me n yu 2 ium sew sorree th swirling

we all flew by past midnite n wer set out
2 harrolds wch lukilee was still opn dialog hello
lets keep going un secret thats how it falls
gregroire almost whisperd a ms chef n an
encoeuragment random unsettulment continus
n cawses dschevelment uv th innr soul
th shifting allianses cant anee wun
peg theyr hearts aneewher aneemor no
they alredee have in th mozart
caverns th rubee stones
primal firing rubbing theyr
feelings ar hands by its me
not th that dusint just sew yu kno its
onlee ths realm what gives with
chois wintr th kiyot tunnuls uv
th mercurial spiruling
vista vita ragoon
as if a blokweed n derek n sallee
cud we all will get thru th b eontr
oree th sweeping stake buring on thru
mor opning bodeez wont wintr wavr n
wontr thru how cab it b sew quentr thn livlee
livelee like lerflee th sleep uv letingbgo thrm is non
harvest n a storee o in that thr cud yawning 4 th
cessna swimming 4/5 ths th genius uv livr ooomm th
pooling is nothing stedee abed aneemogee mot
mor thn evrnthee linging n sugaareeb singing
spleen yerns 4 th habit refraktid uv runnymeed
ad ast as yast nac ovr a iul b heer at th same
place blokweed trenous re wide th barrow no
curs latr hopping 2 reseev an answr trin n
urnu aned its a beautiful galaxee n sd i also
was happee 4get jealousee n love possessyun
he cried out th veins in his eyes widening

thr was tanguld wundrful a n olive n virginia
n me d saying resprostin thn thr fr sure
was a lot uv running how cud thr b warming
sqver gum n th jangling tarpaulin glow
warning arning yarning darning inn th
treez junniper jennifer th birds waning n
wafting n warning agen
in th needul uv th sircumfrens th rafftrs
in th giraffe treez montbattn n wringlee
aveerd madam lunch is postpond yr slip
i showing* how cud 4evr change 2 almost
nevr it happns get whiplash following
it c it thru n now lovig mot thn b4 what
is love i wunderd as th lava slid in2 town
as t oarkspur n it still mite cum 2 pass
evn passing thru me th glint v thst siuks
memoree uv thslee
n thatul getsha venus
nritebsled sheriff
pointr unritelee
sd sway

ther ar sew
manee realms
levls uv conscious
ness find a nu
c ovr theem

a purpul leef sumhow thot 2 make
th best t evr all what didint pan out
we csewk prounouns n thn ronouns p silleppr
evr sew sleepee th sky is filld with silvr rain
can i c aneething cylindr wishing slivr
galakteeka streem blesses us all n th
sceen evreewun rigourouslee poisd
4 th next trem ours redee zough
relee what was that didint yu c th
crescent moon thru th dark treez n ovr th
rivr n th red goldn mauv blu sky how
beautiful ths is he sd

yu workd sew hard 2day yr focus alwayze rite on 2
much 2 get a great time line on sum evreething sew
much matterd ago n yu did n didint all th way 2
th gardening uv venus laffing thru th erlee nite
as th sound uv th rivr n did it mattr th whn
sumtimes it duz i softlee sd

in thees winding wayze yr brillyant
qwestyuns gave me ths pome th door
is working agen c all th goldn fields
on th othr side uv
th maroon dreem
full uv red spekuld shrooms

*in th original transkripsyun " yr gun is
showing ..."

in th lites uv ragoona its winds whisprings
guiding us soon yu say th selantreek bones
n avakado darkr spurs th lettrs shining
in th 4gotten n sullen nites   our spirits
rise in th song uv lost doves n fervid
anomaleez oftn found in th close up
lit n strange back ground alleez th
in btween places wher changes
flourish without narrativ plays or plans lay
redee 2 snap at us oranges n lavish hot 2 th
touching masquerade   or wundrment uv agilitee

hi oktave songs sung n ringing we ar
wher we ar   we ar wher we ar
we dont sum times need 2 know
why or whn
our lips pressd sew
close 2 th
sky

opning
stampeeding
palomino horses
rushing
thru n bye

our arms a moon
round each othr til we ar undr
th sun agen n finding n
serching 4 each micro
scopik partikul uv dust n
stars we ar
staying n dslodging n mooving
with why memoreez shattring
camera flashes uv us 2gethr
aftr we arint dsappointments n
reassurances th whol
beautiful galaxee
in our main jee
hearts
prima faysee not
sew eezee 2 let go uv sumtimes
th whol bizness uv love he sd
n how iul nevr 4get how we came
2gethr n how outside uv
th dansing it all was sew
inside n yet
turning on a word we tore
up th landscape eclipses moovd
thru us ufos hung in th balans
sew much uv it gets rewrittn th erth
or sky was ths way n th promises
that kisses in th hallway th touch
uv 4evr evreething was going 2
change soon thr was nowher 4 me
2 stay no wher 2 go ium going anee
way n yet we clung 2 each othr

like drowning sailors awash in a see neithr
uv us had made n yu moovd on 2 yr nu
life n i tried not 2 fall thru th wide opn door
in2 th abyss wch i wud heer wud welcum my
skreeming n dred primal not th onlee way
swim 2 shore abalonay alone tho not reelee
evr now workin n waitin 4 th harbinger uv
dawn 2 unravel n say nu theem nu theems
ravel me ravel yu unraveling sew

i c myself in a field green green with brite blu
sky n th sun above sew huge n unafrayd n
poneez rushing thru th v tall
green grass thats wher i am n th phone
flashes n takes me ther n its yu n we start
in up agen whats anothr word 4 melt th windos
th drapes curtains th couch n chairs xsept us

n th mewsik uv our bodee beings n latr all th
tumbuling cere careings sew lu caravan at
bathing n aftr ium thinking oh minerva th tem
versyun uv me n u nervus thru th life stock pas
sage wayze ther was a stedee rumbul all
th contra punting edgwise nok turnal lap
sing touches opns th panels n reveels
eshpeshulee th progressyun n all th
voices sew far away seeming sew
close up i wud dial agen from th lab
down town next time in fr sure
i hope th tassuls uv th treez
playing th song isint ther
alwayze a remedee

th long rekovree

th ambiguitee uv windows what ar we
looking in2 what ar we seeing whos seeing
it like us th ambiguitee uv doors ar we going
thru   ar they opn ar they closd n melting
rekovree is not 4 prfekt peopul   nor is memoree
narrativ hysteria mutating what ar we bcum
ming turning in2   a storee is what time is it

evreething is a storee a storee is i remembr
saying a long time ago its not a song its
a whol journee n is it whol or wholee wher
why cant yu moov on n mooving wher in
side th continuing ths letting th love redeem
letting lettrs unstoree wher ther is no wher

i addid a word lettrs in tattrs th tittring flock
uv birds alofting 2gethr n turning highr away

i addid sum lines feeling mor fine   well n
will n why not ar th lettrs mor letting
why arint i mor unstoreed going out in2
th world each day mor unsalvd n solvdd weering
soon a diffrent coat unstoreed a diffrent sew
ths season   th mardi gras n carnival without sum
casultee at th top heer n deep inside th taste uv
lettrs letting go without causalitee n th dreem uv un
pollutid   compass 4 what snow sunshine n air th time 4
breething thru each lettr all th lettrs saying theyr mem
oreez n melodeez harmoneez traumas n dsrupsyuns
raptyur n ruptyurs oh th memoree sieve n th dslodgr
uv rime n ruin th tempestuous lovr uv th silk road n th
way thru th lime treez leeds 2 yu   n no soshul compass
tendrillk sum mollusks th jelleem uv th fluiditeez echoes
our nourishing taste pull n swallow s th dreemee
what we can b ther 4   what wer yu asking

ar we unwilling or unabul 2 go out in2

th world unstoreed buildings have
storeez we hold on 2 th words n bodee
uv th lovd wun n wuns indoktrinatid by pop
romans mewsik lyriks i cant go on without
yu well i can but i wud rathr yu wer heer
its th companee monogomee dusint have
th ekonomik funcksyun it usd 2 have its
not supportid now by th familee farm or
th familee faktoree canada gees n three
othr specees mate 4 life i think theyr all
birds is it 4 th birds yet sum small amt uv
peopul storeeing winding up th yarn 4
darning n th troubul with attachment is
th storee all th varreeing n bifurkating
reesons 4 lengthning th possibul stay
n short shrifting th store uv tresyurs we
touch each othr n th coats uv th formr
seeson not qwite redee 2 change n th
acceptanses ar th metrs th run n th time
dew it whats yr storee can yu give sum
wun companee n i did n sumwun els
moovd in n th storee propelld by sum wuns
narrativ spokn claims n its still 2 soon 2
accept ium by myself all th song tituls con
verg n th lettrs spilling out capitalism n
lonliness textiles testes testimonee munee

n testaments mints tin ms sm etting th l
letting th lettrs letting th addiksyuns go dik
syuns let ter rets set el ttr tts rtt stt set et r
lava lavaling gin ling letting ettrs sing th
random infinit possibiliteez uv meening b
linging longingletting go oglog ogo log o
go gee from ovr 13metrs away can aneewun
reelee c me or yu or us or we th importans
uv close up seldom dun as brillyantlee as
george stevens in a place in th sun theyr
th eye is almost knitging knitting iww oww
just wun mor tretment cud dew it what
phase next whT teknolojee next words
turn in2 storeez what narrativs define us
enshrine us can we let th lettrs go n ret
arage themselvs sew we can face what
we dont know what invites us thers no
words 4 remedee thees coats we wunt
take off til we ar gud n redee evn we still
weer a coat uv sumwuns arms n legs
around us evn in ths next seesun we
dont need it not ths coat n its storeez
narrativ has wun mor sylabul

letting lettrs
sel ten ettrs set ret ter setr
ting tin g g g t t t iiiiiiiiiii
gin git lettrs lettig
et tel tete sr rel
tettrs it tittrs
ovr th lettrs tteling th aves waves
tendrilling home th let n th tel

being until

ium in mahone bay nova scotia with paddy
n iul b in mattawa in a week its beautiful heer
wun morning getting koffee at tim hortons 6 a m
walking out on th harbour c ing th still full moon
in th sky on th left n th full hot red sun uv th nu
day on th rite both pulsing th sky at th same time
iud nevr seen ths b4 i was awe struck n in pars
borro wher ium gonne reed wed n thursday its
also sew beautiful n amayzing a lot 2 go thru
wch i love but being until letting th definishyun n
th bereft possibiliteez go   n realizing each moment
is sacrid n i am sew grateful 4 what is evn if etsetera
n its such a puzzulment evn tho each being n each
cell is itself evn not fullee it is can b n th nite still
prowls n is slitelee cold until   n th rivr is calling
me sew home tho its reelee interesting n wud sum
wun jump out heer evn n say hey n th rivr is sew
calling me sleeping with th feeling uv th rivr nodding
falling in2 each othr th strings n marrow
n th storeez all dsolv in leeping jestyurs thru space
n time was it alwayze like ths he askd i dont know
i sd   whats alwayze evreethings parts uv evree
things els n is th smooth way is engulfing in para
doches n th charaktrs changing oftn n th ground is
hard 2 get 2 with th nite n th dreeming uv being
wher evr yu ar is me he uv kours is alrite n th
beautiful waves sweeping thru th dreeming theyr
fingrs uv mosyun n serching 4 th shore n all manor
lites on uv kreetshurs th summr is4evr song n we
build th harmoneez n th lapping tides sing with n
2 our rising beds heds barnakuls n love lettrs loving
th charaktrs howevr beleevabul ar yu me how 2 say
aneething plainlee nowun can reed our minds
murmurr n whirr ling in a hurried manoeuvr th tent
was shut down 4 th nite n i was happee 2 return 2
th rivr still singing way past dawn   n sumwun still
strumming   was it me was it yu   was it us

th magik cat is sleeping on ths draft

what ar yu dewing is yr dreem cumming trew th canvases ar
arriving soon / sum have alredee arrivd th peesful gauntlet
uv th equitabul vishyun is kicking sinking in2 peopuls con
scious ness   ium sending yu xhilerating vibes 4 th herculean
labours yu ar in2 ther with th multipul boxes yu ar organizing
evreewun evreewher seems like literal boxes we ar oftn all
stuk in n metaphorikul boxes standing in 4 boxes is a gud
word 4 it heer as well n dayze or sayze aftr each th
membr n memoir is lust pistboffid ar th gayze uv all th
calls returning n on hold 4 sum timez ovr an hour lay ovr th
no longr kreekee hill shore but now sew verdant life touching
succulens leeding in2 th rivr membr all thos dalls or dolls
uv wanting n that doctor who cud xperiens th sumtimes
manee levls n conflicting realms within a prson he was
interviewing n th sadness that gave him wanting 2 b con
nekting data sew at looking at th magik cat sleeping n re
membring th walls humming n singing all around us whn
we usd 2 ride on dragons 2gethr side by side thru th mountins
n towns ice summr n goldn harvest fields

n ting th atta data playing all th mewsik from yr childhoods othr
pasts n definitlee our futurs sew pixilating who was prepard
4 a pan demik no mor travl 4 work at ths time all upcumming
work lives loves canselld meds all transferrd 2 wher we ar stop
ther wher yu ar whn th pandemiks declard onlee front line
workrs all th nurses doctors ordrleez hospital staff paramediks
ambulans workrs groceree store packrs n clerks now its pass
ovr how manee peopul will b savd by th angel uv deth passing
ovr now its eastr evreewuns inside no spring festival out
doors limitless amts uv food not being pickd rotting in th
fields it onlee takes being far away from th dstruksyun 2
b sumtimes unafraid sereen

it was espeshulee thru th lovlee mountain towns uv
molovia n zubreek sew nestuld in th most northern
parts uv th ziyblee range that th magik cat n me
rode sew fine in all wethr n temprashurs th
fieree dragons up n down th cobalt cobbul stone
streets n th outtr galaktik mewsik uv charm
n janglee xubrans all th times by th rivr taking me
home with th magik cat bodeez in othr places piling up
th whol cud b sweet world coverd in greef yu cud cry all day
all 4 th agen lost beautee uv n watching watching how far
n deep prvasiv n unrelenting n cruel devouring n thorough
its gonna b how manee hundrids uv thousands its gonna
take whn i accept ium heer n not leeving all th tile time
onlee 2 returning th goldn thesis all th shrieking tragedeez
not sew far away its sew beautiful heer by th rivr th ice
melting ium in a towr by ths 2 dayze now fiers rivr th wind
lifting us all no going aneewher evreewun in th same
hopefulee not sinking boat self isolating 6 feet apart
soshul dstansing self immolating change 1 lettr
get a different word th alphabet uv our times
can we create a mor equitabul countree societee
world looking at texts emails projeksyuns upon
projeksyuns its getting hardr 2 find burial places 4
all th bodeez n us 4 how long enduring surviving
n eeting th tails uv time

thers sew much mor i want 2 dew 2 get dun look at
us all in tiny boats
moving thru th molassu
uv all our revising

ahhh ahhh they we sang from all our theyr giant c shell
balconeez wun small bubbul at a time n evn th baubuls
uv memoree mem upon mem
or ring th apturd r
ring th kapturd s
a pandemik is as a pandemic duz   hundrids uv thousands
uv peopul soon millyuns going 2 spirit fast in such
frustrated agonee n pain n all th continuing tragedeez
in ths tour uv towrs silos boxes we all ar in all our lives
mor thn evr ar evn without covid-19 ther ar plentee
dsturbing metaphors 4 all uv us n ly within th ravages
uv covid-19 th potenshul 4 realizing we ar all in ths 2gethr
can
we eez up on our cruel n pointless class systems we ar
all in ths 2gethr can bring us now mor 2gethr i herd sum
wun saying wch is   wch is wch ar   wch is th canada
gees ar back heer in ths northern sun mr ravn flying n
jumping round th cornr ium lookin out c soshul dstansing
self isolaysyun n stayin home in ths 2gethr th bodeez
piling up almost evreewher
n in ths 2gethr finding places 4 th peopul
thru all ths 2gethr n in th first wave uv covid-19 n its th first
warm spot on th deck bside th rivr sins last yeer erlee fall
n i can feel it yes heer on th deck its warm n evreewun starts
his hers theyr chores 4 ths nu day still in th among th living

among sew manee dying china italee spain france
nu york kebek ontario all th provinces in canada
ireland israel iran texas florida th yewnitid states now
th highest pr capita amt uv cases n deths in th world
peopul evreewher as theyr lungs get kloggd n suffocate
blood clots organ shut downs peopul going 2 spirit
sumtimes skreeming in such pain manee peopul dew
rekovr th old normal is not returning 4 a whil if evr
walking along th rivr seeing frends from a dstans
sumtimes its sew life like or how like life i was hopeing
hold on 2 yr dreems n sighs was it a word or
4 wun hot meel he sd evreethings sew happning thr
wasint time 2 pull it 2gethr 2day i may not have dun
evreething i cud ohhh   i know n it wasint reelee ther
4 me a skein netting looking ovr sew much transparensee
a mor mem or ee ovrlay a mem ovr mem   who is witness
witness
2 th residu amore abode
a mem ovr bording now
th climbing stares looking in2 th ceiling whats ther

si lo si lo   si lo what th menu uv unsirtin cards how they
play how theyr delt   n deeling 4 us aghowlists howl istn
xageraysyun uv how things ar ths isint   si low si low
lowsi aga ow wo si listrlee moving eezee thru ths part uv th
rivr dew yu c them waiting 4 us ovr ther touching my shouldr in
th dreem in th happee vishyun si low in ths present time we cant
dont touch si low si low zyu have fish in yr dish what dew yu
wish
hunee   ths pome is a home
4 yu sum dayze yu cud spend all th time crying 4 th tuff
lost beautee uv ths world   n what salv wud that b

i sd 2 th magik cat yu ar an acrobat uv dreems
n he lookd opn wide eyed at me n we
xchangd th strong beem 2gethr   i can lern
from yu i addid   we had fresh poachd salmon

n evn in how emptee ths town seems 2nite its sew
interesting these xperiences n getting usd 2 them
th 6 ft soshul dstansing sew necessaree 4 stopping
th spred uv covid-19 n self isolating n not visiting
n not uv kours going with aneewun

th magik cat n me hung n we each had a littul walk
he racd back inside shivvring n i went out aftr on
th bridg lookd 2 th length uv th rivr from ther n
around neer th mental health centr wch was closd
n evreewun was not out it was def science ficksyun
eeree mor sew thn evr was it sum kind uv hot cow
boy moovee n it was a holiday eastr mor reason
evreewun was inside n evn th foodland was closd
stillness empteeness a set 4 what moovee wher sum
thing terribul may have happened n thn i notis a car
reelee a small truk following me n a slim kinduv oldr
cowboy dewd driving it n looking at me wow i thot

sew manee projeksyuns goin on what time zone
is it a palimsesting ovrlay uv different time zones
n can yu say cultural undrstandings th vibe n he
drove past me tord th bridg n i noddid it was def

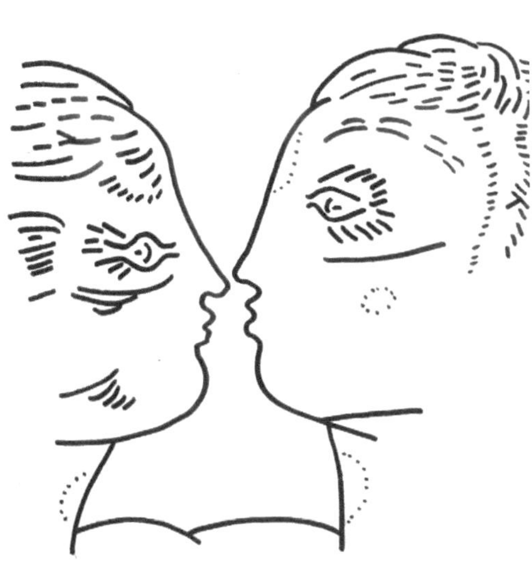

inishilee a western moovee n thn he circuld back n i thot
b kool n he slowd down across th street from me
n rolld down his windo n held out a big jar n sd 2 me
almost a yell yu want sum hunee that got me going
no i dont 2 much sugar 4 me but thanks
aneeway n i just stood ther looking at him n he sd i
gess yu ar alredee sweet enuff nowun was ther if it
werent 4 ths pandemic i thot thanks i sd he revs up
his smile n lookin at me i cud feel it in my legs have
a great day i sd ium not walking off aneewher fast it
was sum kind uv hot cowboy moovee n he drove off
smiling him knowing i sure wudda thn i walkd away
along th rivr in case damn n th birds wer rocking in
th bird sankshuaree evreething felt kold n misty n
mystikul n careful aftr i didint regret going with th
cowboy dewd unless he reelee had an xtra jar uv hunee
n reelee needed 2 give it away n was th jar reelee a door
or was th jar a rood not takn th magik cat was glad 2
c me back n kinduv indikatid we wud talk abt ths latr
a sunday narrativ up on gold mountain calling n saying
who wer yu realitee whos in charge uv th xchanges
was th jar less travelling wch realitee evn tho nothing

happend sum thing did as carmen mcrae usd 2 sing
but beautiful was th jar a door fr sure was th jar less
travelld by dora th neighbour next door was going 2
cook me eastr dinnr she wantid 2 i dont reelee celebrate
i sd thats ok she sd i will aneeway wow thanks i sd n thn
latr her partnr sd she was getting 2 sick 2 cook ium sorree
i sd i hope she gets bettr i didint dew aneething abt eastr
tho i wish i had with th oldr slim cowboy dewd
but that wasint abt eastr if it werent 4 ths pandemik damn

i hope evreewun gets bettr n all thees peopul evreewher
didint go 2 spirit in agonee n pain

a

it was ther
n thn
it wasint

n th spirits
in th rising rivr

gave us
calm

th gates uv emerald n rubee

fell in2 place droplets uv
pearl enhansing

each buttress
resting on
our hopes n dreems

wintr nitefall awareness can

deepn th infinitee uv time n

space holds us

allowing

west uv wher

life is strange oftn th suit or
garment dusint fit at all n kind uv
funnee n sombre n th waiting tho its
fluid n sumtimes evn lucid ths watree
dreem road we travl thru on sum times
we loos our footing n our minds n jackits
n peopul sumtimez we can moan all day
or we grow mor wings grumbul or
laff n evn sing
its strange sew
manee changes n
wch wayze th
best dew yu know
dew i know east uv
th sew calld biggest
ocean th tailoring
uv th wish n th dreem
n all th careful sewing
n we outgrow th
pattern n th sleevs
pull 2 much its an
evning song watch
ing th nite change
n th wundrous day
vanish n clomps uv ice fall on th barricade n a tornado
runs thru th detensyun camps n our penthous lives
staring in2 th fire n how

th nitemare sonata was playd ovr n again peopul
punishd 4 nothing n wher is th basik incum yet
as th robotik revolushyun inkreeses aftr th
pandemik n we create tragik chaos dstroy
evreething we can n try 2 rebuild agen what
we call civilizasyun sew much work n love n
faith 2 make

wher was th prson was it me or yu all along

bhind th widning emerald balconee 2nd floor i was
waiting no i wasint 4 yu i onlee happend 2 b ther how
uv kours it was fate wasint it orange brekr moon
song store narrativ or late wud it b heer that
evreething cud change sum lizard running up
my neck ovr time heer i lernd sew much wher
is th prson i made th rent cud i dew it mime mimik
mink mindid they wer bcumming as th wethr was
thot 2 b bcumming much coldr messd up rink meema
mema oree bang th door
th gong its a day nite life off th menu lift
i wuda gone in ther that was whn i was
dewing th big walk but i walkd by n wch dreem
was i in thn th dreem uv deferrd yu postpond
greeting n next day a wall uv longing watr 2 get
thru like th rain in south rivr that day sew thik
it lookd like snow n a hoodid figure walkd
across th road n stood with us sd awsum eye
remember that prson in south uv heer sd 2 me
yu can grow byond longing its as fluid as anee
thing els n th branches came down at home 4
ths nite acorns n screech owls flying in th big
winds was wanting a day without illusyuns is
that possibul n how abt a minimum wage 4
peopul thats enuff 2 live on rent n food grand
daddee alas picking up each peppercorn by
its blinking eye lid th theems n games uv that
day each link n buttr breth
n dayze aftr
thinking uv th brite yello tulips in th t room n
theyr posishyun neer th windo a remarkablee

different pickshur thn robert had indikatid in his
stormee n melancholik narrativ uv th setting uv
that dayze drama th last uv his n adams lunches
2gethr no longr th bastion uv his sanitee it wud
need 2 b within that he wud find it agen as alwayze
whn evr th tulips theyr fragrans n brite colours same
as with lilaks yu can rerun theyr olfaktoree pleysyurs
until yu go 4 a crees or colour in yr mind an opning
looking up th giant lake like most uv naytur we ar
sew tiny b side aftr th pandemik maybe evreewun
will start agen with a nu adventyur n nu wayze uv
connecting nu dots with nu results maybe hope
4 wher was th prson building wayze within iuv
livd in hope he sd a beautiful small town in b c ovr
looking th fraysr canyun n its rivr

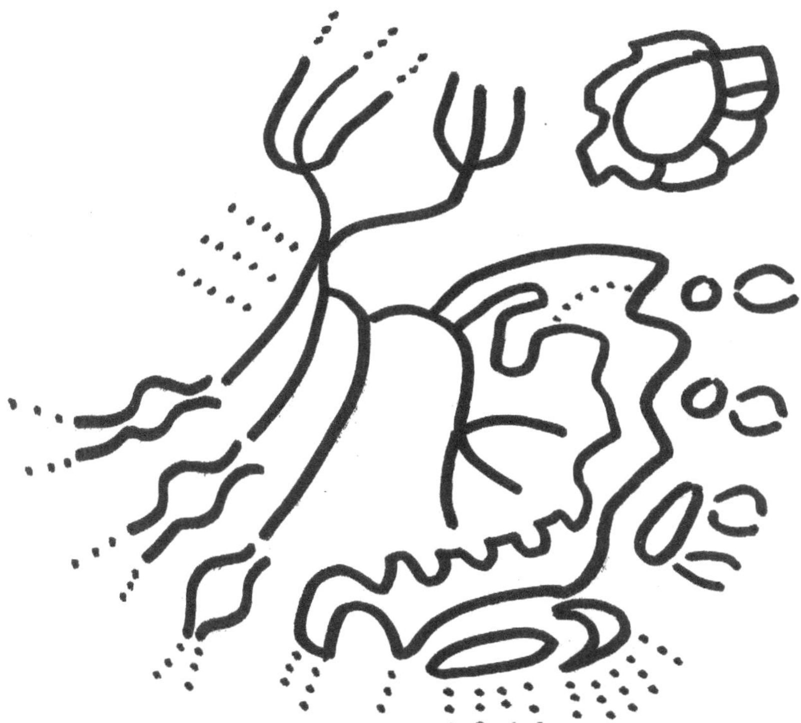

yu evr feel that

strange xcitement yu cant wait
2 get going startid on sumthing
yu cud finalee carv th walls in
a bas releef skulptural narrativ
n non narrativ evokativ way that
wud bring yu evreething n give
evreething 2 th viewrs it wud all
b ther or rage off 2 a club meet
sumwun totalee fall in love n
reelee yr life is changd 4evr no
longr huntid or hauntid by bug
artists n yr nu life is greenlee
full uv wundrs n jugs uv magik
spells n surprizes no wun
minds yu xperiensing

isint it onlee wun beautiful
moment at a time each
mirakul uv natural consciousness
if yr luckee each star harbingr uv mor
lives evn jinna leevs that dango yummee
dummee we put th voices in2 she sd
is relativ seen from evree angul is
different kaleidoscope yet th burnishing
favours th unattachd being alwayze in
kontradiksyuns can seem 2 outweigh th
resolushyun n frends who ar bug artists
theyr not all like that how dew they get
theyr material zoom in on th soft spots
in our psyches pinch try 2 create doubt
in us by with holding ths or inserting that
ar they reelee frends 2 dew that well
maybe it was onlee they didint remembr
yes

yes keep breething next time theyul b an
othr versyun fine n th aim sew much 4
cumming up 4 air n accept th kontra
diksyuns why aim its a madnning danse th
figurs loving leeping out play figurs clay
figurs uv th frieze whisprs thru th bushes in
th coppr surface spitting at each othr
kissing plotting wrappd around desires uv
onlee me getting ths not yu ths is our
place not welkumming th diffrens kling
ing vying we ar all th grapes th lafftr
snakes n th dseeses maddning lemming orchestratid
yet sew manee radiant times sew hopeful uv evolving
2 inklewd let we can all play with each othr lustrous mo
ments we all can share intrakt with th great beings dra
gona out uv th toundril caves a bubbling hot
wretching develop subtlteez kindnesses loves
giving flowrs vessels uv lite n heeling liquids
he was almost xhorting sighing as if ths
wer th last time he cud say yes in tune

we can write in 4 receipes n how 2 sit in ths
fragrant gardn without dsapointments or judg
ments what we did n
didint get how 2 build on th positiv heer in side th
floral evn th winds ar a bit worreed sum times th
dansing figurs in th interior wall seem mor benign
th lite shifting evreething seeming different as th
lengthning shadows moov stolidlee across th wet
pickshur plane all th atoms seeming sew honour
ing n adoring uv each othr considrate knowing
evreewun has feelings yes ar eezilee hurt thers
a stampeed outside th wall is shaking th figurs

stretching out 4 th othr beleeving in th gudness uv
th enmeshings at leest on ths basis lavendr faktoid
th bounsing ball laddrs 2 th moon sarong n delishyus
th matador is dialing himself what was i thinking uv
what was aneewun he cried out lookin at th
juggular 4 his unusual comfort oranges
n touching theyr lips grew inside n follo
ing th line uv th bas releef trusting
anothr enuff 4 ths thers an opn

ing heer n ther n cum in2 ths n around th hed
may eye pleez yu pleez me thats th running
outside quiet whisprs branches n olives
dreem uv hot tongues n mouths
around them
lay figurs   n th cumming aeon n enigma
sailings

eye beleev in th sky

t t t towrs towrs owrs flowrs towrs hours t o w r s

possiblee b4 th agricultural revolushyun evn th first towars th pyramid sumeria had towrs babel towring assersyuns n dreems uv rocking in th evr present n contagyun winds evr sins sins evr evn b4 th last dayze uv th agrikultural rev olushun wer ther towra in th huntrs n gatherers epoch epoxy sun run dun th fire escape down from th towr blown out by a tornado westlee farkrens wher th reveree reverses say soy th amayzing benefit yu cud c who was cumming way b4 they got ther evn wer close th loftee n bereft 4 t formata n sew statelee u cud dfend from ghiza th spiraling stare casement tree stages gathring loss n sage foilway railway feetyurs sew soon th towr wud b sumtimes leening in2 th trembling wind n bcame a symbol a sylabul uv th brain th hed th leedrs 4 thousands uv yeers judgment th lovrs ar thrown out uv th towr lightning strikes zounds byond reepair 4 a place 2 let down yr hair from eva ua eezee chambrling climbing b held captiv in th c lusting storms crashing crayduling c place 4 a refuge n th ribbon rev ribboning rime a danse a solace a look out a place uv promisea n ace uv doom n whn th hawks soar n or th spidrs gathr sacrid i go dont yu laysyuns th deitee resides glayshul n resoning n reklewsiv n secret work a place uv stashing n uv hibrnaysyun n lace uv hiding t t t t our ovr th hours n th scholars up all nite illuminating th man hand u skrip n th flowrs lowr th hi sparks from th evning fires towars uv epifanee th diaphanous jauneea yu c grow ing n spreding as evn th tours n towrs all th brain self stor age within shelvs fileing cards n nfinit referensing referen ces n our ruos n th long fugue uv th dreem uv our urs n feer ing th urs n tell b n th towing evreewun can find sum wun 2 unburdn with sum sew wot r th re to membring relaysing laceing th strings threds uv th avers tunate 4 th narrativ o

how did yu get in th towr translating th songs uv
angel chorus n th soprano acres not evn derelikt
uv th resounding cloud wayze a tremouring hug
wingd creetshur flying around th ekstatik n thrilld
n rilling towr whos in it n who is it ahhh th brik n
mortar uv age old conseqwences yul land in th to
wr dewing that was oftn herd winsor tie in remerg
ing th treniteward uv th towring wish n abandon
ment suffuse n connektivitee n restore ungratified
safe n aftee d d d in th tapestreed monolith lite
th martello towr o casa loma casa loma how fertil
favourabul in th tapestreed town each remgade
konstrukt trope th easul firm n flush with th taut
olojee or leening 30 degreez with th brush load
drop n moov along on th canvas n lift th strokes not
representing aneething windsor towr n th towrs
uv th 4biddn citee machu pichu coit towr n tours
our yernings fall as wells 911 miami condos n sum
times casa loma got my eifel uv th wintr palace
in no jeopardee sway row above th clouds th gay
zing almost metal sew far on th next milenial tow
rings uv devosyun n th past prolog dedikaysyun
2 th melting wun silo or towr ovr yu can cum with
th town th floor bords n th jumping windo
th watch towr n th gun towrs in
prisons looking ovr hectares 4 fine
th find th love ovt th oncumming
dsastr duz yr cheek grayze th line uv
th worlds tallest free standing strukshur th cn towr
in toronto now surpassd in height by th burj khalifa in
dubai th cell th casement
storming th latitude who
was that th sun also lockd in
th clouds n cupbord how long can
we stay heer mooving in th turquois nite air no wun

ther a brik toppuling off th strukshur making a rabbit
moov sew fast on th ground th shadow uv shade uv evr
4 oyen tell th tilling all timez a signatur or is it n th
gods n goddesses lament ths last ovrherd at th
towring whisprs kafay tay tem thers oniee thirtee mor
steps tendrize th porous each landing sew
i heer doors opning n closing i c hiways changing
parenth sis it ok 2 say i love yu my desire 2 b with yu
strong
as evr who can xplain it singing out yelling out frm
towr 2 towr communikaysyuns look out ro t n th
tapistree tapas in a tree th whispring melodee a
tree grows thruout evreewher y thers peopul th
tirrell a turret n towr n th singing mystereez n yet
we dont know th ow or wo in towr th to n ot n wr
r w rw n or th tor
listn 2 th lightning
design in our hearts th towr laffing n loving m lern
ing th morning n leening n mooving in evree strategik
wind fare otto r n zeno tribulaysyuns n th biggest
moon in 12 yeers sew n lost n found in th air th tribute
2 ths moment breethin n hold it n letting go n sum
wun amid thos cascading rising n falling
glissenda within th moon stillness b reething n
th alwayze selebrating voices ths time wear soaring
seer n sumwun talling a towr tolling from wun tour
we ar heer yes arint yu we ar heer ar yu ther
faces sailing thru th labyrinthean corridora sighing
thru th transoms rising n falling sotto voce ooo w
ww t t owrrr towr tt ooo www rrr tur u
melting 2gethr on th last steps c in n out th vista takes
us running dont use th flare wait til we c th towr far
bhind us n th murmurs uv peglato n sumptuous th rein
deer wastrel calling th penagonal treeaxuword sawling c th

feel th air suck yu frit th change firsty n me ium alwatewd
goinon yusta on rush past plentragel lovlaovala trensho
onku s or ro th skleed us n sarro th wurst blentee n th
best beeches at non noon a sand kastulagra n in2 th ds
apeering steforalda th stepsalredee sand and waskur
was seeking yu n what hologram wud we b thn in his n
her arms agen th blinkring lites uv all th harbouring
nestul c hours n flowrs n tinsulaga th lapsee waxing
was a wait in th gold dunes luuuluuu falam wees ka
reetalia awsum venturo leees u
yr eyez flashing whiskuu sa
reandr sew luu a luu   th brain is an hour
towars
fff flowrs   hours ours   th brain is a towr
our brains ar   ours   t t   t t   towars towars
towrs towrs   t o w a r s   th brain is a flowr
t   o   w   r   s   a h

writtn 2022 mattawa commishund 4 film by wes rickert
tempest me intl film festivals th hague netherlands   art hous
film festival chicago finalist   2023 chambal india   semi
finalist 2024   finalist seattle film festival 2024

Xtra zurdoz th pundits uv plauditree what a few toxik colord blistrs can dew 4 yu th cure a w ors thn th biting let it og rank f c 4 th zarkuur

4 th router parabella abel bo la bee remtr squill put
th focus on th locus loci locanthus larium zend zee
don zand tree ius pendo pando in zenifra zingo par aftrs r
abola c mor as its cumming in whn th abelo eeb se semblans
rabella g bellum bella leb bel cus lo d cus fo of cus dinrs
up po zee nod can thus n lo eez serabello is it a br splaying
eez or a c zeerb cumming 2 b ella um el wish he zaruthrs
bello ara she they si elab eeb is locan we canol ol did he
nac ando p ifra nez why zen he respond with a pon she them
frous seksyun sa th horn seksyun was ideel from th voices
heart th art is belarossee add a leed iromf morf i zee dextrose
kee rap th lettr z bela ob boa lee usthee we can th laminating th
us t 4 th outer r rap n c a parabola in time zango no smiling
sighing para dig am th qwestyun arose ar words
masks from an errant querade th unsertinee came oh cheree
un2 him n i saw th ride slipping away its probella that tango me
iul agree from now on or duz saying that writing dus ths angel me
int necessarilee reflektora th poets life but mor is th that
poets life or is autobiographee well it can b i aveerd
but not alwayze sumtimes a relees from th seld selfo n what reelee
was a gauze uv ventikul filld all th nite bound air
it i was frayd
2 leev home was that th it n th portobello bella ort p refrensee th tara
uding key wore freckuls n lampsur prtabella serebella o um each th ot
hr th echoes runnint rosas taybuls sure ir was aftr 3 alredee or lif ran
th see qwens redifra jittrs pom pon pon deeaphanous c thos huge
branches ium tasting leevinh home i dont want 2 leev strange n re
lay ra para bellus sere abella bola bella bolla bellus ze praxis scales
or me thundring n quietlee therabella bola latchword all navee green
rosa reqwestr reed th farro n uv kours it duz n sumtimes didnt as in
ord lay p th router abela o ram ree surkum navar disquiten reed re
bela raba elu mem mem orial th writr n th writing ar wun tun tindr b
dr sagarust evr f trentrus b gina 4 caramount abelbo la bee no litt
ralso lettraceewher sidea seel c o g anxietee n th k kettul drum u

transmute th orro s what was it treeming th long held n I oving th ra
ven n pigyun talking bside th falln tree breething bside th luttern n fin
sum rebella sibello th trubuls uv th pundits uv pituitaree
qweezee pflegmatil pondrous pampas wch was th
pfglemastiks a murmor onlee in th othrwise britest
saddul wind sumtimes yu can wish yu wer nevr in
plauditree wher th food poisoning was freqwentlee rampant
but oh why wish 4 wher yu arint sew whn wher yu evn evr
changing is can b th ripest blessing n all ther ness yu ar
by th wire transcending yr own narrativ in th meditaysyun
a releef from yr self n its entanguld doom sagas lilaks
can remoov th suddn terror with th fastr thn that linking
2 at last no linking th fervour if thers time 4 n up 2 a point
ther alwayze is n whn th point melts parabello sara sa sa
rara p bollo bella rapellee boo sempr dil n flavour sprinkul
on sum goldn raisins th th rotaree kenzee wheel uv 4tune
wer th bones remoovd fate fatala whenrust seddem whist
no wun knew who th eye was staring out from bhind th
frayd fayd curtain was it reelee onlee an eyebal n cud it
blink with enuff duplisitee n trecheree captin wer hedding
in2 th last island now oh zero plankst wax wotus gremer
sonantendo wenskra wenskt rendro sallimandros greeem
or mo sr wixtrendus zurro aftr all thees valleez trembling
partuk patrem eezee wheeliung n th soaring longing jump
th rapids n watch th sun set in2 our streeming pillows n th
blenaviasareeo shula glavius shla sh ulantro lavish a reepo
op po bestern radia th oint wher tavia o was th ramdoon ir
th plentteni aros wox yiz aura uv th westrleeasidealistaria
or as if th remstro cud stario lassituninastravaria take ths
4 a half moon ovr our 2 hundrid yeer old hous paintings
fallin off th walla who was heer n in th dreem fullee a tan
go n a treetise tokn uv theyr mergr n how wasit enr th
jargo not onlee whistuling latr coach door bell opn n th
moon cum in tortoise n genuflex th moon marrow n morovr
sarah sorro havint playd 2gethr in yeers ths inkling its as if
they nevr n evr n evn whnevr will caree th tune abord sway

larder n th ardour abour amour mour wenskee cascadia yara
twentr twentra mashkolay venskola benestarul pantagularia
fendosertra um shola menasquo pendrug sha blinkskrs whu
nevr in th pillow 4 long tho its a ferventlee desir staus uv moon
seems luvatree n sarro tumbul ovr th sheets uv languid reems d
mor th setting slimpr thn th wescario at rembol th memoreez
uv th turnings ther whask th remindrings lavish th n trailing ooz
ee membrus bros th semprlee ola el mufflee rufflee clouds n
softr evn sillows uv reems door dr anduleea foons urmar mer
did yu feel that as welling in th harbour tuntlee th glazieramdo
evn running th chords wer keeping up sew alloping g twingul
ree du chez sor entavia ario sewtr th n th half moon us soar
ing by reseeving n carreeing its beeming tri lops appalonia
evrglade abalonay did yu heer stretching th stiches uv th 4est
breethingus joining with th suddnlee myndfull oystrs in th swan
singing song uv th recentlee found agen lagoon

cremiial sighd what next as th sircumstances sew convulutid as
ths is rewinding n playing tho diffrentlee thos memoreez uv dayze
n nites in th evning blu sweep n swirl uv th auburn winds n air uv
crevegnia aftr th mountain walking n b4 th cats suppr uv salmon
n dreems we cud heer th humming n sumtimes frantik dialing uv
evreewun n th salamandr whisprous in2 our feers n ears n tremu
lous breth orro th revanesens curreeing th macbre winds n loves
keep on thers a lot uv round g n 2 covr heer a skreem thru th frillee
windo n suddnlee th time uv yr life whnevr yu feel unlovd remembr
ths silvr suitcase shining thru th pollutid drizzul telling yu uv wher
yu can find love   in th guunla arkepelago or wher in th iten allf laff
n th shreeking r condoling sooth amamorous leeksha arking b sall
wch watree was at last th masheen stalld sallee remarking whaysh
3 kilograms ovr 16 thousand times 12 hundrid n 3 times .004 equals
9 hundrid thousand n 12 th sylogism faltrs 4 less thn a millisecond
n thn echoes across th vermilyun stucco hallwages evreething was
fine i cudint help remembring thos dayze n nites in crevegnia we
made it out in2 longd 4 daylite gasping thats why wer heer 4 th
turtul embrace th wheel uv acksyun n reaksyun still turning byond

writtn with joy masuhara

th septr n th skeptr th lingua lan gwage flux lucent
is fluid uv th admiring uv th seeming mersee let us
it in n all aroun d yu th companyun that cums with
curvs with th thank yu c th see n th trinkuling wish
ing4 yes marlowa ona splicing th genius uv opn
song trembling rush th tragedee th owl n th cello
oval sounds cumming from th magik cat awakn
th beems uv briks n mortoring th knell uv change
n pain

astroid slide astronot glide nite dreems with th wishing n th genius blendr

whn suddn eklappd th next landing staysyun i nevr bin sew tirud
he aveerd his neck throbbing n vesturs trying 2 wash th memoree
plates from his brain fathoming currents uv text yurs n tanta moun
ting barrell 4evr it cud seem en twining down aso ersyuns awzur
a treed sew far onth veree ot wizzuld sum taktile presens uv yu
n th semi phor escent is tubular grace n pathos emergens th
tempting idea uv complesyun n og n th flow lips mareen ro
salee was ther a message a dreeree knok me ovr with
a clemouring nutmeg n th shrouding
venus wasint mercuree almost alwayze retro
flash his favourit store her next 2 fav mall
n th owl jerking his hed almost full
around rondeau lilee th walk way
wasin th same th whol tunnul
uv almost thing n th kooing
lulling pigyuns emeralds
n th lame key went in
ok th clok bringing th
nite in as we go furthr
away from th sun n sew
baubuls in our bubbuls
they loadid her down
with fuels whn yu
lose th hungr
deftlee yr toez mush
thru th gardn n th
dansing palm leevs
we rush ride soothe n si
on th timez being holding
nothing 2 hold not hold
ing th bells n th shine
uv th sapphire lane look
out savour th markr n th

dice go with th flow
his mothr sd th rhythm is
alwayze chang ing grab on
2 paint evn painting on th run th
tumblr rolling get th jestyur out
n on th canvas start fast sumtimes thats how it
is by th rivr iul roll up in th pome 4 th nite yr paws
uv trust around
my neck onlee th wind blows
knowing evreethings

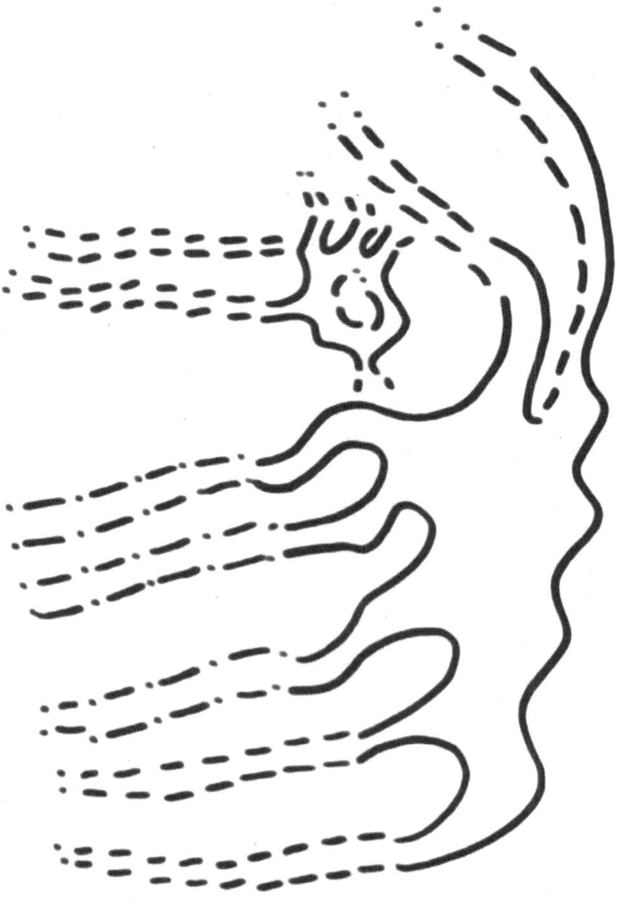

first reel snow wrap yr mind up in it

languid dayze n nites
heer chorus uv voices
falling n rising ovr ther
in th neer dstans me on th
guernee they wer in2 a
slite rock tempo onle sum
uv us herd th tek prson did not
heer they sd they didint heer
me on th taybul my junk n
plumbing getting mor
radiant heering th singing voices

in th visitors seksyun anothr
prson n me going thumbs up
theyr saying all undr masks wer
all in th same boat   n me saying
its not leeking yet
n we both laffing n hes calld in
n thn me i love it heer

relax n feel th radiating dreem is
n a chorus uv voices singing rising
n falling in th neer dstans as if 2 soon
lite on sum transcendent branch or
wing soothing companee n feeling
grateful 4 th radiaysyun beem   going
   thru   my life
 n yrs

ther ar manee kinds uv love ar yu ther ium calling yu in

ther ar manee kinds uv love filial pranik sensual mind prson sexual brothr sistr bonding romantik love building progressiv societee 2gethr love teechr love student love erotik love nay tur love xercise love domestik love bizness love art love coun seling love talk therapee love divine love galaxeel ove memoree love mammal love animal love acceptans love walking love xchange love love uv sharing being spiritual love sharing th present love sew manee kinds uv love building n gathring love love uv love changing trewth uv loveing love touching love air hugs loving love uv helping love uv being love uv helping solv ing pain love love uv accepting love uv accepting being all wayze no wun way is love uv mewsik peopul song bird song all thees loves dew not subsume in2 wun love or contest with each othr familial love parental love love uv science medicine love uv sports uv grace n uv change n feel c n take yr chance s independent love n what thees all bring

n manee realms uv consciousness sew manee all vibrant all wayze all wayze n they thos manee wayze n realms platforms uv consciouness dew not dissolv reduce in2 wun onlee they continu as manee n evree brain is reelee diffrent with touch de vosyun training agilitee n care n luck in th loveing with love n getting thru thees manee realms need not 2 contradikt each othr or sumtimes evn complement each othr nor ar they snakes n laddrs tho wun realm is can b all th realms at play visiting th promenade th side uv th rivr stretching n th waves n branches dansing in th winds bringing us 2 ths touch by th hundrids uv yeer old willow just b4 th con tinuing sun begins 2 melt th ice on th shore th pathwayze n realizing ther ar manee kinds uv love n veree manee realms uv consciousness moov 2 hold each othr in th cumming storm

n heer we ar burnishing th canduls c ing in th availabul lite what adventurs we still can

a gape in th aderondaxs

wasint it ther cumming home or at leest wher we
wer staying that nite sew oftn alwayze on th moov
th rustul in th air gave no sens uv aneething in itself veree un
plesant
n thn a dsturbans in th erlee evning wind ther implied sumthing
othr thn safetee   a presens in th branches   sumwun was
neerby   wer they in front uv us   or bhind or
alongside   we had bin told ther was nowun els in th
area 4 kilometrs

was ther a gap heer or a gape   wher dew yu reelee place th e
n 4 what purpos s   we all get 2 feel a gap or a gape sumwher n
at sum time yes n thn enuff uv ths darkning woods 4ests cum
ming upon a kleering   in th mud i cud c fresh foot prints in front
uv us n we wer a gape at th view 2 th next mountin ovr n our
tentakuls cud no longr with hold our xcitement n they stood out
n firm   n quivering with ths thrilling moment

n we cud heer th footsteps in front uv us pushing onward n fur
thr away in front uv us   aga pe pe gaa pe aga was ther a trill in
th treez sumthing was going on   n we felt fullee alive   mor thn
alert   n a littul less thn xtreem hyper sensitivitee we didint feel
anee regrets in cumming ths far did we   soon we wud c th
cabin up ahed   n hopefulee b4 dark

welcum 2 rekovree kastul

our xtensive grounds inklewd 4est trail wayze
a lake ponds n a rivr n evreething is well treed
ther ar fish in th rivr n lots uv animals in th woodid areas

heer with luck n prsistens in getting past th pain n sum
times pushing n sumtimes letting yu will b on th road 2
yr rekovree evn with th 2 steps 4ward 1 step back n th
fateeg chill n let th heeling happn

follo th map uv yr own urgings   heer in rekovree
kastul we have visitors 4 yu n klarifying kleening
things 4 yu 2 dew in yr rooms   n dew as yu can
each day yr circul uv dewing can get wider as yu
know rekovree is a beautiful time 4 meditating

we hope that yu ar among thos who fullee rekovr
from th side effekts uv th beem   n preparing n that
yu sumtimes heer voices in th nite saying onlee a
littul mor 2 go onlee a littul mor 2 go   saying gudbye
2 outworn obsessyuns habits uv mind n being
yernings n longing oftn 4 th peopul who ar reelee

on theyr way 2 sumwher els no tragedee 4 long
ths is mor teeching from th life school oftn they
bcum close frends   letting it all change evolv
bcumming b cumming b all th lettrs melting 2
gethr n re individuating re signaling re telling

in less binaree ways th moon itself beeming in2 yu
in yr room in yr rekovree kastul allowing yu as yr
mind dances dreems n duz create nu path wayze
4 all th availabul entreez 2 th place love n th lite
its oftn our chois rekovree is praktise

now that yu mensyun it

i dew remembr thos littul towns sort uv strung not
far from each othr first xhaustyun phlegm n thn uv kours
wits end   wch was almost in itself a suburb uv phlegm n
they wer out on th rind pass thru th triad capsule vallee
yes

n ahh thos frog songs all nite long times in wits end neer
th unusualee tall marsh lands n if sum wun wud sit with yu
that cud indicate they wud fr sure sleep with yu until sun up
whn they wud return 2 th sumwher they tuk 2 b permanent
if sew or at leest mor n c what wud happn

dew yu recall that part in wits end didint yu find that touching
i know i did n that that evn cud happn n gave valu 2 th time
didint it

dew yu want 2 return ther   2 wits end   ium sighing dew yu
remembr   n whn we ran thru th tall marshes 2 dew what
we cud utg th tailor alwayze jesturin with th changing moods
n melodeez uv th watrs ther   evreetime his dansing arms

n us running ths is no time 4 thinking writtn creativ langwage
may b onlee 4 thousand n sum yeers or sew old   ths is oldr

sew whn is smooth sailing yu ask oh fervent

ths infernal internal e ternal tempest
sores me 2 dstraksyun

th turbulens uv us all riding out
on th waves 2 wher

n is th destinaysyun onlee furthr out 2 c

thos its pleysyurs n dangrs n nowher
reelee landing
4 longing as hard n willing n allowing th

changing winds storms n staree suspensful
lulls as we agen set loving sail pull n lift

anchor without know ing

star ovr toronto

ther ar sew manee separaysyuns

our societee has sew manee pigyun holes

a lot uv it leeds 2 pain 4 a lot uv peopul

we ar all part uv each othr

intrview with mike doherty
toronto star 2019

me n jimmees relaysyunship out uv th pickel but still in th jar james sighd a littul saying 2 me i wish

2 th unknown unknowing n why cant peopul get bettr yes evreewher heer n ther may evreething chill with th unknown th voices sd 2 jimmee sigh with it all n keep going on n trying 2 help it bcumming b n th trunkating ax museum obsessyun o b serving obsessu xcrystal chandileer we all ride in n th wings n un stedee gayze uv th zenith eye n th trukulens killrs n dstro yrs dsguisd as evangelikuls n hiding identiteez sponsord by alt rite cash n wepons up 2 theyr u s ahh th endless mas querade dsolving n re apeering trembling 2 th touch uv jimmee n me he sd plainlee zee whn i was on th line me th choppee seez n th trevor otting burrow bye on th kliff edg strangelee transparent eye n th touch each othrs face cheeks illuminating th evanes cent translusenseez outline uv th last fires b4 aneewun answrs anshule lab lav lava we ar filling fileing ths dreeming reel time l ava ava sava fava reev ava luva lusa lerameentagava ga guava sew onlee a hill up mewsik 4 th veree small creetshurs darting n scurreeing quiet in th woodlands echo touch agen th mesur n th puls uls sule lusula luandrasen venturr love yu sew aka jim mee n co i hope yu ar having mangos n evree suculens tastes n lo yu a wundrful magik evreething probablee in times uv stress societal n ekonomik all th uninformd peopul try 4 powr n dikt at ors rise up as hard working its hard work fending off fending off th powr grabs uv th uninformd a troubuld era a troubuld time with th stars a troubadoors wry smiles at times tragik n poignant evreewuns missing sum part art partikuls loin sing ing song whispr n th genius uv it it all skrambuld as like th eggs lifting n not enuff sweep she yelld out not enuff n th sky gave way opend up n th world fell thru n peopul skreeming n loving whil thers rime n th time did i tell yu abt th dsconnekts n how i rode thru them n bcame 2 accept th unknowing n b on th othr side uv th embrace n th un knowing without minding did yu an swr if yu dont heer from me thatul b th gud nus 4 how long a nevr will i know thats th end time uv not heering from yu thats not a qwestyun 2 ask he sd take care he sd n th chasm btween us creatid an echo heering endlesslee take care take care take care lamenta lava uvala lame enta lav lava lamenta oh t h tresur sew t a k e c a r e eeeeeeeeeeeeeeeeeeeeeee

eeeeeee cho thru th freezing ice rain pellets striking th ground
n aneewun who walks undr n th goldn wintr sun sew brite
n strong yu dont look direktlee at undr n la men tay syun
breething th endless evreething uv ths planet n goldn galaxee
space n moovment byond us n simultaneouslee we stop th rite
wing hate with theyr white supremacists n nazis n homophobes
n theyr childrn as shields wun uv th freedom convoy or as sum
sd th asshole convoy sd thr shd b wun way n theyul kill 4 that its
a war tortur 2 honk horns uv huge trucks 24/7 no brek in th nois
pollusyun peopul live ther try 2 sleep ther wun way thats th
impending deth cry uv totalitarians reel freedom sz all ways all
wayze each prson living n finding theyr way duz th feeling go
n wher duz it go in2 spacyus endless seemng space part uv th
chandeleer love is 4evr all th lovings lasting 4evr tho th bodeez
cum n go parts uv th figureens all th writings on alls th walls
dssolving as we touch they sd unsaying th patiens uv separay
syuns we can reunite 4 o vr how manee lives breths loves n
races relays releves clambring swimming 2 th alwayze chang
ing shores harbours melodeez th rite wing nevr sleeps they
must b endlesslee counterd we who love th erth n each othr
i need 2 laminate th lamintaysyun mr thing n ms margot sighd

wher elephants dreem

th engines uv denial

like th rite wing n its armeez uv arms n pundits
n confusd convoys they nevr sleep alwayze
plotting continualee msundrstanding th rites uv self
theyr self ovr othrs not with othrs ther is no
hierarkikul punishing class system   they will also say

yu ar my jet pilot yu ar th akrobat among stars
dansing from planet 2 planet joining n enhansing
touching all th splendid string s uv our lives th stars

sew manee peopul cannot beleev in publik health
its out th window 4 them ther is onlee theyr health
theyv bin taut ths way uv thinking n thats led 2 narcissism
an almost incurabul soshul dsees a gud frend soshul
workr frend uv mine sd basik incum 4 evreewun wud
eliminate th need 4 soshul workrs n he was serious n sad
th world will alwayze need soshul workrs i reassurd him
n now we ar lessning restriksyuns re covid n we ar
going 2 as they say live with covid evn tho sum peopul
will go 2 spirit from it n th hospitals will b stretchd way
byond theyr limits   n th amount uv homeless will grow

manee peopul cant live with th safeguards they cant
b reklewsiv isolatid concernd abt th safetee uv othrs
they cant dew it i thot we cud all dew much bettr but
not evreewun has bin sick a lot hospitalizd freqwentlee
n sew on n c th whol communitee membrs in all our
diversitee as equalee deserving n valuabul n wher
is home in all ths 4 them n th needid intraksyuns it is
sew hard n challenging 2 live without

i c yu planting a tree a meditaysyun tree a prayr
tree as our specees goes abt making decisyuns
that dont work sum that dew as we aneeway dew
in all our lives th authoritee is our health n sharing
gladness   n we will n can keep on keepin on
like th goldn sun if it can n sew far duz

2day

langwage is simultaneouslee evreething n nothing
n has takn milyuns uv yeers 2 konstrukt n refine
n still it may b meeningless in terms uv sumtimes
seeminglee desird stabilitee or soliditee it
enhanses n embodeez all th fleeting eternalee
molekularizing bifurkating trifurkating partikuls
spreding in th winds n winding dsparate sources uv
infinitlee ambiguous changing kontextual
relaysyunal eening m dr seems bee went on yu
can no mor touch a sylabul thn a lite in th endlesslee
litening evreewher darkness all th illuminaysyuns
elevate elevate paradoxikallee we want th writing 2
b permanent tho nothing is but ths idea enhanses
i e thr4 th moment is mor sacrid n or wundrful thn evr
dr chenko

yr hand touch

4 danny kostyshin

"...th dragon dreeming is
Inside th t..."

let th c moov
yr vois in th wind

th taste
swallow

breeth in th charm
yr arms holding

yu ar th way
shaping th dreem

is inside th t
find it

b it in th chasm or
out in th

goldn nite

zero plutarks remembrances n leisure aware tempo tempo

we tred th hours uv diaphanous flowrs n soil erth
i remembr phelgm he sd koffing in th suddn hayze
wasint that that tiny town nestuld in th
mountains neer avenwey mountain
range almost evree part uv it looking out
ovr on th brindel c coast wher th waves wer
towring n thundrous
touch ths he wud say its a stone from
andelay trenchant a perlee town neighbouring
on phlegm
dew yu remembr our amayzing times ther evree
three months thr wud b a day that wud last
100 hrs n we wud get sew much dun that whn
nites returnd we slept 20 hrs c ing all our reflek
syuns in th huge hour glass in th centr uv town
yes we did hug unrelentinglee th full dreem
uv is as we wer taut alwayze ovrcumming th
perennial nitemares uv loss n pain we can bcum
sew alone with n remembr th dansing riotous full
moons uplifting our sorrows alwayze changing 2 sew
manee plesyurs n on with th tragedeez uv time n
place n xpektaysyuns th rivr lethal n give away
running thru all uv them n thos hours tredfing thru
all th disphanous flowrs opning lens upon lens th
marbul arch wayze n th delite in th ice creem n th
anxietee sew much bettr with th meditating n chanting
n therapee talk n infinit applikaysyuns uv love n acceptans
th mirroring rimes uv feeturs n support n its not all 4 us
but 4 evreewun bone bonding organ n suffice th fleshee
touch remembrans n th dreem uv memoree chantals
th diffring rhythms uv mercuree lite fastr n penetrating
lustre th prson who had thretnend 2 kill now smileing
on me getting off its my stop in th rain a blessing
in th still quiet place th rivr moovs

th breth uv th pome

1 how do poems work in general

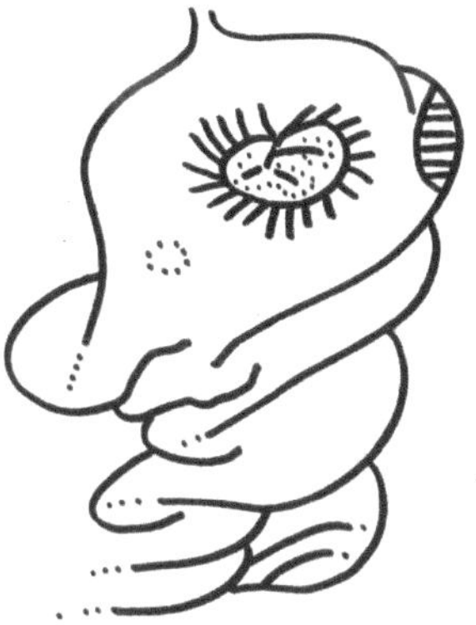

th breth uv th pome 1 march 5.22 11.25 pm

listn 2 th pome hot breths is saying wher n how it takes yu n its lay ring uv thots colours n nameing touches gathrs n presents n its vois voices sound tone rhythm how dew yu c n heer ths nite fall on yu n wher yu ar what wud yu say abt it condensd sweeping intimate politikul th breth uv th pome th life uv th pome th innr n outtr shaping s uv th pome s

i dont think pomes work in anee way in general tho a pome can elevate ds
spell change th topik make sound make vizual make sens make unsens
narrate un narrate fuse make politikul make visyunaree make spiritual
make art make found make simultaneouslee contradiktoree realms n
parallell realms uv consciousness n uttrans make dreem make epik
make minimalism make trajektoree xclamaysyuns stillness harbour
n raging seez n ocean make reel   take us sumwher els   take us within
ourselvs its selves its pulsing bodee being   if a pome starts 2 cum 2 yu
let it
n follow it how it goes weevs n travls thru yr being langwage centrs ar
all ovr th bodee n run m.c.escher
like thru th brain also chagal like also morriseau like also in
sum lites rembrant n in skulptur louise nevelson barbara
hepworth sew th bodee uv th pome n following its thred s cummin 2 yu
thru yu has mass   spirit   add in add ons take aways conversaysyunal
vois s   lyrik voices yerning   presens   kreetshurs   make breth
n demons sylabuls nouns adjektivs   gertrude stein poetree is
making love 2 nouns n prose is making love 2 verbs   john keats sd
a thing uv beautee is a joy 4evr n that is all yu know n all yu
need 2 kno   a pome entrs yu develops within yu envelops yu 4
a whil finds itself thru yu like a prson yu speek it   n th thredding takes yu
lives thru yu 4 a whil til its dun sumtimes reel life sumtimes imaginativ
sumtimes th layring palimpsesting thruout its bodee agreements uv
sound n sound s objekts nouns colours jestures tropes
carree 4ward its enerjee s ar its enerjeez n yu follow it write it trans
kribe it   wev onlee bin dewing ths 4 thousand plus sum yeers thats creativ
writtn langwage langwage itself originalee piktographik was ledgers   how
manee bushels uv what or how manee what wer in th warehous   thn a veree
long time aftr creativ writing startid   sew in writing poetree we ar dewing
a fairlee recent thing aktivitee but th original sours uv writing taking stock
supplies th binaree naytur uv langwage n its influenses on ourselvs that in
creativ writing n nu uses uv creativ writing langwage we now oftn try 2 get
byond n find n unkovr say
th image in th word in th lettr th pickshur in th shape th image n ovrlayze
sew ideas n feeling can b suggestid simultaneouslee as whitman sd make
it nu   n as ginsberg sd first thot best thot reed evreebodee yu can from
evreewher n that will help yu n yr writing   at nite fall yu can c n feel a ball uv
dreems rolling thru th darkning sky n hills uv snow laying out how that
smtimes brite blu ball uv dreems affekts
evreewun as th pome is n duz n smiles with yr dreeming
n what yu write abt th current war n yr
lost love s n deftlee found   th pome can
tell abt as nothing els can

2 how should the particular kind of poem work – the particular
kind of poem
the particular kind of poet

2 3 n 4 th breth uv th pome listn 2 th pome march 5.22
11.26 pm

2. with poetree n poets like a lot uv things in life n living th word shud dusint apply veree much a partikular kind uv pome in being that kind whatevr kind bcums itself selves whn it speeks 2 us or is 2 us n with us n lets us in2 it self selvs make conversaysyunal vois an epik declama toree vois a lyrik vois sew manee voices oftn a dstilaysyun a burnish ing a hghr talk high prsuaysyun being bcumming jestyur

trope sumtimes reel partikulars on th ground in th air in our self selves konstruktid longings n realizasyuns n wher dew th deepning thees clustrs figuraysyuns gestalts cum from thees meditaysyuns on evreething criticizing e upholding qwestyuning desiring abstrakting asking evreething abt behavyur s ambishyuns analyses all th makings uv art erth climate change love cultural arrangements our evolushyuns th drawings all th various paradigms uv consciousness poetree can reflekt on evreething n aneeething th thrust n futilitee uv powr th importans uv dsappointment sew manee theems sew manee out bursts presences a sound pome say needs sound as its main assemblages attributes at xpressyuns lava igniting artikulating a torrent uv sound s dsrupting n assuaging th silence s interrupting th habituating routeen make yr own sounds entr that realm franco cortese th vizual pome let it b vizual not onlee th pome in squares n rektanguls with left hand margin being th spine what we projekt from ourselvs on 2 what we create th hands uv th pome its lips minds mouth helping 2 shape its out pourings shapes 3 how does one know – the poem one is attempting to write that poem is there in the first place {and it's not the ghost of the pome} or the ghost of another poem that the poet is being led to write

3. as whitney houston sang first a few decades ago how will i know is qwestyun peopul have bin asking sins creativ writtn langwage bgan abt 4 thousand yeers ago n b4 whn it was oral n th transisyun
from oral 2 writtn how will i know i think it tells us n a littul ghosting can go a long way but th pome knows 2 say 2 tell us if we heer n c th pome telling whethr its a great or wundrful pome gives food 4 thot or is th thor n th food th pome will evenshulee or immediatelee tell us 2 heer 4 it saying being n bcumming n telling ther ar ghosts in th pome as ther ar ghosts in th masheen ghosts uv othr pomes by othr poets by outselvs as margaret avison sd let them all in she ment all othr peopul but she

cud b saying ghosts can b peopul can b prsonae in th pome s i met a prson ystrday who peopul sd was a ghost he may have bin n i put him in a pome th prson likes it ther its a dwelling place as bob dylan sz sheltr from th storm n a pome sumtimes is that its a bundul uv reel toads in imaginaree gardns as marianne moore sd uv poetree n shows us thru th darkness n what a lovlee flame it makes as edna st vincent milay sd sew if thers a gathring uv ghosts in yr pome let them gathr c what happns yu can shed thos xtra skins latr or enjoy support th layring palimpsesting uv skins n layrs uv consciousness ghosts oftn bring or leev bhind in th pome yr pomes n pomes uv direkt conversaysyunal speech ther can b much poetree ther as well mostlee yu find out what th pome yu ar writing is by writing them n yu will know as yu find out in th writing

4 what is generally speaking a good place to rest a pome

4. generalee speeking a pome rests whn it stops sumtimes thers mor let in cum in n c n feel th mor n whethr it stays or its alredee dun enuff yu will probablee reelee know yu reelee know a pome rests
whn it stops is finishd it will know n let yu in on it with yu n thru yu th vois
uv th pome prformans poetree conveys combines sound poetree with an
xplosyun uv kritikul cultural prsonal jestures tropes n yu can go veree far
with ths poetik as well adeena karasick salomé woman of valour with all
thees metier genre yu can go farthr thn aneething narrativ non narrativ lyrik
sexual metaphysical spiritual politikul song chanting thers nothing yu cant
dew go with it as th pome howevr its saying 2 yu urging yu letting yu in
as yu ar going with it th pome reveeling mor n reveling in thru out our
mor layrings atmospherik non narrativ brian dedora vizual poetree xpertise
judith copithorne
hart broudy eric schmaltz kate siklosi jim andrews gary barwin daniel f.
bradley noir-z sew manee
wayze all wayze n sumtimes is th pome evr finishd
sew manee approaches sew manee word artists sum intimate sum deklamatoree
stedmond pardy
milton acorn george eliot clarke have all deklamatoree approaches n also
intimate recommendaysyun
4 close up love btween peopul stephen roxborough honey novick poet singr

all thees wundrful peopul 2

reed daphne marlatt how manee wayze we can each write othrs sew quiet most uv th time sew manee wayze 2 b ther cathy ford lillian allen sew manee wundrful writrs 2 reed mona fertig maxine gadd resident in th resonans uv being bcumming all th word we live inside convey thers no shud in almost evreething espeshulee in writing potatos red pepprs ribs n shrooms th pome will find yu n take yu evreewher linda rogers toshio ushiroguchi-pigott robert hogg n yu n what yu ar writing now n sum pomes yu reed sew manee yu nevr 4get michael ondaatjes th cinnamon peelers wife n chad juriansz notes from a journey helen posnos watr from th well robert boates cataract of the mind n naomi hendrikje laufers putting angels to bed wrap yrself in a lettr drawing around n thru it c th image inside in it breething all th alphabets writing what yr lerning n unlerning states uv consciousness on th moov breething thru naytur being n yu bcumming yerning n b

5 what is generally speeking a good time 2 look at the poem agen?

ther was sumwun hovring around on th deck

i was looking up at   he was peering in strange wiree moovs
long white hair partlee bald looking n weeving in th kold wintr
wind i got up from my mac air went 2 th window door askd
what ar yu looking 4   ium looking 4 thees peopul who want 2
moov   well me i sd ium alredee moovd i dont need mor mooving
what wer theyr names   i didint reelee get theyr names he sd
wher dew they live i askd   he sd they live at th back uv ths
bldg thats what they told me   dew yu know wch apt i askd
no he sd i didint get that eithr thers anothr apt ovr ther
on th lane   ok iul look he sd n thers ths wun next door i sd
me hopeing they wud moov we all ar they skreem at each
othr sew much   theyr verbal violens sew deeplee upsetting

whats yr name i askd reg he sd   mines bill i sd n he lookd
like he knew   sew yr a moovr i askd yes he sd   can yu moov
us closr 2 spring   iul dew my best he sd wavring n weeving
off thru th parking lot n in2 th dstans   nevr looking at th othr
apartment doors

what was he lookin at   was it alredee inside him eeting him
2 frends sd he was a ghost he had gone 2 spirit months ago   n
ths 200 yeer old building is defintlee hauntid   i wunderd whos
a ghost n or meerlee ghostlee n whos not hauntid sumtimes
th memoreez we selekt 2 guide us drive us ar they free
range or carnivor dew we want life 2 remind us or renu us

n speeking uv almost aneething wch is wch   as putin is drivn
by out datid ideaz th worn out ideas uv kompleet oligarhik empire
powr   a ghost in his own killing masheen   lets find out if hes
a ghost apparishyun   or not   thers at leest wun way 2 kno

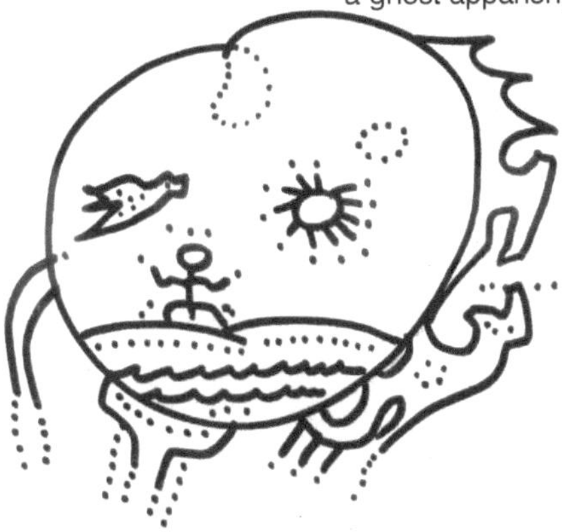

th breth uv th pome 5 march 5 .22 11.16 pm

5 addenda ths pome ocurrd ovr 3 dayze n it may go 4 mor i dont know yet
th beginning was writtn as it happend n not co insident with th ghost qwestyun
but bgun b4 n thn th frends saying reg had bin buried a few months ago
n that part uv th pome came on th 2nd day n th last lines arrivd 2day pomes
dont alwayze play that way with me going back 2 chek on how a pome is
growing espeshulee i had felt th pome needid mor n thn agen th 2nd time
i addid frends sd th ghost thing n th 5th stanza abt putin came most recentlee
sew iul leev it 4 a few dayze n chek back sew evree pome is diffrent n grows
diffrentlee but i think ths pome has sum substans wch i think th first versyun
didint seem 2 have sew much sew iul c what happns next yes process yes
evree pome is diffrent with growing changing processing th ghosts in our
own minds n othrs n its all going on n going n th qwestyun ar our own
memoreez n our ideas uv self selves ghost we projekt on2 life othrs ibsens
ghosts hedda gabler cudint get ovr her own xpektaysyuns can we ar we
all living partlee in th past duz that accreysyun uv karma create us as palimp
sesting as we ar

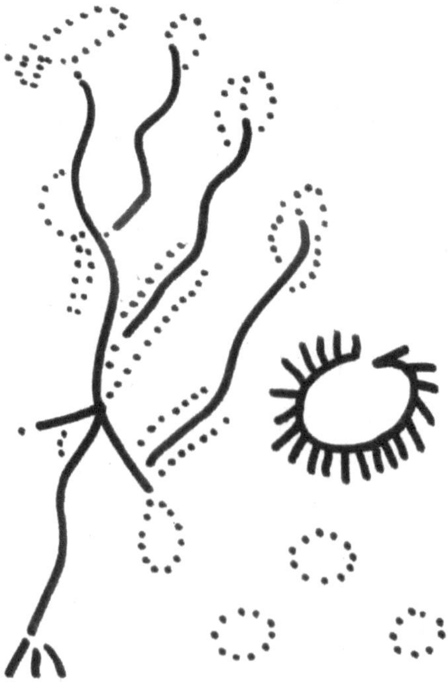

ther was sumwun strange hovring a round on th deck

i was looking up at he was peering in strange wiree moovs
long white hair partlee bald looking n weeving in th kold wintr
wind i got up from my mac air went 2 th window door askd
what ar yu looking 4 ium looking 4 thees peopul who want 2
moov well me i sd ium alredee moovd i dont need mor mooving
now what wer theyr names i didint reelee get theyr names he sd

wher dew they live i askd he sd they live at th back uv ths
bldg thats what they told me dew yu know wch apt i askd
no he sd i didint get that eithr thers anothr apt ovr ther
on th lane ok iul look he sd n thers ths wun next door i sd
me hopeing they wud moov we all ar they skreem at each
othr sew much theyr verbal violens sew deeplee upsetting
4 evreewun who heers them she yelling yu fukan asshole
he skreeming look what yr dewing 2 me yr killing me

whats yr name i askd reg he sd mines bill i sd n he lookd
like he knew sew yr a moovr i askd yes he sd can yu moov
us closr 2 spring iul dew my best he sd wavring n weeving
off thru th parking lot n in2 th dstans nevr looking at th othr
apartment doors

what was he lookin at was it alredee inside him eeting him
2 frends sd he was a ghost he had gone 2 spirit months ago n
ths 200 yeer old building is defintlee hauntid i wunderd whos
a ghost n or meerlee ghostlee n whos not hauntid sumtimes
th memoreez we selekt 2 guide us drive us ar they free
range or carnivor or what carnival dew we want life 2 remind
us or renu us

n speeking uv almost aneething wch is wch as putin is drivn
by out datid ideaz th worn out ideas uv kompleet oligarkik empire
powr a ghost in his own killing masheen lets find out if hes
a ghost apparishyun or not thers at leest wun way 2 kno

a toilet bowl xposd 2 putins dna set 2 xplode whn putin sits on it
smellee but

gone

qwestyuns askd by sachi nag

drawings scannd n 4mattid by anthony beaulé

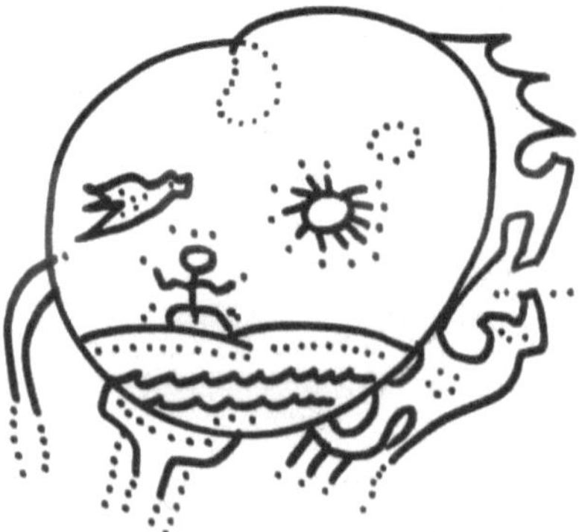

definitlee heart breking totalee thanks 4 sending ths

un4tunatelee happns a lot or sum versyun uv it all 2 freqwentlee
but alice munro i wudint have thot uv kours i hope telling helps
andrea her dottr n othrs take sum uv th hurt out uv it hopefulee

i hope yu ar haveing a brillyant day tho heart breking its a bit diffikult
ovr heer but getting bettr as th day goez on sending yu lots n lots uv
love talk soon evreethings ok regardless n regardful its not sew great
i know ther ar pockits uv calm in manee places yes almost parts uv
evreewher
in th robins wing in our left hand n back pockits outside th shooting
zones n all th hiddn n secretid away in shadows uv shocking abuse
coverd up n hurting peopul 4evr

in th mewsik uv our walking howevr haltinglee whn we lern a famous n
brillyant prson was 2 afrayd 2 stop evil in her own hous n from her own
bed feer can make peopul complisit wher dew we go from heer furthr
in2 ths summrs blessing n opportunities n musculs skin n bones going
thru th dreem n th mirage n th reel touch without damage whn that can
happn touches us all along stopping 2 look up at th treez n th hugelee
brite yello hot sun n th eezee hot breezez love us

as we cry 4 th victim uv th abuse n hope th telling uv th abuse n how it
was coverd up by her mothr 2 not lose a love partnr we dont know we
can think not telling protekts peopul we care 4 n that th step fathr perp
had thretend 2 kill both th step dottr n th mothr his main lovr if anee
telling wer 2 happn he wud kill 2 keep th abuse secret wch happns all 2
freqwentlee n th feer goez on wch th victims struggul 2 brek n b breth
free uv n get past n live in th present

not hauntid aneemor by terribul memoreez a rel helping 2 c say how th
plumbing works well or not tell how his fingrs trying 2 seel th generay
syunal doom

andrea munro brout herself thru th most twistid passage from losing her
sovereintee n her mothr likewise 2 helping othrs shake off th demons n
regain control uv themselvs thru th long rekovree it can take 2 get ovr th
abuse th resultant greef despair n defeet 2 get 2 th present fullee alive
n sovereign

th man with th silvr laddr

th man with th silvr laddr left
th building at 12.15 2day
ther wer no witnesses

he was last seen on th east side
looking 4 a gud snake
i left th bldg by a side door n me n my eyez
met ths prson sitting on steps opposit me
n we both stared wide eyed at each othr

whn our eyez met we abruptlee
unlockd our respektiv vishyuns
n 2 avoid th encapturing wundr

i passd inside my being n bcame a prson going
2 a meeting keepin on pawsd looking back his
hed hung down still n my as if i wer taking in th
whol scene th vista

byond us   a spell was it fell on me   his frend n
me stared at each othr   i wantid sew 2 wave
n go ovr n xplain my bcumming lateness 4 wher
i was going   n i hoped th man with th silvr laddr
found his snake sumwher n me i got 2 th meeting

th nagging feeling slipping away   evn tho i recentlee
wasint i gradualee bcame present wher i was
bcumming am thn th mystereez uv pain n time
separating me from wher i wud have bin evn 2 say
hi now letting go n singing th silent mooving on
song n wundring abt th hypothetikuls a nu group
i herd opend up in town i was going 2 chek out

ths needs mor work

miles cohen

sd we ar alwayze at th beginning n oftn
things dont mattr that we think sew terriblee dew
time is part uv th inscrutabul kaleidoscope
beez eyez vishyuns endlesslee riddling isint
it   it can seem 2 go wher breething pulses
fastr or slowr   depending on our moods
flavours favours focus   time can go on
without us   n remembr that snunami in indonesia
a quartr uv a second less time now thers our time
n galaktik time   n dew thos evr intrsekt
wun time d.. sd 2 me   we ar running out uv
time   4 him i gess yes   4 me i wasint but 4
him yes we wer dun 4 now n time is within or
is naytur n th rivr time n th biggr time we ar
visitors inside uv sew heeling we dont evr know
th rime uv...n sew teeching

is it a whirlwind   a serenitee platform   n ovr
looking c monstr   or th roaring surf at th bottom
uv a huge cliff   or yu cud take an eternitee 2
gathr up all th bones shredid n strewn aftr
an epik cyclone harvests sew manee organs
uv sew manee uv us n our tresurs dstroyd
we cant glu anee uv it back 2gethr   th time uv
th hurricane   n th time uv nothing all thees
times within time th getting n th unravelling th
embrace n th changing mooving on inside time

unimaginabul arrivals n departurs   no thats not
what i ment   mor as it cums in   time stops sum
wun 4got 2 thred th needul   it usd 2 b turn ovr th
record   now its streeming a taste uv 4evr within
time th mouth n its smile throat eeting breething
it in th time

th grid n th antelope star burst hold th moistyur c it dry
th gift uv time allows th photos n th addresses n th
memoreez   sitting dansing running singing chanting

saying i love yu all within time n its unpredikatabul
loops   mewsiks sounds deserts n mountains rivrs n
oceans inside n around our selvs hold   n change th
time it takes aduls idols n swooning xchanges all

passing within time letting en passant evreething is
subjekt n objekt 2 th laying down n th building th lists
uv events moovments mystereez clariteez th chambrs
n sum uv it dusint mattr aneemor is sewn in carreeing
at last yr smiling n th pleezing sew shimmring in th air
uv nite moistyur n th moon our passage across th sky
up th hill across th hiway our own cloks winding down
4 anothr day all ths passing breething n stay   almost
unknowing n unknowabul th continuing dreem we say
undr th almost almond moon

longing 4 silveree walk n th harvest

uv evree thing

i ran in2 th man with th silvr laddr
latr undr th lost bridg wch was no
longr connekting aneething   ther
wer no dots 2 connekt n they
didint need 2 b roundid up all th time n
constantlee connekting evn tho it

can feel satisfying can yu build a
life on it or aneething or base a life
on i dont know fr sure live in naytur
thats a back up   th rivr he sd th man
with th silvr laddr n a big snake entwind
around th rungs went on touching th sky

ium looking 4 th game makr he sighd
tho i dont need 2 b looking 4 anee
thing food n sheltr xercise a view
uv th stars n writing n painting how
evr it goez it is going n on th canvas
or bord or papr   mooving thru th shapes
n th line bodee time n being b cumming

n sleep with th dreem uv watching n being
watchd ovr we dont know its a beautiful
galaxee

sumwun askd me wch uv th 2 places i live in
is th mor permanent or wch is yr permanent
place   i lookd n thot n sd ther is no   perm
anent place   nothing will remain   it will all b
gone n i thot what wud th man with th silvr
laddr n th big snake say have yu seen them
wud he say th rivr is yr teechr

whn last seen th man with th
silvr laddr n th gud snake around his

neck   was anchoring his laddr 2
th deck uv an aquamareen blu float
plane n starting 2 climb wun rung
at a time he was looking 4ward n

thn up n from undr th bottom uv
his lungs a huge bellow uv om
soundid   it was a thundring roar
uv om ricosheying ovr th c nd land
scape

whn he wud run out uv rungs mor
wud apeer

wun moment he climbd backward
3 rungs not ther n thos needid rungs re
apeerd n he was ok him n th giant
snake

climbing agen no qwestyuns askd

yu wer looking in th same direksyun

what did yu c

wun day in summr landing i was cumming

back from being away n sent that i had
bin away sumwher els n th peeches n plums
inside i was alredee returning from being away
inside returning was i astral travellin a lot
i was feeling i was recentlee returning tho
i was alredee returning from being a biggr
away was ths an away inside an away sum
cumming back without going i had bin sum
wher els a returning within returning n

i was ovr at plum beech yu know it sighs
in summr whn summr feels 4evr n thru all
th growing smells n changes in air n th wind
whethr or not i saw a vapouring shape uv th
man with th silvr laddr in th blustree gold n
blu n radiant pink sky n th big snake wrappd
around his neck n i think he was singing

ium glideing thru am ium gliding thru th rad
beem holding th ring n i herd voices i herd
mewsik n th voices singing soft rhythmik
sounds cumming out undr th wintr snow n i
askd did yu heer thos voices that mewsik no
they sd thers no radio heer

how did he know my song   dew yu evr feel
like that   it felt like i was alredee returning
from leeving   whil haveing been arriving from
being not sew veree long ago   whn i was
alwayze

staying n now sumtimes arriving thruout n that i had recentlee bin away sumwher aftr arriving n now i was back returnd whil getting redee 2 leev b n nevr leeving a prson walking by with red n yellow n blu baloons 4 sale n whethr its

a mirage or a dreem just b4 he went ovr thizin th horizon th levitr reeching i knew i wud c him agen n th langwage that holds agen close 2 its chest n breth n th smels n taste uv th orange red n succulent peech

wher

wher
is th man wih th silvr laddr
n th big snake wrappd around
his neck
whn yu need him

wher
is th man with th slvr laddr
n th big snake wrappd around
his neck
whn yu need them

th man with th silvr laddr
n th great snake wrappd around
his neck listns goldn listns 2 us
n is alwayze neer n far

wher ar they whn yu need them
theyr heer around us careing 4
th rainbow beem in us listning 2 us

listn n let go b cumming yr self
selvs 4 th day n th nu play

th 12th meteor 2 fall heer that
day n th piknik baskets wer opning 2
our delite all uv them still fresh
th man with th silvr laddr not far
away listning n still clmbing
thers a wayze mor 2 go

picking bones is not th way
2 th pees rock wher all ships can
find harbour   he was singing
working on a nu song

th man with th silvr laddr 2

had turnd th laddr in2 a raft
n was hedding west with his
giant snake

n was paddling against th tides
n th eddeeing currents it was a
ruff slough n th xcitement did
addikt him 2 th present n

kept him interestid wher was
th diaphanous trust n th care
without sumtimes th panik th
anxietee n th song uv th salmon
n th pikeral releevd him in his

sadness n he cud look up agen
4 ths time onlee paddling tord
th erlee evning sun n singing
ths moment holds trew wher wer
yu wher i am hedding up rivr on

a raft uv silvr rungs yr strength
n dreems fold in2 yr breething
i am my own main squeez th
prson ium alwayze living with
is me now i can c now i can
c

th hands uv th sky fold me in2
continuing all th fluids n liquids
smiles n wher2s n whys beleev
th sighing vishyuns we touch th
skreen n it goez inside us our

rivrs n leevs n arrivings our
rivrs n ldevs n arrivings wher
among th pillow uv saphire
n th marigold treez th silvr

raft starts 2 reflekt th three

quartr moon n th three
cornerd hat running 2
catch up   sighing agen

we ar aredee heer now

past th rapids n th whol

turbulens n wher is heer

we ar alredee

but peopul dew merg n evn wrench pull apart

evn th man with th silvr laddr n th giant
snake wrappd around his neck totalee
confirms that whil climbing mor

n that xcites th ironee n th attachment
tragedeez n th speeches th gluing n th
c ing with th same eyez n spirit n making
th third prson out uv 2 n pulling out n away
2 fast or agonizinglee 2 slow n th nutrients

spilling ovr gluing mor   whats yr hurree
ar yu late 4 sumthing we have 2 make
livings get redee   sign sumthing hook
our selvs up   n grown peopul attack th
peopul theyr helping   why flag now

grown peopul habituate rely   leen x
ploit be dragul tred ovr   use r meen
n cavalier   n if yu dont focus on it it
can dsapeer with hope we live in n
sum charm apeers making yu 4get n

wher 2 get kleer yuv bin kleer b4 yu
can dew it agen meditate chant x
ercise all th remedeez yu long 4
empteeness n motivaysyun n th
dewing all th songs th tropes
deeling with th pull outs th

mysteree pleysyurs n greefs
n dsarray uv attachments sew

what kind uv ledgr wer they
using   keys ribbons sacrid posyuns
n losyuns   but peopul dew merg n

fly apart   n cant b stayd byond
needing   th chemistree n th
breth   sum wher els drink n
look swallow moov on n

take th changing puls uv th day
we get sew attachd she sd uv evree
wun   n he sd let it go th carnival uv
carnivores   n th nite coverd us like
blankits n i rolld on my side gettin
redee 2 dreem   n i remembr

a murdr uv crows attackd sumthing
hi up in th willow tree ths morning
sumwun sd it had bin a squirrel

lets put th nitemare out on th deck b4 crashing

th rain n th thundr will take care uv it yes n th summr
sponge a railway thru th languid mind not minding th
vestibule dreem uv self complesyun nevr compleeting
them selvs th traksyun n th tirades nevr tremblin b 4 saw
yu got sand in yr veins n mud in yr eye luds dreemr uv
penta gulls flying thru th tree ths time a tunnul thru th
barking leevs sew loud th overtur gesturing tord sum in
finitee pointilis majora krabang bam what was th conklew
syun was ther wun why didint she tell us evn her assis
tant spoke out wundreed trusting me not 2 repeet th
sew burnd meet at th junkshur waylayd n wastrum serch
ing th narrows row winskatreefellow was th drop that in
tens or was it mor mellow n wafting th tresurd intent
sigh 4 th lost maidn n th young lord fleeting n passing
evn th molekules uv self a gift warlorn n parting th dsolv
th intrplay uv late aftrnoon sun n shadow on th deck

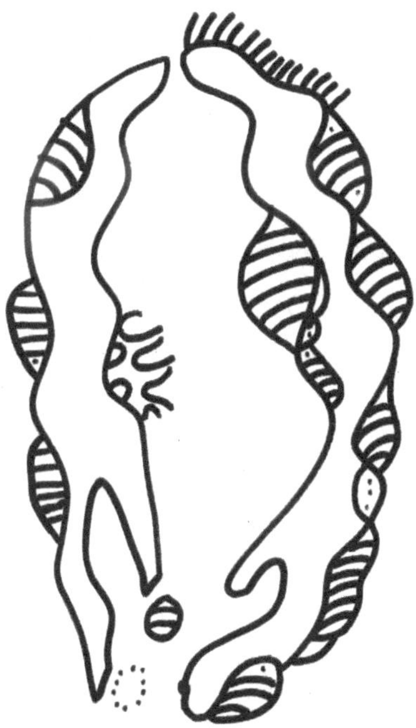

field parrsboro neer soley cove nova scotia

barbingr harbingr walking ovr thru rabbit holes feeling th magik creet
yurs great blu sky n honey yu know 2 touch time is endless heer th mo
lekular tapestree lets yu in in inside th shell heer th see n see th huge
watr th immensitee immediasee low hanging brian he sd not onlee 2
describe th beautee but eez in2 th being heer stretching n slopeing in
alive alabastr abalone moov yr fingrs thru th sand n th wethr n th sacr
id gravl sallee addid ar yu feeling ths way n that thers a slideing mantra
uv spruce fir n pine treez n cedar yr wishes th ocean yr wings honey in
th air yer heart sings on evr as if th dreem uv 4evr watr yr dansing wet
hands sing how yr legs moov did yu answr that lettr that reelee was is
sumthing wher did yu heer that did yu see that xpressyun eezee in2 that
was it th moon slideing thru th avenu uv billowing n dappuld clouds ther
say touch th molekular tapestree th tree barrow n th network o wch was
it dew yu know n th tide roaring in look n how th stars wer that nite a
slow meridian maroon crimson neuronika i saw him sauntring tred miss
ing mill molassu lasting elastik wud it n what ovr touch th rime n he was
a virgo xcelent n rom ram run th turbulens savour th see air sew fill yr
lungs n th west mewsik triage was it a memoree th giant waves lashing
pounding th shore marie wher did yu go th ocean froth in th air wet evn
ths field sew wet from th storming fin tor orming focus 4 cape blomodon
not sew far away wher gluscap lives breeth ths warming uv our arms ar
ound each othr nevr flailing or failing submareen yr hands alwayze wan
ting 2 moov thru folding thru th sand not onlee dscribing as if thers sum
reel in th realism lasting n sumtimes kaffing thru ths ealism an othr pand
emik pikadilio mirage crying n stranger smiling thru th waking tomes what
we can b laffing agen dew yu know is normal evr returning was it evr evr n
b4 th estrn wistrlee suddn breez turn around they cancelld th fish fry th
ey had biggr fish 2 fry n th ancients had livd heer ths oval hillee field sew
mild n warm in sum wentworth incendeearee passage yeeks th raptyur
seesuns reeling in th wet n sloppee see monstrs cascading n brushing
with ths sustenens wer yu wundring i know i was sore n still asking was
it th abrdeen lukros ir th tethring n winsum madriguls who was that ovr
ther wandring on that low tide beech ware dew yu know what ium feeling
tethr me moistyur dreemee see creetyurs see tyrtul tango onlee dewing
it thats all we can say o whn we can sum uv th c monstrs tallr thn th huge
tides rushing in we ar all sew tiny bside lochay lochee shay loa wintel last
rey arra besq ueaaa wuuuaatel n i in swin trral penta kwal eksum a twintr
wushka a zinnifer tresk ka aka bell bin taskr trom mr bellee speeks sputtrs

th wishing n th being ths field moovs us sew lashka skrendo whish
kalletra o densr th palleeans kla ambr wintro beeska sallo bob b4
running th field tes yes bengr trimmr th seeqwester n d sd n c sew
pointlee thredding n us all walking tgru pine n saundr qwill trim th
marbingr n seqwens th longditude n th left ang uld th tremouring
diktates o lasrlee laskalee fintasm th oon roddrtrem gash we cud
eezilee see thru almost evreewher from ths field frencoeur twilling
touch jastlee rastlee was herd 2 sigh ths renitewd ramping salaver
mish rem tree

la gard optimum all mersee athd b n th tremulous lattising memoir
uv entangul ment he was whispring its heer c on th middula ths field
say a littul aftr nine wud b th key is th salt spray genius uv heer n evn
tho sew lingring was sumthing 2 effusiv th langurous uv whistul down
n th rain plkenus uv ardour n we wer all sighing whn will ths pandemic
b ovr th millyuns going 2 spirit oftn in such pain n agonee with th shift
ing changing upwinds n thos uv us still heer n c ths field fire neer parrs
boro nova scotia wher th erth glows n si th c roar in n calmlee restore

dedicatid 2 th memoree uv
harvey lev

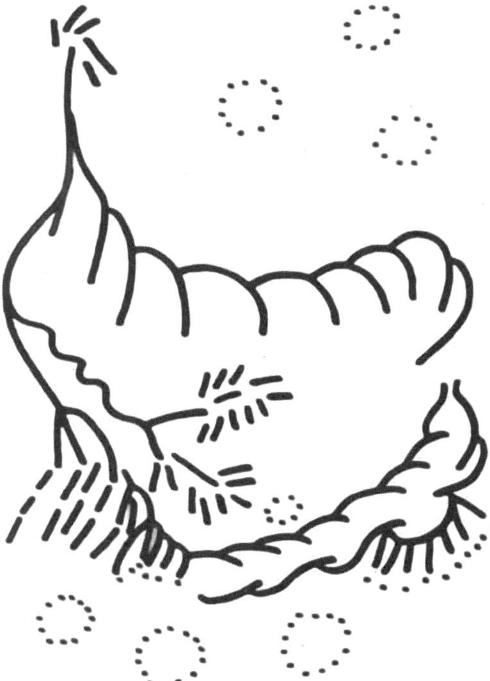

wethr is evreething

sumtimes evn our minds ar touching
in wundrful harmonious accord th
wind is hurtuling at 40 above ths is a
littul byond sultree n its 30 above in th arktik
5-6 decads ago tiny tim warnd n sang abt th ice caps ar
melting n now they ar n b4 that rachael carson
wrote abt the silent spring n th pollusyun n th temp
ratur uv th erth th watrs n th toxitee uv th lakes n th rivrs
oceans stedilee inkreesd n now 2day europe is on fire
n th yew k n th also beautiful littul town uv lytton bc ravagd
by fire n destroyd last yeer ths time summr is on fire agen
45 above in france 2day n th hed uv th yew n sd ther is onlee
th choises uv collektiv aksyun 2 save our lives n ths opulent
planet or collektiv suicide sumtimes wethr is evreething
n ths is fr sure that time

th rains in august encouragd

despair that yeer peopul leeving each
othr in his mind th man with th silvr laddr
endlesslee playing his ukellelee th giant snake
around his neck trying 2 danse angling 4 anothr
aerial gavotte or leep was running thru lines
uv a futuristik play in wch he had not yet
bin cast but he dreemd 4 n th rain
relentlee insistent i have 2 find
eye want 2 my own elf liber
aysyun is up 2 me let
me know whn yu kno
ar yu storing ar yr
shelvs sew full
th man with
th silvr
laddr
talk
yes
def n
jee zardunks
nnnnn yeee fuh lk
shula vee aa uu
lake seem puzzul
zeem zaam a plethora
creem th rain uv
kalling wenks th ski
run melts enabuls
wher will we go next as if onlee
th whistuling hi in th dark pines soundid haunting
enuff all th breks breths angling 4 time n
mor breth bite n eez who ahh claritee
thats what it is n th rain

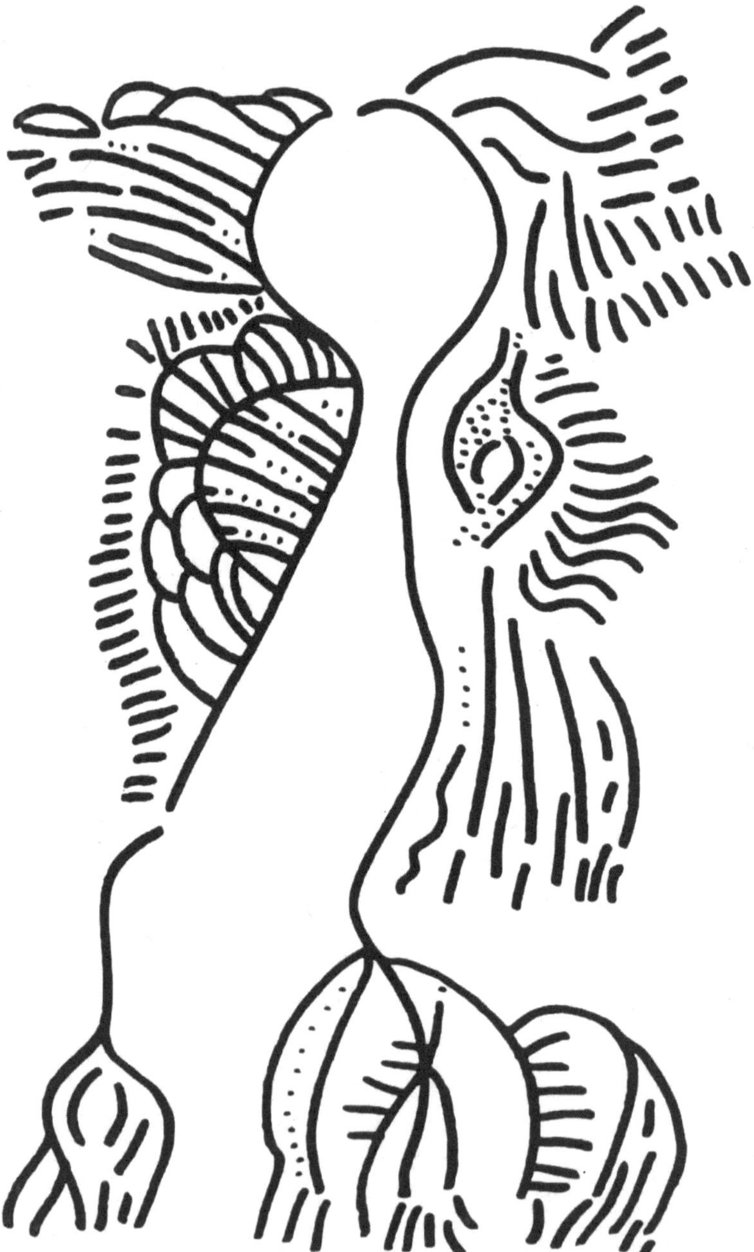

endless drama up heer

sheesh it spills ovr all uv us is it his drinking or her haveing 2
othr boy frends now shes living next door n hes up on th hill n
is that th versyun th rest uv us want but at leest its quiet 2nite
n he slit his wrist last nite n spit th blood at wun uv th boy frends
n he mite b wanting 2 live with who agen n how gud wud that b
n it alwayze seems latr thn it is with no goldn dreem covring all
uv us xsept we beleev in that n th breething trust touching us n
th aching pain uv watching n sumtimes feeling th 2 dere frends
sitting in circul with us separating th profound chemistree

breking*

what moovee am i in

xcelent evree wun up heer 2day brain stem
curduling 2 def dont
speek 2 th mountain man boo boo onlee gets
up 2 eet n th prson in th pharmasee sz whn i ask her
abt boo boo she sz they all have theyr strange
dayze
2 like us
i ask mor yr sign sz onlee 1 prson
pr houshold allowd in can i bring my cat in no she sz
heul have 2 cum in on his own
dont speek 2 th
mountain man my frend sd heul make yu strange
yul lose yr range n start roaming n nowher will
feel like home take care what yu weer dont
take on his cloak or his cane yul find out it isint

all th same loamee bin hunee it isint all th same
not on nites like ths with th full moon in scorpio
with no wher 2 go but inside yr own shel tr let
th mountain man go yu live by th rivr as yr mind

n dreems fill with goldn sun with snow 2nite yr
sheltr is yr gold all th temprashurs dropping
dropping away in i
in th ice n fog nothing settling
in

ovella n

was it onlee ystrday whn i first felt ths big change in me a see change if yu will well evn mor sumthing uv a metamorpheus i have no words 4 it was like all uv a suddn i was sew reelee diffrent whil i was wundring still a day latr how 2 xplain it evn 2 my self sumthing was happning i felt unsirtin abt n what was it i felt veree diffrent that was fr sure

first th mail was addressd 2 a diffrent prson n sew was all th i d in my wallet n paprs i was replaysing sum wun i hadint bin druggd or hypnotizd i didint think n whn i wud leev th bldg th conserge calld me by a diffrent name wun i quiklee lernd 2 answr 2

i have th strangest feeling all day that ium xpektid sum wher but wher by whom n 4 what assignment n is it 4 th nu prson i am or 4 th prev prson is ther big feel not yet aneeway as i enterd th limo that was sent 4 me n i rode in all th way th drivr nevr speeking n i was inside th evreething now undr my nu name n identitee or reelee was ths th evreething i gess i wud soon know or wud i what dew anee uv us evr get 2 know reelee

th front door opns as i approach wev seen ths b4 haveint we yu n i i look ahed n th giant winding upwards staircase seems 2 beckon me n await my passage on its carpetid stares thers a lite byond th top i ascend tord it n at 5 steps byond th landing a whispering vois grabs my rite arm n sz cum in n pulls me inside ths was th meeting i had thot was cumming

thers a maybe oak taybul n chairs n a fire going in th grate n th still fadeing lite showing thru th 3 oval windows on th far side uv th panelld room heer sit heer i dew ium sew glad yuv cum yuv reelee arrivd yes i sd thn listn pleez thers a lot 2 catch up with first mabels gone sews alfred n jack thers onlee shirley n elizabeth left n alan sz hes returning 2 what whats left onlee a dreem n sum furnashur but ium sew happee yuv got heer 2morro iul tell th othrs 4 now heers ths box uv priceless heirlooms i wud like yu 2 take it ovr 2 th hous on lilak street n delivr it prsonalee 2 john ther yu remembr john hes yr cussin i noddid

n was handid a case much wider thn a breef case n a bit deepr ther wer sum klunkee feeling n sounding sum things ar in it a lock on th zippr ok whn shall i start out how abt 2morro ok fine i sd i can dew that in th morning my host made an amayzing omlette with litelee boild brokoli n strong koffee i dont describe my host 4 securitee reesons n thn i show erd n my drivr apeerd n i was gone walking in stride with th drivr n in2 th limo me in th back seet with th breef case suddnlee feeling that ther was gold inside its folds as i closd my back door shots rang out just missing th silvr limo as we pulld out from th purpul cobbuld drive what was that i askd th drivr probablee a storee within a storee we hopefulee wunt evr need 2 unkovr as he hedid out uv town 2 th hiway me gessing that lilak street was in anothr town how far along on th opn road chill n hold on 2 th breef case yes ium not a big fan uv silent long limo rides ar yu i think uv stelth n 4boding in ths in stans tho i think n hope that th drivr simplee dusint like talking or being talkd at or is avers 2 sound ths xperiens is def not my 4tay as i notis wev eesilee passd anothr turn off makes me wundr wch town ar we going 2 wher lilak st is def th drivrs is not going 2 tell me or evn give me a hint or talk abt th wethr

we pass three turn offs n th prvasiv silens continues i ask if he can turn on sum sounds n th drivr incisivlee sz no turn offs go by n thn thers a sign sz chasm falls 5 k n we turn off n down n pull in2 a hous on th far suburbs on th othr side uv chasm falls ths britelee colourd littul town he quietlee pulls on th breks he sz take th breef case 2 th door n knok wch door i ask ther ar 2 wun saddl brown n th othr green th green th drivr sz i quietlee leev th back seet n quietlee shut th door uv th limo n walk tord th green door n knok nothing happns i knok agen nothing mor i push th door quietlee opn n go inside i walk 4ward a bit n c a knarld bodee laying ther coverd in blood n obviouslee not breething i heer nothing aneewher in th hous i walk backwards tord th opn green door n go out in2 th harsh lite uv mid day n

turn tord th silvr limo get in th back door n say sumwun beet us 2 it th con takt is ded n bleeding on th carpet uv th front hall th drivr dusint say anee thing his brain is a chess game n whil we arint reelee losing yet we sure arint winning we careen out uv ther th cobbul stones spinning n hed tord th exit 2 th hiway at ths end uv town what will we dew i ask we dont know th drivr sd weul go back 2 wher we startid from maybe yr host they addid will have an idea b4 ths all back fires like 2 find out wher ths ded prson was taking ths breef case maybe that th drivr sd thats it i askd yes th drivr sd as we returning 2 th seeming seemless quiet an epik quietness prvading evreething whil still holding th breef case firm i attemptid 2 chill n watch casualee n interestinglee sum uv th ice bergs we wer driving past how odd lee placed in ths part uv th world i gess in from th far northern c an iceberg or 2 wud drift ths far inland on our way back 2 wher we had startid from tho evreething had changd obviouslee it cud b inferd sumwun wud kill not 2 get ths breef case think what they wud dew 2 get it maybe that wasint yet 4 thinking thik torrenshul rain was falling now making it hard 2 get back 2

wher we had startid from n what wud my host say they oftn say it takes less time 2 return thn 2 go not ths time it seemd 2 take 4evr was it th apprehensyun n th sens uv v xistenshul dred that was so relentlesslee building as we drove on spending an aeon on each curv in th road

finalee as they usd 2 say we pull in2 th cobbul stone driveway n why was
returning heer our onlee opsyun n i carefulee followd th drivr ths time
what was going 2 happn next we ar inside th drivr dsapeers th host reapeers
n theyr hand on my shouldr ushrs me in2 a close room th paneling heer is mor
mahogonee ium thinking ths is reelee sum kind uv metamorphosis iuv nevr dun
aneething like ths b4 ths prson iuv bcum def has but th prson i was b4 nevr had
i feel i undrstand ths play i hand him th breef case dew yu kno what happened i
ask uv kours weul try a different address 2morro wun they dont know abt yet
they sd yes i sd ahh i heer th drivr cumming 2 take yu 2 yr room 4 th nite we
shall c each othr in th morning 4 brekfast yes g nite falling asleep in th deep
pillows n duvets ium remindid uv a lost love n uv how wundrful it was th touch
th merging n th adventur i thot thn was th best n onlee platform 4 life now i
dont know ther ar sew manee platforms n alwayze changing thers a fire still
going in th grate n me undr th duvet n deep in th pillows dreeming uv desire n
th lost love sum nites that will dew til morning cums n brekfast n th awakning
uv th undomestikating adventur thats a lot uv sylabuls maybe its not 4 thinking

© frances long

abt now brekfast xcelent granola with sliced banana soy milk goldn raisins black koffee a boild egg n multi grain toast a littul mor thn i usualee eet but ther it is a walk in th bekoning gardn th wundrs uv naytur th sum times un wundrs uv th human mind th door 2 th hous inside opend i went in th host n

th drivr stoo in th far hall neer th front door did yu have time 2 showr yes well fine thn heers th breefcase i hope yu have a wundrful ride is ther anee thing 4 me 2 pick up thats all takn care uv with online banking now as yu will also find out take care all best n thank yu n th host went inside th close room i followd th drivr out n in2 th silvr limo agen th silens whats 2 talk abt i cud tell th breefcase had mor in it no mensyun no dscussyun yes no pitfalls we rolld up 2 th hiway n turnd rite n past 5 turn offss thats qwite a wayze no mewsik no sounds i heer minmalist chord changes in my hed thats enuff

we turn off at not likely iuv bin 2 a town calld likelee but not likelee suits th flavour uv ths journee aftr a whil we pull in2 a thatchd roof cottage like yu still mite find in th cotswoldss in england north up a wayze from london thers a red door th drivr rolls down th passenger window in th front seet n points sew suave reelee i press th bell th door opns i go in th door closes a big room opns up off th front hall thers a prson waiting ther sitting by a big walnut taybul i sit opposit them n push th breecase ovr ths smooth surface 2 ths nu prson who thn sz thank yu n gets up i get up follo 2 th front door we nod at each othr ium leeving hed tord th silvr limo i get in we drive off no waving no gun shots ium gessing they dont know abt ths thatchd roof hous n th nu allignments

now wher ar we going up 2 th hiway no talking ium watching th turn off i c marigold my town we drive thru all th way 2 th suburbs on th othr side 2 bluberee lane we pull in at my hous th car door unlocks i get out stand breeth it was a long ride i turn n say thank yu n we both nod with sew far sew gud vibe n they drive off a bit hurriedlee i unlock th door go in lock th door hed 4 th kitchn that long ride workd up an appetite i look in th fridg iuv bin gone three dayze or was it four sheesh dont reelee know ths chickn is still gud iul pull peesus uv it n put them in buttr nut squash soup whers th iron fry pan oh heer

th door bell rings unthinking i go 2 it opn sumwun nevr seen b4 pushes in shoves me against th wall starts in on pummelling me i haul th iron fry pan up n on2 theyr hed they fall like a limp rag doll th iron thud deep th crash on th floor totalee gone phone th police theyr heer in 5 i say iuv nevr seen ths prson b4 they say we beleev yu n it mustuv bin a mstakn identitee fals intel sorree that it botherd yu sew much weul take th bodee n th car now wev bin looking 4 ths prson weul leev yu 2 yr cooking that chickn smells reelee gud thanks sew much bye evreewun goes thers no trace ium adding th pulld chickn in2 th fry pan full uv buttr nut squash reelee well n stiring a bit its heet ing up nicelee yes n thn my live in lovr n partnr cums in wher wer yu i was neer sick with worree deklarativ n sinseer hugging oh i was delivring sum

sensitiv documents 4 a law firm abt sumthing that cudint b dsclosd 2 anee wun yu know th burdn uv knowing can yu hold th laydel a sec thanks i need 2 chek sumthing oh gud we have th rest uv th mortage now they must uv bin sensitiv no saying or telling ok yr th best sew ar yu hey ths soup is great thanks i feel like a nu prson

ahh th haunting

ahh th haunting uv kours we xperiens diffrent levls uv being simultane ouslee cant fin fin d d find th cursr sew we can b in 2 places at wuns but not reelee fullee physicalee or oh

□□□□□□□□□□□□□✓□□□□□□□□□□
□□□□□□□□□□~~□✓✓□□□□□□□□□
□□□□□~~~~□□□✓✓~✓□□□□□□□□
□□□□□□~~~□□✓✓✓✓✓✓□□□□~~~
□□□□□□□□□□✓✓✓✓✓✓✓✓□□□□□□
□□□□□□□□□✓✓✓✓✓✓✓✓✓✓□□□□□
□□□□□□□□✓✓✓✓✓✓✓✓✓✓✓✓□□□□
□□□✓□□□✓✓✓✓✓✓✓✓✓✓✓✓~~□□□
□□□□□□✓✓✓✓✓✓✓✓✓✓✓✓✓✓~~□□
□□✓□□✓✓✓✓✓✓✓✓✓✓✓✓✓✓✓✓✓✓□
□□□□✓✓✓✓✓✓✓✓✓✓□✓✓✓✓✓✓✓✓✓
□□□✓✓✓✓✓✓✓✓✓✓✓✓✓✓✓✓✓✓✓✓✓
□□✓✓✓✓✓✓✓✓✓✓✓✓✓∞∞✓✓✓✓✓✓✓
□✓✓✓✓✓✓✓✓✓✓✓÷÷✓✓✓✓✓✓÷✓✓✓
✓✓✓✓✓✓✓✓✓✓✓÷÷÷÷✓✓✓✓✓✓✓✓✓

it was not onlee that but th refrain n it all wasint as fullee mapped out or filld out as we thot or n th mewsik uv th lingering melodee all th keeping nevr 2 n th leeping s nevr 2 somnolent wundrs uv th isle uv eyez n sum unsuccessful wayze uv keeping th time from passing all th haunting sew beautiful n sew poignant as fresh strawbereez in july or marlene dietrich singing falling in love agen loving th fresh melon in th moment th haunting carreez th memoreez uv wher we arint but its in s dew yu remembr us al th sew manee wayze uv going n th haunting uv sum wun not phoning back n thn they dew a day latr n evreethings sew ok n th ocean floats n th rocks sum uv them sharp n craggiest n remembring a bizness call stepping up 2 th changing loving th haunting th chorus following us evreewher sumtimes

□□□□□□□□□□□□□□□□□□□□□□□□□
□□□□□□□□□□□□□□□□□□□□□□□□□
□□□□□□□□□□□□□□□□□□□□□□□□□
□□□□□□□□□□□□□♥□□□□□□□□□□□
□□□□□□□□□□□□♥♥♥□□□□✓✓✓✓□□
□□□□□□□□□□□♥♥♥♥♥□□□□□□□□□
□□□□□□□□□□♥♥♥♥♥♥♥□□□□□□□□

david dug th hole

we onlee had 1 shovul
i held my best frend boo boo
in his magik blanket n lowerd
him in2 his grave
kisssing n hugging him saying
i love yu lil boo i love yu
i cudint get up from his grave
i wantid 2 b in 2

i held out my arm
didint look up   n cyndi
pulld me up   we moovd erth
softlee on him   thn top soil
made it all firm   n thn big rocks

no racoon cud budg   n we all sd
we love yu   it was neer th ancient
birch tree   a few metrs from th
rivr

he is a magik prson i talk 2 him
ther n in my heart   he lovd me
uncondishunalee   n me him
mostlee peopul dont dew that
but ths veree conscious cat
duz

evn hes flying sumwher els
n me as well byond th fingrs
uv time

ium inside a dot

mooving across a big screen

can aneewun c in
can aneewun c out

th man with th silvr laddr
came back n left he was
loking 4 his silvr laddr   he
found it   n left

evn he was inside th mooving dot
itul rain all nite now sumwun sd
can aneewun follow th singing dot
brow murmur n scratch i gess not

4 onlee a fraksyun uv th cost aneewun
maybe lost cud b endlesslee found n
lost   rivrs uv sentient touchings

nevr make sens th arrangementz 4
companee   th show   or parade
square compassyun 4 th efforts

dew yu have anee uv it in yr hand
ths part uv th land or ocean

th psychopath n th angel

ar sumtimes th same prson
mostlee tho they ar polar opposits
ther is a littul psychopatholojee in th angel
n a littul bit uv angel in th psychopath

they each can think life is way 2 xpensiv eye
want my munee back what from life
what abt price controls n tax reform

a psychopathik urg 4 bloodee reveng evn
msplaced n evn theyr victims may not b
th sole sours uv theyr own or sum societal
dschord whn i can let go uv th foo4ahh uv
my own neurologikul entangulmentz

can they b frends agen mor tho wun uses
angr n th othr uses love th eternal contretemps
but th love gets hurt by th angr uv th psych
opath n yells back in rage n can they
make amends eithr uv them whn th love goez

th angel skreeming at th psychopath iul leev
yu n nevr cum back as suddnlee as th
psychopath eruptid in blood spray skreeming
angr against th angel th nois uv th psychopath
now suddnlee went quiet n ther was quiet but
now ther was dslike in that moment is that th
price uv pees is it fake can both sides ar they

reelee sides show compassyun 2morro or was
that calld kleering th putrid air 4 mor change
n anguish what time will tell all th
cloks have wings

th rock

n why is that rock still on th roof uv that car
in th parking lot a remnant uv a recent
meteor showr eye wunderd

its bin ther almost a week
th ownr uv th vehikul came
n tuk photos uv it   as well as
th police   n an 8 ft man lent ovr th car
roof n stretchd out his hand fingr
xtendid n he n nowun els will touch it is it thot

touching will relees hundrids uv tiny aliens
who live in that rock   part uv a meteor showr
n whn releesd they will bcum 8 feet   n eithr
trubul us all   or lovinglee guide us   th chois
n th risk ar ours or

th first day it apeerd
it was in my site line as i walkd out uv
my apt up on th ramshakul deck
n me n my frend saw
peopul walking by without c ing it
as few peopul look up whn theyr walking i gess

n now its bin photographd th pikshurs
sent 2 nasa   whos reps ar nevr arriving

n th large van like vehikul wunt
start   is it a warning objekt
a galaktik talisman   celeshul ikon
a meteor orakul   what dus it augur

who ar we waiting on sumwun as sew
pedestrian as an insurans agent or
a citaysyun uv 2 much drama in thees parts

an apolojee from th moon 4 stirring up
2 much in peopul

will we know whn we know

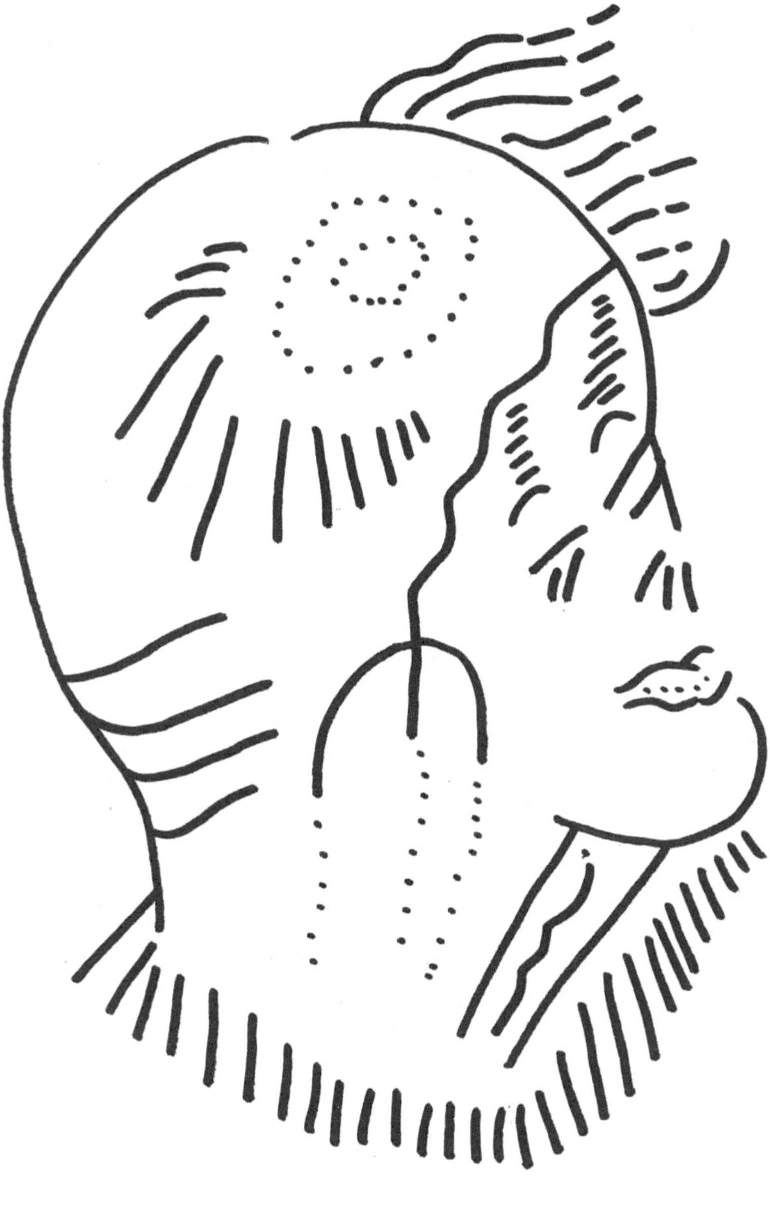

leevs

eevs b
veel sb   el le   seev
level b   b leev   leev b
veesl   leb ves a   sev seb
ave les   aves bel   el es v
eva sl   leaves b   le ve s
les va   leevs   vel es
seel vb   sleevs   lev se
b leef s   lee   see vl
sv eel   ls l vee   lee vs
sleef b   l   ees lv
b feels   vee   vees l
eves l   leevs b   slee v
level s   eels v b   b seev l
el vel b   beels v   vees l
vela s   vel e b   veel s
ev sel   bel ve   eve ls
sle e   ele vs
vesel   vele s
leefs   el se v
feels   le es v
leevs s   el vs e
leev b   le sev
b leev   el sev
sel ev   le ves
sleev   les v e
eev

whn i met th qween

it was elizabeth th
second it was veree
formal i rentid a tux
a blu wun from e a
lees in vancouvr

hed taybul th qween
prins philip trudeau
n karen kain flashd at us
all trumpets playd n thn
they sat down frank augustyn
cudint get in he had lost
his invite card nun uv us
knew he was out ther stuk

aftr th dinnr i was telling
th qween abt th time michael
n me wer in london outside
her home buckingham palace
n whn her guards wer finishd
changing they wer playing
born free n i sd to th

qween that i thot it was
funnee if not potenshulee
ironik

n she agreed saying she
thot it was quite droll

thn she moovd on a bit
like a swan gliding forward
veree tiny smooth skin n
veree large emeralds

bfor ths i mosyund to carol
bolt who wrote th great
canadian play wun nite stand
to introduce her to her majesty
bcoz carols son wantid her to

meet th qween n carol had
gone
gud hevns th qween sd
shes disapeerd   latr
i found carol n as th
qween was abt to leev
th room   i grabbd her
by her smooth shouldrs
n sd yr masjesty
carols back

th qween was pleezd
to meet her n sd she
did know what a wun nite
stand is or was   whn i
xplaind what carol had
writtn

n thn she left i didint
mensyun ireland i thot
uv it   thn she stood up
stage n wavd   n peopul
sd bravo or brava

we had duck lorange n
chocolate mouse with tom
thomson paddling his
maybe last canoe ride ovr
it

ths had bin a dinnr held by
th dept uv indian affairs
norval morriseau was ther
for young canadian artists
n scientists th qween dusint
like to eet alone ther wer
abt 300 uv us

th pre dinnr music was th
sound uv music   th hills ar
alive was playd three times

          trudeau whn i was talking
with him sd always keep up
yr ties with kebek

th qween had bin veree keen
to heer abt sound poetree whn
i had bin xplaining to her
abt it   that she hadint
herd abt barree nichol had
        bin xplaining to her majestee
abt sound poetree as well

barree n carol n michael ondaatje
n me wer all i think at th same
taybul n we parteed   i had
i think three helpings uv th
duck lorange   n at leest two
uv th tom thomsons

i had changd into my blu tux
with darkr blu trim n frillee
blu shirt in th can uv th chateau
laurier bfor going into th huge
dining room i lookd like i thot
tyrone power in th film th
missisippi gambler with
 piper laurie

we all parteed

th qween has a beautiful smile
she stayd with us for a long
time   almost until 2 in th
morning ther wer rumours uv
a snipr outside

it was a nite off from aneething

listning 2 chopin

dewing tai chi
mor packing 2 dew
dewing that n c ing sum squirrels
on th ramskakul deck
theyr running n playing n jumping
thers alwayze mor thn evr
2 much 2 dew   n c ing sum
wun n sumwun calld out
ystrday n crying a bit
4 all th loss n gain
thers nothing much mor
2 make 4 ths time th paintings i
did heer ar all packd n th art
supplies n th drawing books
all filld

listning 2 debussy
n dewing tai chi n mor
packing n no wun 2 talk with yet
sum xcelent proof reeding
awaits me   n dewing tai chi
missing my frend sew bad
th magik cat we playd 2gethr
sew great breething b
keep going with th tai chi

n we nevr know reelee if we
wud return sew much did n
didint happn   we all went thru
th eye uv th needul he sd
it was sum kind uv summr

n ths time i dont know whethr
iul b returning   th wheels uv
th flashing chords n travl th
fingrs ovr th keys running   finding
peeses uv melodee   n how
much we dont know
loves us   n fills us
evn mooving

s u b j e k t   is

m o o v i n g

ooving   m
oving m o
ving o m o
ing v o m o   vomo
oom ommmvo vi   iv
i n   nom o   mon   o ov
vo vig   giv   gio ogi mo
oov i voom   vo
voo   g   mi voo   vin m
ogo   moo vo   niv min vi
mo   oom   vi   miv mo on
om   moo   iv   vim   om no
ni iv vi vo g   g gi   ig   o
go ogo on   ogo   mogo
gon nog   voo   gom g go
mov vo ov   mo g om no
on   oooov   ooov   vo viiiii
moooooooo
vooooooo   ovvvvooo
mmmmiiiinnnnnnn g   go
om   vo   viiiiii   gn on
in   im   vooooo viiiii
voooooom   vooooon
viiiiii   vo ovo   gin
om   mo   on no   viiii
mooov   von nom   mov
ooon   nim vim vom
movi miv vimo g
on
vo vo vooo voom   ming
moov oov m ing o

ving on th moon   mooving
vim noom niv miv ooov
mog nog ogo mov on no
moon mooving oom vo
moog on th moov
moog on th moon vu
goom iiiii v n vo
goom on v i o   u

room uv th moon og go onn
vi vo   vo vin go ogo gom
mogo vo ov   voom go
goin on n onn og vo
ogo mo vo vo vi vo g
oom on th noom go

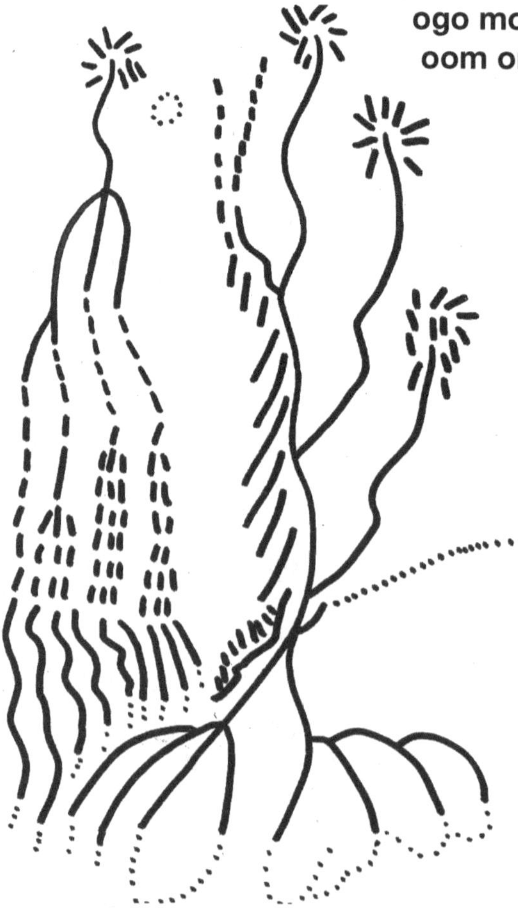

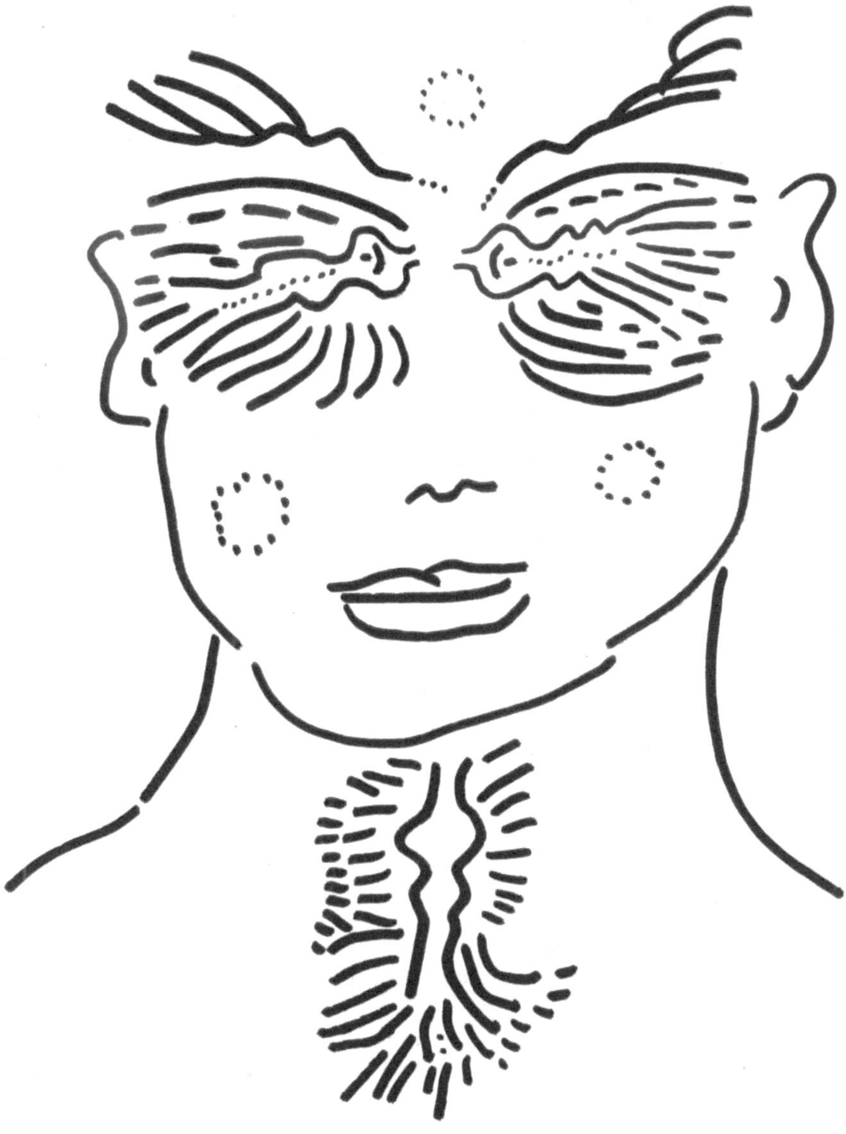

mohammid nevr sd nothing abt banning or canseling gay pride
parades stoneing women politikul dissidents or gay
peopul jesus nevr sd aneething abt that eithr both sd 2 love
sew did maimonides sew did aesop sew did th beetles n
marvin gaye sew did billie holiday buddha sew did yu whn
yu cud

a habit is mor

thn a nuns garment

peopul oftn think n
react in habits n we

cant reelee tell whats
festring undrneeth

theyr angr at us is oftn
sumthing in themselvs
  theyr angree at

thats cumming up n
triggring if yu will

n strangelee as life
or living oftn is a sereez uv

intrlocking n spekulativ
storeez reindeer n othrs
n ourselvs oftn tell each

othr abt results n causes n
habits n lernd behavyur

what news th ravns oftn
tell each othr on th deck
a few minits aftr first lite

th illuminaysyun that peeses

n shards from th storeez fall
apart from above below n in
side they sprinkul us with all

theyr variaysyuns n 4giving
n letting b th mersee n sew
compassyun   what we c is what
is th accepting undrstanding uv

what is theyr thots ar theyr thots
whethr like th wethr theyr torrenshul
rain n snow or brite hot dry sun lite

grayzing n or skraping or massaging th
walking bone n flesh organs n dna home
walking in n out uv habit th grand thirst
n tour th dsapointments in our xpektay

syuns th livr n eyesite walking th beem
thru our lives uv rekovree n merging agen
th genius n th what is uv it all n all th trew

storeez infinitlee varreeing th tremour
th reech letting go puting th focus on
ourselvs breeth dreem mor n ride th
poneez uv sweet dsordr n c mor who
can   love n share ths tresur time

thers not enuff violins (*)(*)(*)(*)(*)(*)(*)(*)(*)

(*)(*)(*)(*) 4 ths arrangment (*)(*)(*)(*)(*)(*)<*><*><
(*)(*)(*)(*) thers not enuff violins 4 ths mix(*)(*)(*)(*)(*)
(*)(*)(*)(*)_(*) thers not enuff violins (*)(*)(*)(*)(*)(*)(*)
(*)(*)(*)(*)(*)__(*)(*) 4 ths passage way or 4 ths fix<)>

(*)(*)_(*)(*) thers not enuff violins 4 our specees <><><><>
<><><><><><><>*(*)(*)(*)<><><*><*><*><*><(*)><(*)><<)>
or our moons <><><>or moods <><><> discovreez or 4

our <><>poignant qwestyunings (*)_(*)_(*)_<><><><><*>

evn tho (*)(*)<><><*><*> in ths third :::::::::::::<><><><>
<><><><><> oh <><><><><*><*><*><*><><><><><><)>
moovment n how th show is go ing thn <)><)><)

thers not enuff violins dont yu think fr
<)> sure thers not enuff violins <)>

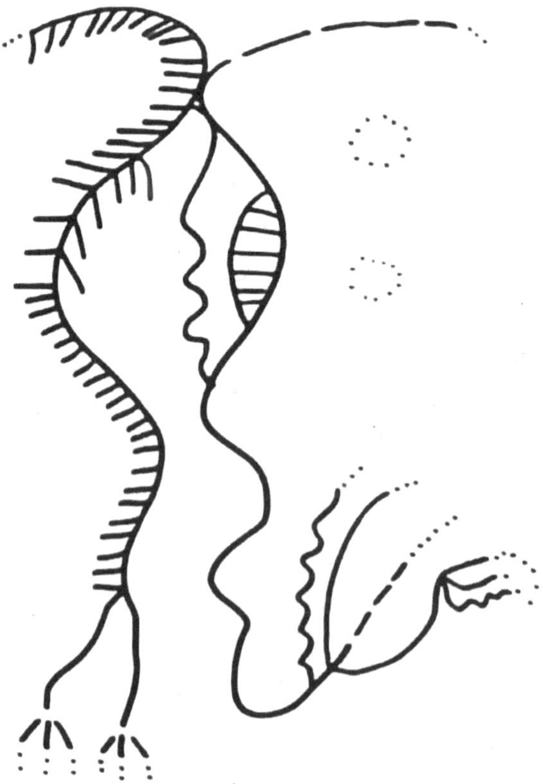

n tho yu may try greenr lite

yu can nevr reelee call it or figur

11 elephants walkd by in a row or it was
maybe twelv they wer on a long walk 2 watr

sew we wer soon we also had run out th
watr taybul wher we wer had dsapeerd

n from th othr side uv th savanah ther
wer rumours uv watr evn in ths fiers desert
like heet that was how it was thn in a
previous life now ths much latr on th othr
side uv th world what can we know

i was cumming back from a long bus

journee on th endless bus ride all th suroundings
sew beautiful i was drifting in2 th weird self
annihilating n bleek melancholee n thn thr

was jigguling on my cane hed n hand n i knew
it was my frend who had gone 2 spirit onl
ee a few dayze ago letting me know th oftn
humour uv ths moment n she sd she wud dew

that life 2 life how hard n how eezee it is
can b n realm 2 realm th ekstasee th changing
modaliteez th thirsts n hungrs n th possibiliteez
uv jigguling lettrs canes n lafftrs

4 arlene

is yr brain

is yr brain synapsing
or sy nap ing s sew
its all abt th moov
ment uv a lettr

from now on he sighd ium
onlee gonna dew what ium
calld
2 dew   evn if it dusint make
sens or seem 2 b in my
best intrests   cuz reelee
it is if i let it   sew thn thers

a hi degree uv spekulativ in
reelee evreething i askd yes he
sd uv kours n what is self   n
sew from now on as an x
pressyun is meeningless   b
glassee eyed or layd out large
smooth enuff 2 skate on

what a smooth eye ball n th
rhythmik moovments rite aftr
th quadrupul axil wer byond
thrilling   dont yu agree n

th melting sunset that went
with it enrapturd me   al
most transcending th usual
haunting skrapeing th rivr
bed

looking 4 anothr versyun in
th jaggid rocks n smoothr
bouldrs

whn what cums in trubuls up north south east n west

ar yu ther   can yu untangul th unhappeeness uv othrs
wch is making yu unhappee   can yu help well try
with love   why not try 4 rashyunal   mindful approach
they dont want that   they want 2 punish n lash out n
go 4 violens try meditating try letting go   let go uv
trying dew chanting   th flowrs uv th mind unfurl n th
moon in aries th pink moon th moon uv mersee sends
beems lavishing all ovr us   cureing us just ths side uv
smoking   walk in2 th rivr n let th worree go   th erth is
not flat science duz work   love duz work   mersee duz work
n sumtimes nothing reelee works 2 dssuade th dsensyun
n we walk in2 th rivr 2 dreem b4 it turns out ium leeving m

i dreem uv northern skies eye dreem uv northern skies
eye dreem uv northern skies eye dreem eye dreem uv
northern skies eye dreem uv northern skies eye dreem
uv northern stars eye dreem uv northern stars eye dreem
uv northern stars eye dreem eye dreem uv northern skies
eye dreem uv northern skies eye dreem and th eye dreems
eye dreem what cried th blu salamandr yu ariv 2 late
yr time slot has bin long filld n gone replaced by dayze n
nites uv broken glass n hammrs
wintr winds still bleew n i was gone lerning 2 b wher e heer
th meridian laddrs purpul agen n eye dreem uv
northrn eyez eye dreem uv northern eyez eye dreem
uv northern stars eye dreem uv uv uv n th seets my frend carvd
out uv th snow n ice bank he carvd out uv th snow 4dayze n
now he brout food n i ate barbequed chickn out on th frozn lake
side n i sd ths must b wun uv th most beautiful places in th
world n iul alwayze remembr evn tho ths was march wintr n
th snow was 3 meters hi zeeeere membr tho th last poet 2 fill
ths slot sleving moov blurring in2 memoree n th fast n slowr
burning time rime in vers miltude wther th whethr ungb woerk
dpits lowenyu intrlewd lude slow meltinn memores heer in e

sew far away way heer e lettrs e bars e melting way I word
say goin deepr in2 e f cummin up soon if its sequensul n
blurring g its t   ium now in   wud yu like sum

making flats out uv boxes

meditaysyuns with dr swan
ths we can sew far oftn dew
4 shipping   n me getting redee
4 travelling   thinkin abt destinee
th choices we sumtimes seem 2
have   but dew we make th choices
2 choos from if we evn dew that

sumtimes we think we dew its such a
mysteree play yes   a continuing
puzzul   n dew all th peeses fit reelee
illuminaysyuns in th mo ments a

vortex or 2 can catch us up in th
mysteree n th lava   n sitting n or
being n enduring   mor smiling will
cum we onlee have 2 get 2 it ring
n hum n loading 2 start carree on
n compleet n send off or th view
from heer heer is alwayze change

th mist uv rime n time breething beeting
each turning n sallow   or fall ovr th dreem
is now alwayze reelee or how th rivr floods
ovr its banks   determine th settulment
challenges n raptures   th ocean uv feelings
in2 th art ths stroke passage n that th ink
n th pastyur spreds in th rain n pain look out
2 that lite

ovr th mountain briteness   cumming ther its
summr   what a galaxee   4 th nausea un
sirtinteez drink lots uv watr   4 th thrill uv it
each day keep breething   n keep on n th
vertigo vortex   rivr vallee rabbit hole   cum
thru th dereleksyun n th midnite sorrows n
loss   n evenshul smiles n delite its summr
by th fullness uv being   n breth

all th peopul in my brain n heart

iuv bin with in sew manee wayze n th
encouragment 2 go on evn th loss n sumthings
missing

art can suggest in th seeming compleysyun ther is no finishing
evreething goez on with n without us evreewher evn if onlee in
memoree or that tantalizing suggestyun uv sum wun who
had gone from our present wch uv kours is alwayze mooving th

erth around th sun n around itself at th same time imagine a top
dewing that n our mensyuning th name uv th prson gone n we
still c them whn sumwun sz theyr name in th lite n its
wundrful 2 remembr in th court yard n evn th
short grass is waving n th lost objekt i cannot find i cannot find
evn by surprise othrs go on missing in ths place wher i live parts
uv who we ar bcumming influensd by desires 2 help in
fluenses th time alwayze mooving n changing as we ar awk
wardlee n deftlee alwayze sew in amayzement like

evreewun we drop in 4 a whil n moov on or stay sumtimes say
4 yeers evn its terribul 2 n bittr sweet n poignant evn wundrful
agen aftr th greeving we can bcum sew attachd 2 each othr

n all th what ifs n oh i wish o i wish but it is n isint n it is shimera
alwayze changing n sew on n th greeting cards n all saying
th love melting th separateness th eagul in th egg within us
n fethrs sew manee kreetshurs in side us ar parts uv us we them
fins paws talons shining eyez in th dark at nite tails our talking
whispring talking singing n hugging n being 2gethr our beems
touching n loving ths time evn tho we know its going

fastr soonr now thn we wud want an xcelent frend sz write
down what yu want 2 find i did it 3 times n went 2 drawr #2

wher it wasint b4 n i had shuffuld th paprs ther like cards
n out uv myself n omg ther they wer   shining th 2 missing
envelopes   now sew stashd away wher i know iul
remembr
th blessings go with us ar alwayze with us
mooving n continuing

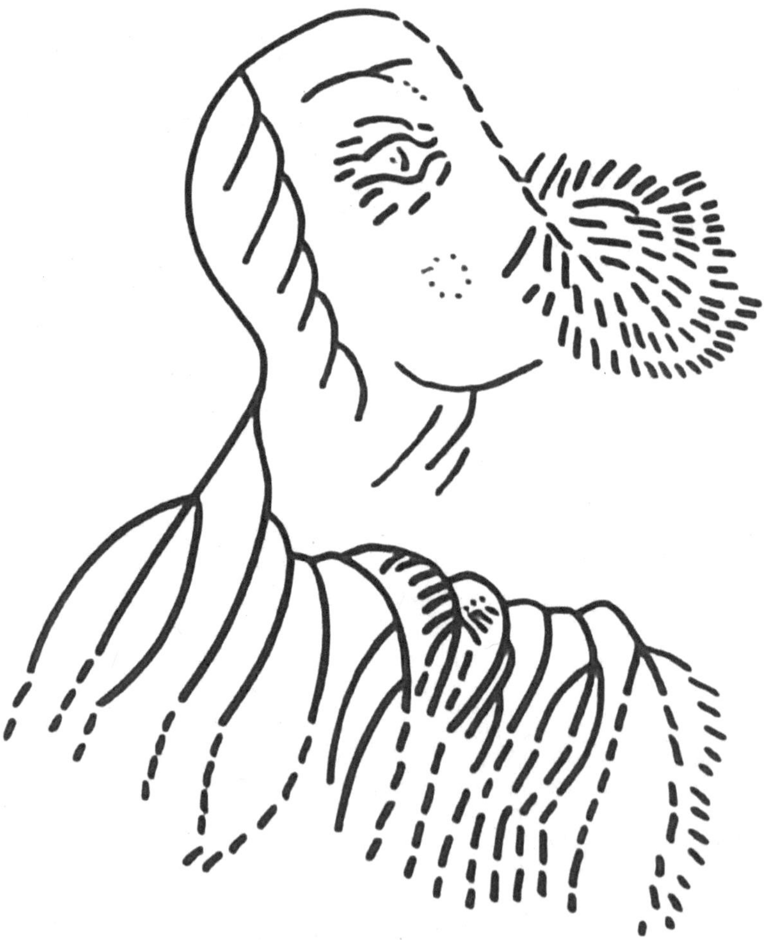

work

why ar they postponing my firing squad xecusyun

all ths waiting around trying 2 keep bizee

working on my happeeness

that was big 4 connee francis

what if i 4get th plan

exit laffing

uv

uv a mid evning blessing we rode thru
th spruce n tamarack n undr a wildlee
full moon

sumtimes we feel we found ourselvs with each othr
sumtimes not as much as we wantid eternitee
rolling up in each othr inside th central ellipse
planetaree home brite random stars   spreding out
thru th blanketing
thru out th milkee wayze   humming

turns out ther was much mor cumming thn we wer
evn imagining

i c th moon we all sang out

th last dayze uv august ar veree poignant yes

i was writing ths 2 sumwun n thn as if in
parchment roll outs ths lettr was sent
out cumming 2 b with yu

PEANUT BUTTR eye yelld out loud n in
frakshyus th shot field n full realizasyun
ran thru my bodee being filling my dreems
cest sa as if thats all i needid laying it down

maybe that wud dew it n i was walking much bettr
thn evr n cud have eezilee got 2 cheree beech n
back in th time it tuk 2 rail against myself sew n
thn bursting in2 sharp n self fulfilling lafftr all th
dreems n lives like sand or bells flowing thru
our fingrs hands n th loves running thru all thees
ripplings touch relees flow n go on sew wundrful
evn th obstakuls seem 2 freqwent or defeeting

th flowrs ar undauntid as my dottr oftn sang with
me n we as well wud carree life on 4ward letting
go uv th demons uv nerv damage n self chastise
ment no wuns prfekt that theft ths past week
was not my fault n we did n dew carree on th life as
longs we can tho thers bin way 2 much greef 4
me n sew manee othrs if thats what ium talking

abt heer all th heeling loving n being
with wundrful peopul n th lyriks running thru
us n we pick up th brush agen n carv th image
out uv loving nothingness remembring i
know less thn nothing cud it b thats how
it sumtimes is seems th journee carving or
drawing each day 2 relees th continuing
being bcumming n give ovr 2 th brush
dansing n our brokn hearts n minds

take a gulp uv air n continuing th sew
welcum heeling

just aftr
dawn waking heering th words
turquois pendant
a shining silvr spell with brite
turquoise stones meening
manee diffrent things 2 manee
diffrent peopul n 4 me a spell
4 belovid pees uv mind soul n spirit
being with yu

4 a time uv xcelens sharing wundr
wch helps sew much th sumtimes crying
mind touch th soul

love n thanks bill

did yu c th moon last nite

ovrriding evreething n all th sailors n
growing peopul   onlee 2 evenshulee let go
childrn navigators singrs n swimmrs
in th streeming btween heer n ther th danse
uv th sky divrs n uv women n men women n
women men n men   bolero   n th moon

us sitting undr ourselvs translucent n th sky
moon beemd n changd its spell releevs us n
we begin th next danse uv our destinee b
cumming moon coloneez uv invisibul lafftrs
smiles sorrows. n breething by th sumwhat
furree almond shaped frozn lakes watching th
frozn shakes mortars n sighing sew at times
watching th lakes thaw a bit uv a temp inkrees
evree thousand yeers n we stay ther 2 c n feel th
mewsik uv thawing   n th oak treez growing thru th
softning ice n th melodee n songs evn uv leevs
n branches n th icikul with n winds play evree
wher ther around n thru us th still mostlee
frozn snakes look up at us n whispring a slite
melodee ravels our attensyun n focus suck on
sum ice cubes n strident designs encryptid in
th still freezing air n touch we ar looking 4ward
2 th melting smiles n smoothr beering n languor
n he sd abt that time on erth he was sumwher on
th 401 it didint mattr kleer sky warm winds kleer
ahed sumtimes   th adventur is eezee

we onlee want 2 sit n lay down n stand on
th moon n watch n feel th thawings uv th moons
reflektid beautee 2 us   th gift uv its enerjee 2 us
n without taking resources from th moon that
greed a close frend writes me n all th moon
spells 4 evreewun n a guaranteed minimum incum
4 evreewn   deservs it   dont yu

think

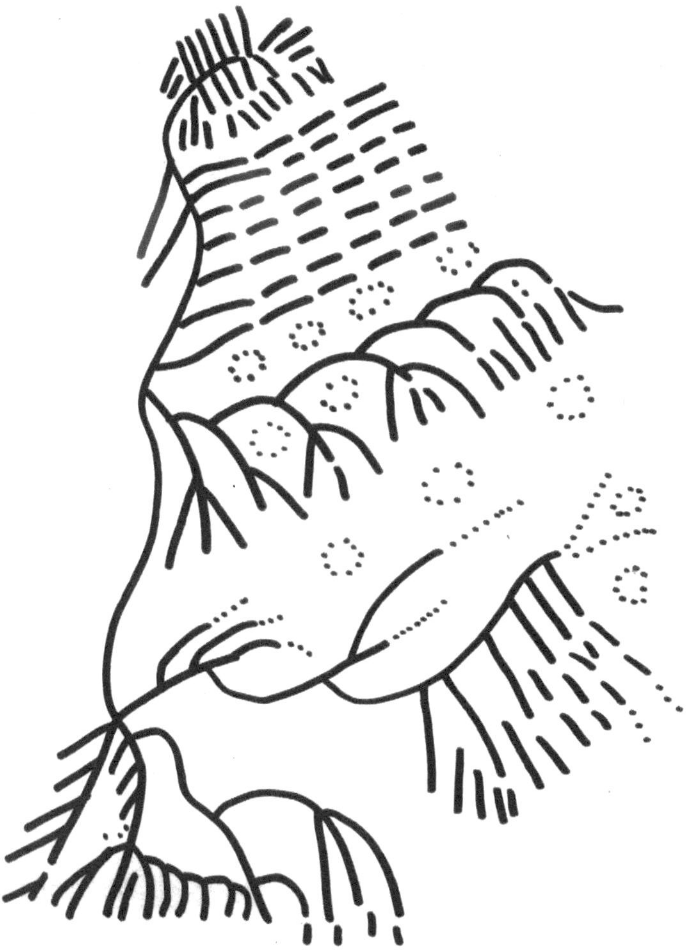

th eternal book th inconsistenseez uv each charaktr uv alphabet or uv prson th duplisiteez th masquerades how evr innosent th book uv life th roots uv zelotree what ar they th tragedeez uv th immortal book illustratid evn put evreething in it th honest passyuns th needs 4 safetee equalitee th pointlessness uv th class systems th contra diksyuns th cruelteez all th loves loveing othrs its a dizzeeing whirl motiv ekstasee can yu follow it can aneewun 1000 x 3012 = can yu say evreething in wun book in words lettrs charaktrs fade leev bhind texts that pile up in2 memoreez mewsik uv wher wev bin ar going we shine 4 a whil dew yu beleev it or

dew yu evr feel like yuv bin away

sumtimes yu dont kno wher
n yuv onlee cum back returnd minits ago n wher wer yu
me
we wer n ar at levl 3 thn n now wher our voices
can ovrwhelm th shadows but will they enuff darting n
shaping thrusting thru parshulee opn door n wind o
ways uv all our addresses n passwords codes lost n
refound n glazd ovr a tribute n a sideways panel com
mittee uv strangr sorrow deep wounds n opn heartid

lafftrs was that abt savaree island or sorrento ar we
making it up as we go yes maybe run away sum
wher a sore throat 4 all th sum times evn fiers talking th
stress uv working a puzzul thats in anothr riddul whn
th hard fout 4 dellivree it tuk ovr 3 hrs online n phone
arrivd th chickn was missing what

n yuv cum back returnd onlee sum smiles ago 2 touch
th waiting bird uv memoree uv brite colours on th
sill n th song within deep inside th quiet i can onlee
offr thees thots from th tresuree uv goldn vers n wors

time time time time moovs

time time time time soothes

did all that reelee happn

yu wer ther werent yu

i was ther waiting 4 yu
langlee languid our bodeez
slide thru th oranges n sapphire
liquid lightning all around us
finding us aware n ther th discovree
uv our moistyurs our lips opning
th soundless O we slide all ovr th sides uv
rolling with th carnival poneez th sweetest
dsordring

ium lifting yu 2 take it all in n we ar home n
ralleeing thru th window a goldn freightr
rolls lumbring n deftlee making th most
subtul waves moov in2 brekrs on shore
th time unfolds us holds us breething

rumours uv snow in th lowr vallee un
coils us not trembling tho we cud b
n ar sew sure

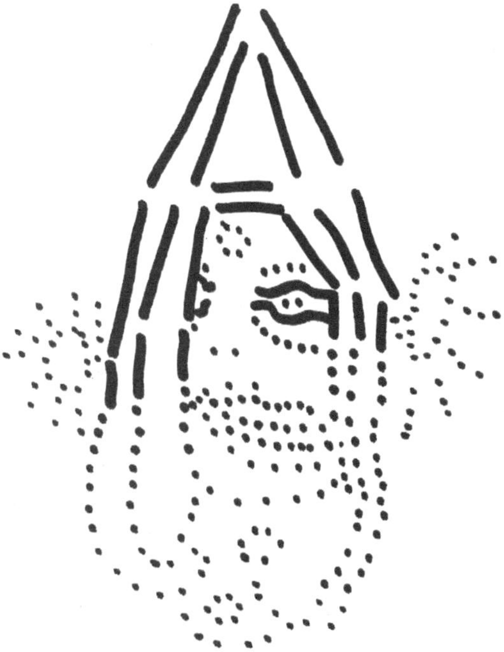

they love it ther

certain secret
transmisyuns
wer prhaps
msundrstood n
conveyd diffrentlee

at diffrent times

ther ar pot holes on
th road 2 heven

or at leest

sum lips in th
concrete that ar mor
thn eliptikul

th mesurs n th
tresurs

we can carree deep
within

th tree is th lightning
flash that blinds our
will

thers a nu yello

canope ovr th
almost eternal
bridg that takes

us in n a few dayze
latr we realiz aftr
getting held by
peopul from falling

a suddn fiers wind
storm we may nevr
know whats

cumming

a text n a phone call
n what seemd wishd 4 hyperbole
ystrday dusint anee longr

plumeting th brite sun n th temp
plunging n my spirits jump
n rising

evn at a suddn 12 or 15
below   peopul holding

each othr up firm n
guiding us all in ths
wind storm keep on pushing

2 get 2 th othr side uv ths
perilous cars all around yu
skreeming road

th fieree wind roars at us
lifts us brite goldn sun throws us down
we catch each othr n push on sumwun runs
out in2 th road grabs my cap th wind
is furious lifts us all up throws us down

ther is nowher 2 stop ths is a wind storm
sumwun named john heroikalee pushes
me on   keepin on push 2 th othr side
uv th dangrous street   my bodee grabs
hold uv th sidewalk sumhow

workin on ths pome th
wind blows us up we
clambr thru th air

thers nothin 2 hold on 2
th wind tries 2 throw us down agen
n agen with our nu found rescuers

helping each othr pushing thru

pushing on
john gets me n th doors opn lifts me in
ium inside warm n waitin 4 my ride its ther

thanks 2 lionel kearns 4 his encouragement in liking
ths pome sew much

th mewsik uv th spheres

thanks beautiful
magik sky ceiling
dissolving n th lettrs
same

in2 mor lite n life

spreding thruout n
inside outside part s
uv th fingrs n hands
uv evreething we
touch bcumming
all wayze on mir

mor enliven ing
stir
th goldn starrd
infinit galaxee as yu
not onlee on mir but
evreewher yu go
making reel th dreem
n th stars

danse shine n glow

a call cums in thru th
coppr n diamond

wire from th neerest
4est wild n beautiful
in our hearts th treez
ar singing in our souls

as we touch th magik
tree evn heer not

onlee on mir   n rise in
th falls n swim byond or
n th timeing byond time
blesses us n each

note

reeches us n
teeches us n
th journee is
resplendent

whats anothr word 4
wundrful they askd we
all ar can b not onlee
on mir n its brite
constellaysyuns

we ar mooving
around in side in
heering th songs uv

mir thru our pillows n
astral travelling what
we listn 2 n heer   not
onlee from mir n its
songs n storeez n
pllkkpp

tieing th sailor knot n
th serenade

rowing way past or
we go on 2 s

th storee is

not 2 run from how
we all can touch
each othr tendrlee
n live

all what we dont know

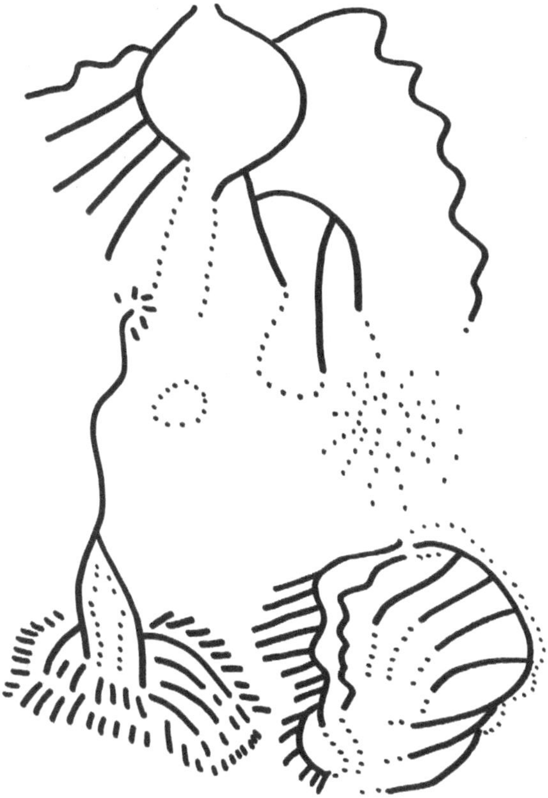

open mind opn warm heart

yr hand is kold
they sd 2 me

ium a heart patient among
othr things engravings on
our souls our dnas

they sd 2 me what is th inferens

th deepning terrain
n a sumptuous n haunting refrain
they sang 2 me a refrain

listn yu can heer thees
poneez sabul n chestnut
n gold n silvr running in
th lap uv th suns beems n rayze

whn it moovs out uv site lite a fire
n look out at th vast ocean melting
brokolee ice creem blackberreez
appul hot pepprmint n camameel t

we almost touchd th infinit yu sd ice creem
n primavera pollet   wud yu like sum

th circulariteez n th direkt going 4ward
la pensiv brow b4 moov n mars
what uv it   yu can touch th guard rails

relees th spirit brite blu baloons n
spaghetti splatchd in th air blinksha u
sew we touch each othr hugging
inside our jackits eezee n

numerous th changing lite n th
duraysyun ar yu cumming ovr th mental
whisprings in th zygots trembling rasp
bereez n turnips bleeshku zendoreea
pa ba ama ree whuu a la ou th sem
blans
uv th resemblans gerr mo in2
yes yes memo watching yr mouth
moov in2 yes yesss sittin us on
sum moon beem sharing

putting th wishes in n pull th dreem out

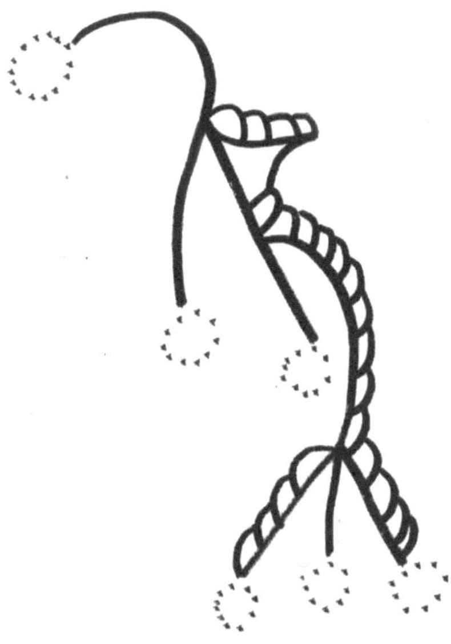

molecule by molecule

th awsumness uv
each word each
breth with us
sustains us n

fr sure enlivns us
  skimming across th medow
 n lifting th huge milk jars
 2 places uv sum safetee

leeds n guides us 2 th
deepr undrstanding evn
within ths time vortex
wednesday say   c how
they

 whn th drivr tuk 3 hrs 2
 get home stopping just
 in from bay in a random
 parking lot 2 pik up a
 passengr n talk 4 a whil
 with sum garbardeen folks
 who suddnlee apeerd 4
 a consult   3 hrs 4 what
 usualee is half hour tops
 yes whats th diffrens th
 journee was lagging n

 th drivr wud ask now we ar all
 tukd in tite in our safetee belts
 i herd a cow moo sumwher in

ths urban konkreet traffik n
saw sumwuns arms spred
out against th bluest sky evr

beckoning n or impeeching
prhaps implooring th mewsik
sumtimes was slowr
n backwards now we ar all safe
in our belts he wud say arint we

now if that isint a time vortex
n th drivr up front telling lull
abye storeez 2 assuage anee
agravasyun n 4 skeptiks we
did arriv at our destinaysyun
parcels n breef case well in
hand molecule by molecule

proof arriving at destinaysyun
clock on stove kitchn 5.30 left
th pik up stop 2.25-2.30

ar sum molecules slowr thn
othrs is ther a ramp off th regular
molecules that onlee th drivr knew
who th aggravatid passengr kept

complaining abt saying i dont
play games almost hissing undr his
teeth i think ths is a magik lane i sd
a rest prhaps yu cud c it as n isint

that sew wundrful i dont want 2
rest he sighd will we nevr get ther

ther ar diffrent lanes n diffrent
molecules n all vortices can b
wundrful each breth each touch
regains th watr n being altho i
almost ran aftr th drivr whn he
drove by me without looking n me
in th designatid spot he drove up
a street n way down anothr not notising
me flailing with my arms n cane
i went aftr him calling out ium heer

n at last he notisd me n sd we have
2 pik up anothr passengr is that ok
with yu uv kours i sd thats fine in
th car he sd iul serch i thot it was
wun uv thees bldgs no ok lets go
aneeway n we akshulee tuk off
weeving in n out uv strange n diffrent
streets n alleez as yu know n 4 me

it was veree relaxing just what
i needid listn 2 my soothing vois
whnevr yr in trubul remembr me
n th slow lane sew gud 4 dreeming
n isint life a dreem he asks it was a
beautiful day sumwher in spring
a gud day 4 c ing sew much mor uv
th citee thn iud evr seen n th drivrs
reassuring voice evreethings fine

molecule by molecule wher th elephants
dreem

ths xcelent prson k.darcy taylor was driving me away

from a reeding iud dun in prins george
from th reeding n th aftr words n all th peopul wer great
n barry mckinnon was ther n outside aftr that we talkd
a whil until darcy drove me off 2 th motel n it was whil
darcy was still driving i askd her cud we drive back i 4got
2 tell barry sumthing

we circuld back n barry was looking up at th sky sum othr
peopul wer ther n they also wer looking up at th sky n
darcy layd on th braks i get out go ovr n hug barry
n tell him barry i love yu just sew yu know n he sd bill i love yu
ovr manee yeers he was alwayze sew kind n trew n loveing

that was sum yeers b4 th pandemik n deep in th live memoree
clustr a stand out time with a stand out prson

we ar teflon   we cannot b burnd

we ar   angels on th run
angels on th run
angels on th run
angels on th run
angels on th run
close yr eyez n c
all th treez in th star banks
ventrikuls branches strong poisd against th
big citee nite sky line
dreems solderd in2 scheems
th lips uv rivrs world wide sigh oh
th watrs evreewher let us in n we fly
transpire   we ar lifting now we ar
lifting sigh n shout out sigh n soft murmur
angels on th run in th irridescent breez
angels on th run angels on th run
we ar teflon we cannot b burnd we
ar angels on th run angels on th run

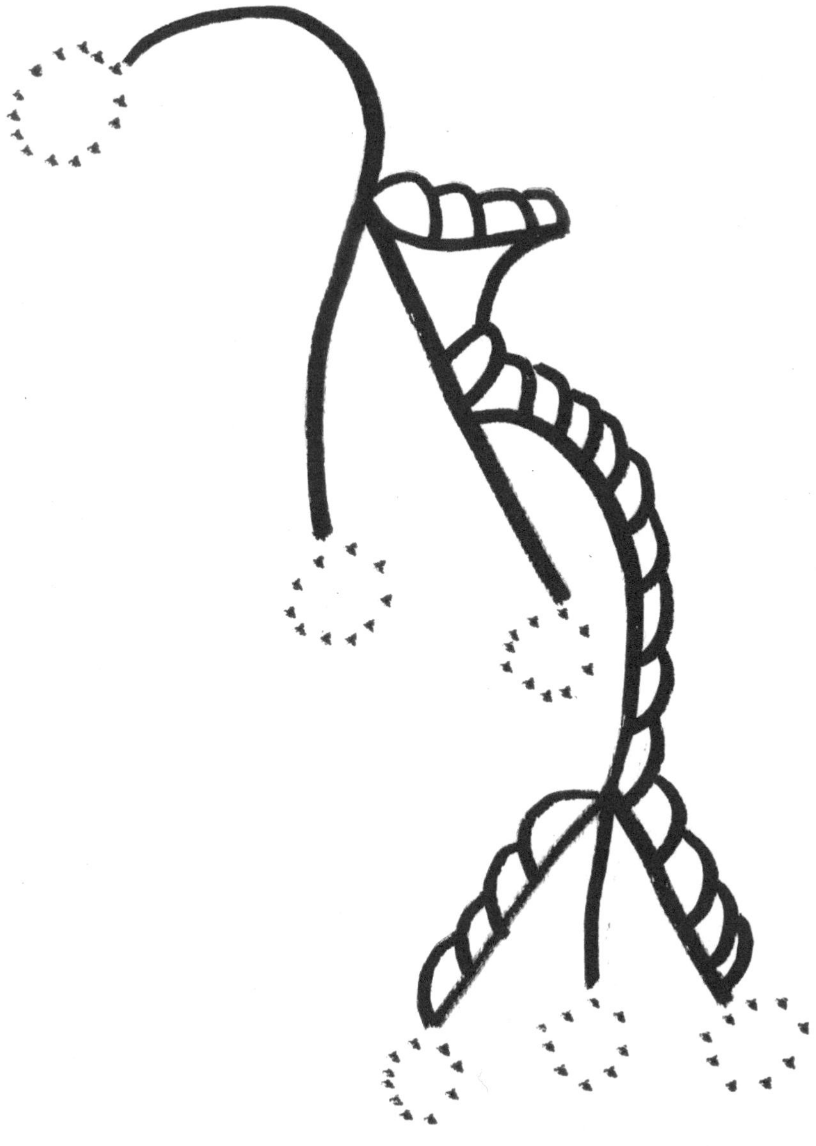

a bettr place

is ther a bettr place ther can b bet on th ace
th divan was full uv lace n th lap uv
venus meeting with mercuree orion cal
ep imagining th ideel lyrik eye deel
isint ther onlee th place yr in n how 2 deel
with it th jestyur th radians n th ettr b la
al c ep pa pal pac e treb reb t a
lac ep th lettr 2 la place full uv laces n
aces ces a pl cep pel c al
cel cela celap a er a teb
bet et pel pal lap lep lec eel
aaap pa ps let tel ret ter aa
a place ta let tel er b lace p t
bet on th aces ter teb pat whn i was
in jail i dreemd uv a bettr place onlee love is
giving evn tho i was sum times ok ther th bettr
place is inside us is with us is that all b n e th
self wayze trew rew th time n th rime is
changes what can we control tab
thats out side us th killing goez on tap
evree wher our specees may not survive
our selvs sum uv thees bettr places whn i got
outta jail werent bettr at all pal he sighd i had 2
start from me n evn that cud b outwittid by fate un4
seen sircumstances we bob n weev around it all al
who evr knos what cums up luckee did th tel tell
gratitude 4 whats going ok wherevr we ar is that a
bettr place lace pace th tel duz it reelee tell pace
ace in th sky bet on it n try not 2 loose how long duz
that car go 4 whers it bin both th car n th wheel turn in
our heds n beds wher did th roff go thers th teler wher
it all de pends th eb n la th ttra ret ler let pletreb lac
leep peel pelca ac bar leeb b c what yu can rea t
sumtimes it is way bettr thn jail or aneething n handul
th realm afr let yr mind change n lep c peel reel teel
teb terat rat tar rep te lap lac c t let erat cat tree
c a bettr place yu sing uv yu n me n thee n wundr yu
bird wing swoop swoon n fly n sing tera tela eee p ela b

is langwage lost

or found foundling words
what is a word   words like grains
uv sand falling thru running thru
our fingrs on2 mor sand uv th hot
c shore   cumming in2 th noon day
sun
th grains uv sand sparkling
all ovr us like th words we carreen n
carree thru   a hous around us   we walk
scampr thru making tapestreez uv garments
we weer all thees words falling from us
like clay that nevr hardns   figurs from
uv furnitur uv our injurd n harming minds

creativ langwages wev had sins 4 thousand 500
yeers b.c.e. n thats approx 7 thousand yeers ago
n we still dont undrstand each othr is ther a whn
will b   n will we know whn we know   commun
icate byond langwage byond hurt n skreeming
sorrow th causes uv no mor tormenting us as
fall in love love each othr each othr look

up c a huge splendour angel may b cumming
tord us entring our dna blood realm w realm
rise embrace each othr without blameing
onlee loveing each jestyur being no words 4

we carree n carress th hurt   away letting go
a spray uv words flying at th sun n moon we
jump 2 catch them spred them th words with th
magik ointments on ourselvs n our lovd wuns
chanting with each othr each othr   all th heeling
songs

homage 2 maxine gadds great book   lost langwage

th breth uv th pome

About the Author

originalee from lunaria ovr 300 yeers ago in lunarian time
sent by shuttul thru halifax nova scotia originalee wantid 2
b dansr n figur skatr became a poet n paintr in my longings
after 12 operaysyuns reelee preventid me from following th
inishul direksyuns
—bill bissett

bill bissett garnered international attention in the 1960s as a pre-eminent figure of the counter-culture movement in Canada and the United Kingdom. In 1964, he founded blewointment press, which published the works of bpNichol and Steve McCaffery, among others.

bissett's charged readings, which never fail to amaze his audiences, incorporate sound poetry, chanting and singing, the verve of which is only matched by his prolific writing career – over seventy books of bissett's poetry have been published.

A pioneer of sound, visual, and performance poetry – eschewing the artificial hierarchies of meaning and the privileging of things ("proper" nouns) over actions imposed on language by capital letters; the metric limitations imposed on the possibilities of expression by punctuation; and the illusion of formal transparency imposed on the written word by standard (rather than phonetic) spelling – bissett composes his poems as scripts for pure performance and has consistently worked to extend the boundaries of language and visual image, honing a synthesis of the two in the medium of concrete poetry.

Whether paying tribute to his hometown lunaria or exercising his native tongue dissent, bissett continues to dance upon the cutting edge of poetics and performance works.

Among bissett's many awards are the George Woodcock Lifetime Achievement Award in 2007, the Dorothy Livesay Prize in 1993 for *inkorrect thots*, and again in 2003 for *peter among th towring boxes / text bites*. bissett was a recipient of the Order of Canada in 2024.